"*What's Good about Feeling Bad?* is the most thorough treatment of pain and suffering I have ever seen. With the skill of a reflective person who has been there, Thomas and Habermas lead the reader through a thoughtful, practical, sensitive journey through no less than fifteen different aspects of suffering. The book closes with a powerful set of guidelines for working through life's hardships. This book is not only brimming with practical guidance, but its breadth of analysis will also offer the teacher and scholar much food for thought when grappling with the problem of evil at a theoretical level."

J. P. MORELAND
Distinguished Professor of Philosophy, Talbot School of Theology, Biola University; author of *Kingdom Triangle*

"Ever ask God why? We all have. *What's Good about Feeling Bad?* helps you wade those waters. With a solid biblical foundation, you'll discover how God uses suffering to benefit and bless us all. Best of all, it will help you understand how to answer the difficult questions and comfort others as Christ Himself has comforted you."

DR. TIM CLINTON
President, American Association of Christian Counselors

"Forged in the furnace of trials and hardships, this book is both a brilliant examination of suffering from a Christian perspective and a practical handbook that guides the reader through God's purposes and promises for the formidable journey. Learn through its pages how God can use pain and suffering in your own life as means of grace for personal transformation."

CHAD MEISTER
Director of philosophy program, Bethel College; author of *Building Belief*

"John Thomas and Gary Habermas have wrestled with the issue of pain and suffering and now share what they have learned, providing a wealth of practical steps for dealing with the unpleasant situations in which all of us at times find ourselves."

MICHAEL LICONA
New Testament historian, North American Mission Board; author of *Paul Meets Muhammad*

"As a psychologist leading a ministry to the separated and divorced, I found *What's Good about Feeling Bad?* to be a valuable addition to my recommended reading list. John Thomas and Gary Habermas have given us a compassionate but realistic overview on handling the difficulties we face. While most want to 'get on with life' as quickly as possible, this book encourages the reader to see God in this process and to use each experience for spiritual and personal growth. I found the book to be insightful and encouraging."

THOMAS WHITEMAN, Ph.D.
President, Fresh Start Seminars

WHAT'S
GOOD
ABOUT
FEELING
BAD?

Finding Purpose and a
Path through Your Pain

John C. Thomas · Gary Habermas

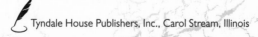

Tyndale House Publishers, Inc., Carol Stream, Illinois

JOHN'S DEDICATION

To my beautiful and amazing wife, without
whose support, love, and grace I would not
be able to fulfill my God-given call in life.
Katie and Stephen, thanks for bringing joy and
excitement into my life.
To the glory of God!

In loving memory of
Nathaniel David Sours
December 2, 1991, to June 7, 1998

GARY'S DEDICATION

With much love to our nine grandchildren:
Austin, Madelynn, Ethan, Kaitlin, Jackson,
Hannah, Tyler, Lilly, and Elam

Table of Contents

Melt in the Mouth

A headache—the kind that takes up residence behind your eyes and throbs with the rhythm of your pulse—overtakes you. Seeing you squint, your boss asks if you are feeling well.

"Yes, I'm fine, thank you." You rationalize that it really isn't so bad, that you've had worse—although you can't really remember when and don't really care. You have other things on your mind, namely the mess you will face tomorrow if today's work is left undone. You manage to remain conscious through your boss's rant, muttering "That's interesting," and "Of course, I'll get right on that," at the appropriate moments. You are dismissed just in time for lunch, where you settle for your daily ration of over-the-counter painkillers, each branded with the recommendations of "Four out of Five Doctors," and each promising instant relief. Unfortunately, your headache fails to confirm the claims on the label and you begin to wonder about the fifth doctor. Barely managing to muddle through the rest of the afternoon, you hobble home, pull the shades, and retreat into the darkness, hoping that the combination of sleep, silence, and luck will make the unbearable pain subside.

Now suppose that the pain is not centered in your head, but in your heart—the kind that comes from betrayal or loss. On the surface, the two may be similar. When asked if you are feeling well, you would most likely reply with the same "Yes, I'm fine, thank you" that you gave to your boss. And as you did with the headache, you might rationalize your grieving heart by minimizing the pain, medicating it, or hiding it—or most likely some combination of all three. Unlike your headache, however, heartache isn't so easily dismissed, and its pain can be (and usually is) much more severe.

As a college student, I (John) experienced heartache when I was rejected by my fiancée. In the deepest recesses of my pain and emotional poverty, I remember a good friend putting his arm around me and saying the most profound words I had ever heard: "I guess you are gonna really hurt for a while." My initial response was "Duh!" But weeks later, as I considered his words, I realized there was much to what he said. My friend's comment had conveyed three truths that provided encouragement during that heart-wrenching time.

First, he reminded me that it was "gonna really hurt." In other words, what I was feeling at that time was normal and, in its own peculiar way, proper. It was comforting to know that I was not heading down the road toward insanity. My feelings of loneliness, rejection, and grief did not indicate weakness, but rather the fact that I was a human being who experienced human emotions.

Second, his words "for a while" communicated that although I would hurt and hurt badly, I could take comfort in the fact that there would be an end to this turmoil. The winter in my heart would pass and yield to the promise of spring. I did not know the timetable for when or how it would lessen, but I knew that eventually, somehow, the sting would fade.

Finally, my friend's comment assured me that he knew how deeply I hurt. This was perhaps the greatest comfort. In a time of utter isolation, I had someone with whom to share the hurt. Of course, there was no way he could fully understand my internal chaos, but merely knowing that he sensed my pain was enough.

Perhaps you are agonizing over a wayward child or living with the sorrowful reminders of bad decisions. You may have learned that a loved one is terminally ill or anguished over the untimely death of a family member. Maybe you have lost your job or your dreams have been shattered. Perhaps your past has been marked by the dreadful reality of sexual abuse or the chaos of an alcoholic home. Maybe you have lost your home and all your possessions in a flood or hurricane. Or maybe your future has been radically altered by a spouse's decision to leave or the irresponsibility of a careless driver. A multitude of things in life can harm us and steal our joy. Regardless of the reason, our experiences with suffering all share one common denominator—the pain is beyond description. It doesn't matter whether you brought it on yourself or not. It doesn't matter if your response to the circumstances is common or not. Whatever the case, the ache of suffering still screams out for relief.

A quick reading of the Old Testament reveals many examples of the children of Israel crying out to the Lord. As slaves in Egypt they continually called out to God for deliverance, yet year after year passed with no answer to their prayers and no reprieve from their bondage. Eventually, the harsh reality that no relief was coming hardened their disillusioned hearts. God had turned His back on them. He had neglected His own children for no apparent reason. Or so it seemed.

But God *had* heard them. What the people of Israel did not understand was that mere men could never hinder God's plan and that their increasing affliction was also part of that plan. According to His own timetable, God prepared and sent Moses to liberate the people from Pharaoh's oppression. And at just the right time, He turned their cries of desperation into songs of celebration as the jubilee of freedom rang through the streets of their city. No longer did the future seem to be a bleak continuation of the past. They had hope for a new life as they prepared to embark upon an unknown, but welcome, journey.

This festivity was short-lived, however. They had barely begun their journey when trouble started. Some of the Israelites had developed such a negative outlook on life that they criticized Moses at every opportunity. In fact, on one particular day when they were hungry from their travels, some of them accused Moses of rescuing them only to let them die in the desert. Now, rather than defining their suffering as being in bondage, they pointed to the poverty of their provisions. Who could question their logic if they had said, "If God is trying to help, get Him to stop!"

The real problem for the children of Israel was not their circumstances but their attitude, which led them to test God.[1] In spite of their grumblings, the Lord graciously provided water from a rock. Whether the Israelites were in Egypt or the desert, their perception of their circumstances blinded them to the grace of God, and they melted under the heat of hardship. As slaves in Egypt they had cried out in anguish to God. But in spite of their pleas for deliverance, their suffering continued. Yes, God did deliver them, but *in His time*. Then, just when they thought they could trust Him again, it seemed that God had abandoned them once more. "Where is God?" they shouted. Time and time again, they allowed affliction to distort their perception of God. Though led by the pillar of cloud and fire, they neglected to truly follow God with their hearts. Put yourself in their sandals for a moment. As difficult as it is for us to admit sometimes, we often struggle with the same questions the Israelites had: Where is God? Why is He allowing me to suffer? What did I do to deserve this? Indeed, the questions are sometimes so unsettling that we begin to doubt the goodness of God. One philosopher concluded, "If there is a God, surely He is the devil." In other words, if God is in control of the universe, He must be evil to put His own children through such misery, adversity, and affliction. The Bible says that God is a loving Father,[2] but what kind of father would see his children hurting and do nothing? The only logical conclusion would be that God must not care. Maybe He is too consumed by His personal business to give us any attention. Whatever the case, our suffering continues.

A Tale of Two Realities

The Diet Mountain Dew was a perfect chaser for my (John's) midnight snack of spicy buffalo wings. With my tummy full, I searched for the remote while comical M&M's danced across the television screen to the confident and cheerful refrain, "Melts in your mouth, not in your hand."

I stumbled to bed and snuggled down into my favorite feather pillow. My stomach began to rumble and turn over and over as the commercial slogan became a sweet lullaby to my tired mind and nauseated gut. Soon I drifted off into a dreamy world where I found myself in boot camp. But this wasn't just any military camp. By now the commercial tune had taken on an army cadence, and to my amazement, I was a peanut M&M!

As a green recruit, I struggled to keep up with the other enlisted candies as we were put through our paces. The drill instructor, or DI as we called him, bullied our mission into us. On command, we trainees bellowed in unison, "Melt in the mouth, not in the hand, *sir!*"

The DI was brutal throughout our training, pushing us to exhaustion and calling into question our ability to succeed—whatever it took to hone our skills and prepare us for our mission. All the while, he told of veteran M&M's who endured the heat of battle without failing in their duty.

With pronounced bravado and a strong sense of optimism, I graduated boot camp and was dispatched to fulfill my orders—"Melt in the mouth, not in the hand!" Finally, the moment of truth had come. The bunker was ripped open, and we were thrown onto the battlefield. As we rapidly attempted to form ranks, I braced myself for what was ahead. But before we could fall into position, we were thrust into darkness as a hand closed over us.

This doesn't make sense, I thought. *It is not supposed to work this way!* I mustered all my determination to stay cool and calm as the heat of battle intensified. Eventually, my resolve evaporated into overpowering dread as I realized I was melting. I had failed to carry out my orders. In that moment of panic, I awoke in a cold sweat.

Though this tale was nothing more than a strange dream, it illustrates an all-too-familiar struggle. As Christians, we are indoctrinated with the message that we are to trust God in the midst of hardship and endure as good soldiers. With the fervency of drill instructors, some ministers dogmatically preach that we are to bear trials with joy, thanksgiving, and an assured peace. We are expected to be heartened by the hope-filled words from Romans 8:28 that God works out everything for good for those who love Him. Whether the message is in sermon, song, or script, our orders are clear: Trust God. Hang on to your faith. Be joyful.

Yet these orders seem to pose an impossible challenge. Our hearts say something radically different. Logically, we accept the truth of the Bible. We know that God is in control and that He is good. We believe that He is trustworthy and faithful. But there is the other reality of our emotions, which make it really tough to smile and praise the Lord in the midst of tragedy.

While some Christians struggle to maintain their composure

under pressure, others cannot make sense of God allowing us to suffer in the first place. When we see suffering, or more particularly, *experience* suffering ourselves, the hard reality of the pain nags us to question how God could allow so much hurt. Where is His protection? Why didn't He rescue us? How could He have let something so unfair happen? We conclude that God can't be good or loving, or trustworthy or faithful, because if He were those things He would have protected us from unnecessary pain.

On the other hand, if He is good, suffering must be a punishment for some hideous sin. A pervasive sense of shame and guilt begins to move in as we wonder, *What did I do to deserve this pain?*

It is extremely difficult to reconcile the realities of God and suffering. One reality has to be wrong. Either we must change our theology or we must deny the force of our emotions. For most of us, the reality of our hearts rings louder and truer. Instead of sensing joy and peace, we are confused, angry, and despondent. And in the heat of battle, we begin to melt.

The Purpose of This Book

In this book we will examine the age-old question of why God allows His children to suffer. When I (John) shared with a friend that I was working on a book about suffering, he jokingly replied, "After reading what you write, people will know what true suffering is!" In his jest, my friend actually hit upon one of our goals: that you will have a better understanding of the pain you have or undoubtedly will endure in this life.

As we will show, suffering comes in many shapes and sizes, and it can serve many different functions in our lives, as well as in the lives of others. Similarly, God's responses and the type of relief that comes our way can also be quite varied. Having preconceived ideas about how God "must" act in a situation, particularly when we are all too ready to quote and claim Scripture, often leads to disappointment or even anger with God.

Sometimes God might deliver us *from* our suffering completely. Needless to say, this provides a certain type of relief. But on other occasions, He might hold our hands and walk with us *through* the hurtful situation. Although it's natural to prefer the first response, there are times when the only way to gain blessing, insight, or growth is to face adversity. We must be willing to trust that God evaluates our circumstances differently than we do.[3]

Some of the clearest answers to the questions of suffering are spiritual in nature. Of course, no matter how hard we might search the Scriptures during and after a trial, we might never know why we suffer. Since God's ways are beyond our finite understanding, we may never wrap our minds around suffering. For that reason, our purpose in writing this book is not to give glib or neatly packaged answers to the mystery of suffering. It is too complex a problem for pat answers. Our goal is simply to use His Word as a guide in an attempt to bridge the great divide between despair and hope. We hope that it will deepen your understanding of the will and purposes of God.

Once you've read through this book in its entirety, you can refer back to it again and again during times of suffering. As you grow in your understanding of what the Scriptures teach about pain and suffering and God's role in them, you can go back to the purposes and promises contained in each section. We've tried to organize the book so that you can easily review it in order to glean information for a particular circumstance or situation.

We've divided the book into three sections: "The Pain of Suffering," "The Purposes of Suffering," and "A Pathway through Suffering." The first section provides a basic theology of suffering and deals with the impact of pain on our lives. In section 2, we'll look at fifteen of God's purposes in suffering culled from the pages of Scripture. Within these fifteen purposes, we'll see that God's purpose is often to move the sufferer in one of four directions: inward, forward, outward, or upward. Finally, section 3 provides scriptural and practical advice for moving through suffering. If you are hurting, we resolutely pray that you will find direction and a road map to Christ through this writing.

As the authors of this book, we come at the issue of suffering from different, although complementary, angles. John is a professional counselor who has had vast experience in private practice and corporate psychology. In his current occupation as a professor, he also directs a graduate counseling program. Although the details have been changed considerably (except where permission has been given), most of the examples in this book have been taken from John's many years of experience.

Gary is a former pastor, a distinguished professor, and an author in the areas of philosophy and apologetics. Over the past thirty years, his chief areas of study have been the questions of religious doubt and personal suffering. He has written several books on these subjects, in addition to having more than four hundred informal discussions with hurting individuals in the course of his study.

In the following pages, it is our prayer that you will come to see suffering, not as something to be avoided, but as a significant part of life. Although pain and difficulty are tied to our fallen nature, they can still be God's tools for transformation.

Moreover, we pray that you will come to the place in your spiritual journey where you not only expect suffering but learn to use it. If our desire is to be like Christ, we must persevere through suffering, seeing it as one of God's anvils to hammer out His image in us.[4]

THE PAIN OF SUFFERING

It is very unpleasant to consider the tragedies that could happen to us. Yet suffering comes to all without prejudice—the Christian and the non-Christian, the destitute and the prosperous, the weak and the strong. Jesus said that God sends the sun and rain on the just and the unjust.[1] Nothing will protect us from experiencing the suffering of this life, and when we are faced with the heartache of rejection, the emptiness of loss, the bite of physical pain, or the betrayal of being violated, pain is the natural result.

The reality is that this world is broken, cursed, and fallen. Pain, heartache, and adversity are to be expected. God's main objective is not that we live pain free, but that we are holy and acceptable in His sight. Our joy is not to come from the ease of circumstance, but from Christ who has overcome the world.[2]

In this section, we will examine the nature of pain and suffering. We all know that suffering is a reality that sometimes creates internal confusion and chaos. In order not only to face these conditions but also to grow through them, we'll need to begin by exploring some deeply held assumptions that cause us to feel suffering's sting to a greater degree.

CHAPTER ONE

The Perils of Pain

Dave and Teresa Sours were high school sweethearts who married shortly after graduation. Soon thereafter, they brought their first child, Ashley, into the world.[1] She was a blessing to her parents, and today Ashley is a nineteen-year-old blonde with a big smile and an even bigger heart.

Like most parents, Dave and Teresa looked forward with energetic anticipation to the birth of their second child. In the twentieth week of pregnancy, however, they were told that their unborn baby boy had a very serious medical condition. Three choices were offered to them: do nothing, which would result in the inevitable death of their baby; abort the child; or allow a potentially dangerous and experimental surgery to be performed on the unborn child. Even if the surgery was successful, there was no way to assess the extent of damage already done to the baby's tiny lungs and whether or not they would be able to support life. Further testing revealed that their baby had only a one in four chance of survival. And if he did survive, he would probably suffer significant brain damage and deformities. With the odds against them, Dave and Teresa decided to do everything humanly possible to give their child a chance to survive. They would risk the experimental surgery and leave the results in God's hands.

The operation was performed, but the results were inconclusive. Over the next few months, doctors closely monitored Teresa's pregnancy. Then on December 2, 1991, complications dictated an emergency C-section, and the delivery room was filled with

medical professionals ready to respond to the needs of a dangerously unhealthy newborn. There was complete silence—a combination of anxiety and fear—as the tiny infant was lifted from the
open womb. Then the world's most beautiful sound filled the room
as the tiny miracle child let out his first cry. Dave and Teresa gave
him the name Nathaniel, which means "gift of God." During the
course of the following weeks, the doctors discovered that Nathan's
brain was not damaged, nor were any deformities detected in his
lungs. He had, however, sustained significant damage to his entire
urinary system.

Nathan's care demanded much of her time, and it didn't take
long before experience and research made Teresa a very medically
astute caregiver. The next few years were spent dealing with frequent hospital stays, numerous infections, a number of surgeries
and medical procedures, much blood work, and countless visits to
the doctor. These were indeed trying times for the whole family.
Their faith was shaken and hopes were dashed time and time again.
And yet they repeatedly found the love of God and the common
grace they needed to make it through the trials.

Over time, Nathan became more stable and was finally able to
attend school to address his developmental delays. At two and a half
years of age, he began attending an early childhood class, where he
blossomed into a promising student.

Unfortunately, over the next several years, Nathan's already limited renal functions began to fail. It became evident that a kidney
transplant was necessary. The Sours family became local celebrities
as the community organized a "Nickels for Nathan" campaign to
offset the expenses of the pending transplant surgery.

A persistent pattern of complications delayed the surgery, and
in August 1997, peritoneal dialysis was begun. As the dialysis tem-
porarily managed the kidney failure, preparations for a transplant
continued. Dave was found to be the perfect match for Nathan,
and as soon as Nathan was infection free, doctors planned to do
the transplant.

The church organized daily prayer vigils to intercede for the
family and physicians and to pray that God's will would be done.

Church members and friends prepared to help the family through Dave's one-month recuperation and Nathan's equally long hospital stay.

After years of anticipation, the day for the transplant finally arrived. The waiting room and hallway were filled with family and friends who gathered to await the outcome. After eight hours, word came that the surgery had finally been completed. Father and son were fine, and Nathan's new kidney was functioning perfectly. While Dave had a difficult postsurgical experience, Nathan amazed everyone with his smooth recovery.

Two days after the transplant at the University of Virginia Medical Center, Dave was in a wheelchair by his son's side and Nathan was using a remote control to find the Cartoon Network. I (John) went to visit them and was delighted to find them well. We laughed at sleepy Nathan's struggle to keep his eyes open and his treasured attempts to cuddle with his mother. After long hugs and encouraging words, I left with the promise to return soon. News quickly spread that Nathan and Dave were doing well, and we all gave thanks to God for His continued blessings in the life of this family.

When the telephone rang at four o'clock the next morning, I knew something must be wrong. Teresa's shaky voice confirmed my notion, and in the space of mere seconds, the joy we had all felt evaporated into fear.

"Nathan has taken a turn for the worse," she said. "The doctors are working on him, but they don't expect him to make it. We need you to pray."

"Oh, Teresa," I muttered. Years of psychological and theological training had provided me with no words of wisdom or comfort. "We will pray, and we will be there," I said. As I hung up the phone, I was still in a state of disbelief. Everything had been going so well. Only hours before we had praised God for what He was doing in and through Nathan, and now this!

That day at the hospital was a long one. At least thirty people sat on the floor or stood against the walls outside the pediatric intensive care unit. Apparently, Nathan had had a serious reaction to one of the antirejection medications, which led to breathing difficulties. He was placed back on the respirator. Shortly after that, he had had a massive heart attack. The doctors worked passionately for over four hours to revive him. Unwilling to let him go, they put him on life support. Because artificial resuscitation does not efficiently provide oxygen to the brain, a neurological consultation was ordered. Unfortunately, the neurologist was unable to find any response. Hoping that medication might be hindering his ability to respond, the doctors decided to discontinue the medication and wait for four hours to see if Nathan would show any signs of neurological functioning. And so we waited, only in the end to be convinced of the worst. Late Sunday evening, on June 7, 1998, Nathan was pronounced dead.

Dave and Teresa's initial response was like that of almost anyone who has helplessly watched as their world unfurled around them: *Why? Why had God allowed Nathan to die?* It was as if a priceless string of pearls had suddenly broken and scattered across the ground, lost forever. The miracles that had caused Nathan to survive—and even thrive—during his short life brought glory to God and hope to His people. Certainly, God had many opportunities during the pregnancy to keep Nathan from being born and thereby absolve the family of such pain. What purpose could He have had in Nathan's death? Is such a purpose important enough to justify the agony that Dave and Teresa were experiencing or the loss that we all felt?

The Reality of Suffering

On a vacation once, I (John) learned of a cornfield maze the size of three football fields that had just opened to the public. Since it was patterned after Noah's ark, I joked with my family that going through it would be a "spiritual experience." So after being given a clue to help us navigate the maze, we excitedly entered the cornfield and began our quest.

As we wandered around the heavily trampled paths, I couldn't help but think of Stephen King's short story "Children of the Corn." Hopelessly lost in the maze of maize, we quickly found that heat and fatigue were giving way to frustration. At times, we thought we were heading in the right direction, only to find ourselves face-to-face with people we had just passed. After taking time to regroup, we set out with a new strategy. But before we had traveled far, we met the same group of people again! My children began to wonder if they would ever get out, let alone find the next watercooler.

Suffering is much like being in a disorienting maze; it produces the confused and desperate feelings of being trapped. And we don't have to look far to see that suffering is a disturbing and inescapable reality that we all must face. At any time, tragedy can zero in on us and without notice turn the world upside down. Other times, suffering develops slowly over seasons, eroding away our resources until there is nothing left of us and the happiness we seek. Suffering comes in a variety of shapes and sizes. Regardless of how we experience it and what wrapping it comes in, suffering always redefines our reality. To better understand this phenomenon, we need to examine six realities of suffering.

Reality #1: Suffering is universal

Until modern times, suffering was assumed to be a constant of life. Today, with improvements in medicine, radical advances in technology, and significant progress in so many fields of knowledge, suffering has come to be seen as an anomaly.

In spite of our accomplishments, the signature of suffering is written on every human heart. All people suffer, regardless of their race, gender, intelligence, financial status, or faith. A casual glance at the six-o'clock news or the daily paper provides ample evidence that people all over the world are experiencing hardships of many kinds. Since we live in a fallen world, the sources of pain and suffering are plentiful. Natural disasters, random accidents, and physical illnesses result in pain. Mental anguish, family dysfunction, and criminal behavior inject adversity into an otherwise peaceful life. Economic downturns, political unrest, and war bring distress, as does the fear that these things may befall us. Even the knowledge that we cannot ensure our future or control our destiny brings about suffering with greater force.

Reality #2: Suffering is painful

Pain. Just hearing the word brings a feeling of discomfort. In fact, the word *trauma*, which means "wound," uniquely captures the idea. There is nothing more central to the human experience than our capacity to feel, and no aspect of this is as deep as our capacity to suffer. To some degree, every person has experienced a wound or hurt. Yet as frequent as physical and emotional pain seem to be, we react as if trouble is unexpected and alien to our lives.

Sometimes there are no words to describe the excruciating pain that grips the soul. The agony is so intense it seems to envelop our entire existence. Pain can be like acid, rapidly eating away at us from the inside out. It's difficult to see beyond our own misery when we are consumed by the enormity of this kind of pain.

Emotional pain can also bring about a cascade of other symptoms: a loss of concentration, fatigue, changes in sleeping and eating patterns, profound sadness and depression, crying, agitation, and anger. Enduring such great pain would seem to be beyond the scope of normal human capability, and therefore it requires a supernatural Healer.

Suffering arouses pain and fear that are so intense that we naturally demand relief. The prophet Hosea saw this when he described God's people wailing upon their beds.[2] Sometimes the compounded effects of suffering produce a pain so intense that we feel desperate, wanting relief at any cost. When people are repeatedly traumatized—as hostages, victims of chronic family violence, or survivors of war atrocities—they may actually remain trapped in the trauma long after the events have ceased.

Reality #3: Suffering is personal

There is no correct way to suffer. Although certain aspects of human suffering are common, the experience is truly an individual process. Your reaction to pain is influenced by many factors, including the nature of the suffering, previous experiences with suffering, your personality and environment, and present circumstances. It is critical to remember that many of the situations that bring about suffering are outside the realm of normal experience, so there is no "normal" way to respond to them. Suffering is an intensely personal, privately lived, unique experience.

Of course, some people might have some notion of what you are feeling, especially if they've had similar experiences. But no one can fully grasp the reality of suffering in someone else's life—the plaguing questions, the pain, and the ongoing battles that only you can understand.

But pain should not be experienced in a vacuum. Even when those around us don't understand exactly what we're going through, we can still share our hurts and our needs with family and friends who love us. Pain is personal, but that doesn't mean it should be experienced in isolation.

Reality #4: Suffering is unnerving

The unnerving reality is that with one stroke of the clock, our worlds can turn completely upside down. From that one point in time, our minds, hearts, and bodies will never be the same again. In fact, research indicates that severe suffering can permanently change brain functioning. Seemingly cruel circumstances often leave us feeling stunned and blindsided, and we experience a shock to the system, a laceration of the soul, and a wound to the spirit.

In her book *The Waves*, Virginia Woolf struggles to define her pain as she writes, "For pain words are lacking. There should be cries, cracks, fissures, whiteness passing over chintz covers, interference with the sense of time, of space; the sense also of extreme fixity in passing objects; and sounds very remote and then very close."[3]

Despite our attempts to devise a world where we can predict, contrive, and control the outcome, we find that our best efforts most often fail and we're reminded once again that life is beyond our control. We see the suffering of Christians who have perfect church attendance and seemingly perfect spirituality. However, the problems and turmoil they encounter seem to contradict their Christian lifestyle. How could such godly people experience such problems? To alleviate our confusion, we sometimes assume that beneath the righteous public persona there lurks a dark side. It comforts us to believe that as long as we are as "good" as possible, their suffering will not befall us.

Suffering is also unnerving because few people have any preparation for or understanding about suffering. To some extent, the shock of any trauma is a function of its novelty and unexpectedness. Hence, the more unfamiliar the experience is and the more unprepared we are for it, the greater our shock and the greater our difficulties in working through the pain. In essence, we fear anything that is beyond our ability to control.

Suppose that you are driving down a road when you happen upon a severely damaged area of pavement. Having expected smooth sailing on your journey, you are not ready for such an obstruction. Your car bounces about as you slow your speed to accommodate the perilous pavement. You might complain about high taxes and miserable roadways. You might belittle the government officials who seem to ignore the problem. If, however, a road sign had warned you about the impending problem, you would have curtailed your speed in preparation for the road conditions. Of course, you would not like having to deal with such conditions, but knowing that it was coming, you would have had a very different emotional response. Yes, you would still feel the bounce and jostle as you crossed the rough patch, but having anticipated the trouble, you would have readied yourself for the experience.[4]

Reality #5: Suffering is mysterious

Suffering is a mystery, a puzzle for which we do not have all the pieces. Much like being in a disorienting maze, suffering produces the confusion and desperation of being trapped. Answers often seem to lie just beyond reach. Like a maze, it is difficult to find one's way out of suffering, and the inescapability of the pain can be overwhelming. Days seem to never end; the future is only an extension of the tormenting past. Hopelessness and despair often become our only companions. Our wills become paralyzed, constraining us to passivity. Although we yearn to feel normal again, we know normalcy is forever lost.

Initially, suffering produces a sense of disbelief. *This can't be happening to me*, we think. *There must be some mistake!* The experience feels unreal. It is more gratifying to swim in a vague sea of possibilities than it is to see reality clearly and face the deep hurts and fears of what is happening. Eventually, the unreality of the situation gives way to an overwhelming sense of bewilderment, and the suffering intensifies when it creates questions to which there are no ready answers. Confusion plagues the mind. Our gut-felt responses to suffering often override our theology. Our belief systems are undermined, and our faith is called into question. We doubt everything that we once believed about God. Oh, we know that He sent His only Son to die for us and that He has done miraculous things in our lives. But in the grips of confusing suffering, He is, in essence, only as good as His last benevolent action toward us.

Cries such as "Where is God?" and "Why is He not helping me?" seemingly fall on deaf ears. And when our faith in God is ruptured, we turn to our own reasoning in an attempt to make sense of the jarring turmoil. Such confusion is particularly disturbing when we believe that we do not deserve the ordeal. We are dumbfounded by the way things have turned out; it just doesn't make sense. *How did I get into this mess?* we wonder. *What did I do to deserve such misery?* We get caught up in the unending questions, but usually the repetitive, circular thoughts that bombard our conscious moments have no apparent answers. While God seeks to use suffering for our benefit, Satan seeks to use suffering to create doubts about ourselves and the character of God. He convinces us that God is treating us unfairly. So in order to find answers to unanswerable questions, we tend to fill in the gaps. For instance, some people choose to find fault in someone or something else: *He made me do it*, or *If I had different parents, this would never have happened to me.* Sufferers attempt to understand the problem by ascribing the problem to something beyond their control; that is, they believe that they are victims. By attributing our calamities to forces outside of ourselves, we hope to protect our sense of order and control.

Some sufferers seek to make sense of the event by blaming themselves. Taking responsibility for suffering puts control in our own hands. But if this is only an attempt to make sense of the problem and not to resolve it, we end up feeling even more powerless. Of course, when we *have* brought about our own misery, we often become guilt ridden. Rather than having a God-given sorrow over sin that leads us to repentance and wholeness, we become intensely self-focused.[5] Compare the different responses of Peter and Judas to their betrayal of Jesus. Peter became broken and repented, but Judas was so self-focused that he committed suicide. This tendency to become self-consumed leads to hopelessness because it keeps us in bondage to our failures. In the end, blame only compounds the problem and confuses us more.

Reality #6: Suffering is biblical

It should be no surprise that Jesus Christ suffered. His beatings and crucifixion were necessary in order for Him to accomplish His mission of redemption. The writer of Hebrews put it this way:

> For it was fitting for Him, for whom are all things and
> by whom are all things, in bringing many sons to glory,
> to make the captain of their salvation perfect through
> sufferings. . . . Though He was a Son, yet He learned
> obedience by the things which He suffered. And having
> been perfected, He became the author of eternal salvation
> to all who obey Him.   Hebrews 2:10; 5:8-9

These verses drip with truths about suffering. First, "it was fitting" for God to use suffering to perfect His Son. In other words, it is consistent with the character and nature of God to use pain and suffering to achieve His purpose. Jesus Christ became the perfect captain (literally, "leader" or "pioneer") of salvation because God was willing to allow it. It seems almost sacrilegious to say that allowing suffering is consistent with God's character. But before you turn your back on God, keep reading. Our goal is to know God; and if allowing us to suffer is indeed acceptable to Him, we must at least try to understand why.

Second, suffering teaches obedience. Pain taught Jesus Christ obedience to the Father and submission to His will. It is an amazing thought to consider that Jesus, God Incarnate, could learn anything, but according to this verse, such was the case. Christ was not spared hardship and pain. Through suffering, He became our Redeemer, the High Priest who felt our infirmities, and through it He learned the costs of obedience. Moreover, because Jesus was wholeheartedly committed to do His Father's will, He willingly accepted pain as part of God's agenda. Perhaps there is no greater key to our ability to deal with suffering than to accept our circumstances and suffering as part of God's redemptive and transforming work in our lives.

Many of the early church fathers experienced suffering for the same reasons Jesus did.[6] The litany of horrific circumstances that Paul experienced are genuinely valid reasons to moan: imprisonments, beatings, shipwrecks, and deprivation. But Paul simply accepted them as part of his Christian walk. In fact, in the book of Philippians, Paul was bold enough to say that he deeply wanted to know the "fellowship" of Christ's suffering. Like readers today, the recipients of that letter may have thought, *What is Paul thinking in saying that he wants to suffer?* We're sure, however, that Paul knew exactly what he was saying.

The great heroes of faith from the Old Testament typically earned their commendations through suffering.[7] Abraham, Moses, David, and Isaiah were "put to death all day long" because of their faith.[8] Certainly, these believers' testimonies run contrary to the notion that the Christian life is to be easy, convenient, and smooth sailing.

Suffering has no value in our economy, except for those who profit financially from the hardships of others. We do not like the inconvenience and pain that trials impose, but God values suffering. In His economy, suffering is a wise investment because it bears the potential for greater things. Like any investment, it carries with it risks, but God knows that the advantages far outweigh them.

The Bible makes clear that we can expect suffering. It cannot be avoided. We will hurt and be hurt. Pain will surround us. Though this sounds pretty bleak, there is hope. Though the basis of our hope is in the past work of Christ on the cross, the realization of that hope is still in the future. God has assured us that His Son has overcome the world.[9] The grip of death could not hold Jesus.[10] In overcoming death, Christ defeated pain, sorrow, sickness, and suffering. Our hope rests in the truth that we will follow in His victory.[11]

Jesus said that life would not be easy. But we can take confidence and find delight in the hope that we have in and through Him. Christ's triumph over Satan is cause to find peace. Because Jesus conquered pain, He can use our pain to accomplish His plan in and through us.

CHAPTER TWO

The Bedrock of Suffering

Have you ever wondered why some people respond to trauma with resiliency and others become hopeless and helpless? Why is it that events can take such control over our lives, even when our Christian beliefs encourage us to trust God? The answer to these questions is found in the bedrock of human nature: our attitudes.

I (John) remember getting a secret decoder ring in a box of cereal as a child. On the back of the box was a map that was unintelligible without the ring. But by using the secret decoder ring, I was able to navigate through the map and find the hidden treasure chest (a mission that made the purchase of the cereal worthwhile!).

In the same way, we all have an internal decoder ring that we use to navigate the journey of life and make sense of everything. In essence, this internal ring dictates our perception and understanding of life. This ring is our attitude. An attitude could be described as a relatively consistent way of thinking, feeling, and behaving toward an object, person, group, or idea. Our attitudes involve our personal theories about ourselves, the external world, and the interaction between the two. Because we interpret many of our experiences through our attitudes, our responses have little to do with the actual situation. Our attitudes determine our responses to a situation, not the situation itself. In other words, suffering is in the eye of the beholder.

For example, when we label an event "catastrophic," we are revealing our attitudes and the way we perceive the situation. I (John) once provided counseling to a group of employees who were being downsized. Two of them merit attention. Both men were forty-five years old, married, with two children; each had one child in college. Both employees had been with the company about twenty-three years, and on the day the layoffs occurred, both men were shocked to learn that their jobs were being eliminated. Both of these employees had a stellar employment history, were well-regarded, and had assumed they would not be on "the list."

I met with each of them following their termination meetings. At that time, both were still in shock, but that's where the similarities between these two men ended. One man believed that God would take care of him and his family, and that somehow they would come through stronger than ever. The other man could not move beyond the shock of what had happened to him. He spent most of our time together listing other employees who *should* have been terminated but were not. He railed against the manager and the company. He feared that he and his family would not be able to survive financially. He lamented having to tell his daughter that she couldn't stay in college and that his son would have to quit martial arts before earning his black belt. Our entire session was dark, bleak, and unproductive.

I met several times with each man as part of their separation packages. After several months, the first man obtained a job with another large firm. Though it required a move, his compensation and benefits were equitable. He expressed gratitude at the way God had used the worst loss of his life to bring his family closer and strengthen his faith. The second man was unwilling to look for a job outside the company. He continued to query other divisions, believing that the company owed him and would give him a job somewhere. Month after month he grew more depressed. Eventually his wife left him, and shortly thereafter he committed suicide.

One event, two completely different perceptions of the event, and two radically divergent responses. Attitude is everything.

One main problem when it comes to suffering may be that our theology is inadequate. After touring the United States, the well-known theologian and pastor Helmut Thielicke of Hamburg was asked what he saw as the greatest deficiency among American Christians. This great scholar said that we have an inadequate view of suffering.[1]

The bedrock of our attitudes is a network of beliefs that we unwittingly build for ourselves. Some of these beliefs are global and abstract, while others are more narrow and concrete. The belief that you are a good tennis player is more specific and less global than the belief that you are a good athlete. But the belief that you are a good athlete is less global and more narrow than the belief that you are a competent person. The most significant and pervasive beliefs are those that are more abstract and general. While you may rethink the belief that you are a good tennis player, losing several matches in a row will not necessarily cause you to believe that you are incompetent. You can believe that you are a competent person, even in the face of evidence that your tennis game is abominable. This is because other beliefs comprise your attitude about your competence.

Though beliefs are the foundation of emotions and behavior, they are so embedded within us that we seldom consciously think about them. When challenged, however, people are usually adamant in their resolve to maintain a particular belief, even in the face of contrary evidence. It is this strong bias to preserve what we believe that allows us to make sense of a complex and chaotic world.

From very early on, we observe how the world operates, and we make conclusions about what we see. These conclusions then become part of the lens through which we continue to perceive the world and make further generalizations. We live our lives as if those conclusions were both well-founded and binding, continually reinforcing them through our interpretations of new experiences and observations of others. Although our conclusions may not be biblical, healthy, or accurate, we resist modifying them. We seek to interpret all of our experiences in such a way that our fundamental beliefs are essentially unaffected.

A person's beliefs about what sort of world this is, how he or she should be treated, what to expect from life, and who God is will predominantly determine that person's reaction to adversity. Based upon years of clinical experience, I (John) have identified three key beliefs that make up most people's attitudes and determine our reactions to adversity.[2] These beliefs are:

1. I deserve ease and comfort in life.
2. I deserve a predictable world.
3. I deserve a fair world.

You may assume that these beliefs do not apply to you, but do not quickly dismiss them. Our beliefs are emotionally laden assumptions that operate instinctively, mostly outside our awareness. What you actually believe may be quite different than what you *think* you believe. Since adversity does not create our attitudes as much as it *reveals* our attitudes, the best way to know what you truly believe is to examine your reaction to affliction.

I Deserve Ease and Comfort

Since the Garden of Eden, humanity's goal has been to derive as much satisfaction from life as possible. Our sin drives us to pursue the good life and to find fulfillment for our deepest needs apart from Christ. Sigmund Freud spoke of the "pleasure principle" as our primary motivation; namely, to maximize pleasures and avoid pain. Obviously, there have been many times throughout history when a person's exclusive purpose has been survival. But when our basic needs for survival are met, a passion for indulgence is not far behind.

As Americans, we are told that we have been endowed with certain inalienable rights, among which is the pursuit of happiness. Homes, jobs, money, family, friends, sex, health, and social status are supposed to provide us with that fulfillment and happiness. When any of these things are threatened or taken away, we typically react with fear and discomfort.

We have created a world in which we savor comfort and immediate gratification: think microwave ovens and drive-up windows for fast food; ATM machines for on-the-spot cash; one-hour dry cleaning for prompt laundry. We love our remote controls and automatic appliances. While the Son of Man had no place to lay His head, we complain if we don't get a king-sized bed at a hotel.

You might ask what is wrong with these things. In and of themselves, they are not wrong. They provide entertainment and convenience after a long workday. They are humanity's attempt to make a fallen world orderly and comfortable. It seems, however, that comfort has become one of the most sought-after idols of our times. Rather than being pilgrims on a journey through a foreign land, we have become settlers. Instead of feeling out of place in this sin-laden world, we have become accustomed to the thorns and thistles that mark what once was paradise.

The problem is usually not the source of comfort but our passionate pursuit of it. There is nothing inherently wrong with creature comforts. The problem occurs when we have an attitude toward life that demands comfort. When that happens, our self-serving nature compels us to manipulate life to get what we want.[3] We persistently seek and sustain those things that provide the greatest sense of comfort. Hence, we unwittingly make contentment and happiness idols. Yet no matter how hard we try, we are rarely satisfied and seek to fill the void through materialism, alcohol and other drugs, pornography, and violence—all self-designed strategies to numb a chronic heartache. Confession, repentance, and trusting in God typically are not seen as the most effective way to handle problems. In fact, our earnest demands for comfort usually compel us to find ways to elude the undesirable consequences of our actions. Lying, abortion, and divorce are but a few ways to escape the pain and suffering that result from poor choices.

When confronted with the painful reality that life is adverse, we typically assume God is not good. In other words, God is good if I am comfortable and happy.

In addition to counseling courses in graduate school, I (John) took several classes in apologetics (some taught by Gary!). It was there that I was first introduced to the work of C. S. Lewis, a well-known literary scholar and one of the twentieth century's best known popular writers and apologists on Christian theology.

Although I had heard of his work, I had never been inclined to read it. But over the course of two semesters, I devoured most of Lewis' nonfiction. In one of his better-known works, Lewis tackles the problem of pain. He describes the typical view of the nature of God when he writes, "If God were good, He would wish to make His creatures perfectly happy, and if God were almighty, He would be able to do what He wished. But the creatures are not happy. Therefore God lacks either goodness, or power, or both."[4]

The Bible says that in due time God will make His people happy and make things the way He desires them to be.[5] For most of us, however, that seems a long way off, and when life is not what we desire, we often react with intense emotion. Job poignantly captured this idea when he moaned, "I was at ease, but He [God] has shattered me; He also has taken me by my neck, and shaken me to pieces; He has set me up for His target, His archers surround me. He pierces my heart and does not pity; He pours out my gall on the ground. He breaks me with wound upon wound; He runs at me like a warrior."[6] Imagine that testimony coming from the pulpit.

I (John) once counseled a kind Christian woman who lived her life in a noteworthy fashion. She was persistent in serving the Lord, had a caring shoulder for others, and seemed to be the model wife and mother. Her world was rocked to the core, however, when her husband of twenty-seven years informed her that he was leaving her for a younger woman.

"How can I possibly compete with a twenty-two-year-old?" she asked, weeping almost uncontrollably as she poured out her painful story. In a later counseling session, this woman's hostility began to emerge, not just at her husband but at God as well. "I thought if I did everything I was supposed to do, God would take care of me. I don't know what else He wants from me. Christian service has been my life, and this is my reward? When I get to heaven, God is going to owe me an apology for the way that He has treated me!" This woman may not have realized it, but she had a deep-seated commitment to comfort. It wasn't until she experienced the real press of life that the true nature of her heart was revealed.

Another woman told me (Gary) that God was responsible for the fact that she and her husband had never been able to have children. Pulling promises from Scripture, she lashed out at God for allowing "everyone else" to raise children and to "enjoy the good things of life," while she never could. Finding a soul mate in Hannah[7]—the mother of Samuel the prophet—she tried to pray similarly, but without the results for which she had hoped. To her way of thinking, God was responsible for all of these problems and at least owed her an explanation. I knew she would never find peace until she faced and corrected the many misbeliefs that she had regarding the Lord, His promises, and her situation.

Today Christian books and videos, support groups, and seminars on a wide array of topics meet real needs with biblically sound counsel. Sadly, however, some of these programs actually promote further self-indulgence. We have become victims to be healed rather than sinners to be sanctified. We believe in solutions that are simple and easy, whether they're "eight steps" or "ten ways" or "a simple plan." We have even turned the Bible into a self-help book, using its words of inspiration to help us feel better about ourselves. Holiness, sanctification, and self-denial have been replaced with healing our wounds, personal growth, and improving our self-esteem. Rather than being the central theme of life's drama, God seems to be nothing more than the curtain puller.

In essence, we've replaced serving and glorifying the Lord with seeking the good life. We live to make life as comfortable and convenient as possible. It is this self-consuming nature that makes understanding God's purposes in suffering unreasonable.

Contrast this response with that of Corrie ten Boom, another Christian servant who also traveled a difficult road. This famed survivor of Ravensbrück, the dreadful concentration camp located just north of Berlin, knew much about adversity. Corrie suffered from hunger, sleep deprivation, appalling living conditions, brutality, and the loss of personal possessions. She lived under the constant threat of extermination. Though she had moments of doubt, these circumstances actually fortified her belief in the goodness of God. Years after her release, she perceptively wrote, "Often I have heard people say, 'How good God is. We prayed that it would not rain for our church picnic, and look at this lovely weather!' Yes, God is good when He sends good weather. But God was also good when He allowed my sister Betsie to starve to death before my eyes in the German concentration camp."[8]

Common sense nudges us toward the fact that the world is ill equipped to provide constant comfort. Consider the opening sentence of M. Scott Peck's best-selling and controversial book, *The Road Less Traveled:* "Life is difficult. . . ."[9] Comedian Jerry Seinfeld once said that perhaps the road less traveled is less traveled for a good reason. He was right, since our natural drive for pleasure leads us to choose a different route.

Perhaps drawing from the words of Jesus, the apostle Peter instructed us not to think that life would be problem free; in fact, he said we should rejoice because problems let us partake of Christ's sufferings.[10]

When it comes to living, most of us prefer a riverboat ride to a roller coaster. Our self-centered drive for comfort wants a smooth, steady ride. But as long as we assume that life must be comfortable, we will never come to accept trials and adversity as normal, especially those hardships that we deem to be undeserved. When people think they've been dealt a bad hand, they often attempt to make that hand work. Rather than depending upon God, they rely on their own power and strategies to maximize pleasure and reduce pain. If unsuccessful, they fold, throw up their hands in despair, and wonder, *Where is God?*

I Deserve a Predictable World

God created our world with natural laws to provide order. For instance, I know that a ball dropped from a roof will fall toward the ground. Physical realities such as gravity make it easy to predict outcomes and therefore control circumstances. In science, events are intelligible if they fit accepted physical laws. Likewise, events in everyday life are comprehensible if they fit accepted social laws. Because we know that the world operates according to certain physical laws, we similarly assume that nonphysical realities are also predictable. We believe that people and events should make just as much sense as the natural world.

The belief that the world must be predictable is based on the assumption that misfortune is not arbitrary and that events are mostly positive in outcome. Of course, we know of misery and oppression in the world, but we innately distinguish between the world in general and the world in which we live. The people and events that touch us constitute *our* world, and it is these people and events that shape our attitudes.

Our fundamental belief in order and predictability deals not only with why events happen in our world but, more specifically, why these events happen to particular people. We seek to understand the distribution of good and bad, and in the service of order and predictability, assume a cause-and-effect relationship between people and what they experience. The assumption is that we can directly control what happens to us through our own behaviors. Thus, we believe that if we behave in an appropriate, precautionary way, we will be protected from negative events. Similarly, if we engage in appropriate positive behavior, good things will happen. Because effort, exertion, practice, and planning generally affect outcomes that we can control, we often believe we can control chance outcomes as well.

This attitude leads us to believe that if we train our children right, they will not fall away from God; if we are good workers, we will not lose our jobs; and if we take care of our health, we will not get sick. Certainly such behaviors may decrease the likelihood of the negative outcomes, but they will not reduce the probability to zero. Good parents have rebellious children, good workers do get laid off, and generally healthy people can have heart attacks.

It is our embellished belief in control that contributes to our blaming victims for their tribulations. Research on trauma victims has shown that people naturally look for an explanation for negative events. In one study, two groups of people were given different scenarios of a woman leaving work and going home. In one scenario, the woman arrived home without incident. When the participants were asked if the woman did anything that posed a risk to her safety, they were unable to name anything. The second group read the same scenario, but this time the woman was attacked before entering her home. When these participants were asked the same question about the woman's cautiousness, they reported several things that she could have done or not done to prevent the assault. In order to protect the illusion that our world is predictable and thus controllable, we are strongly motivated to place blame. If we do not or cannot blame someone, suffering becomes more frightening because it's random and unpredictable and we have no hope of controlling life.

Ben, a man who prided himself on his work, had devised a strategy to succeed. As a child, Ben learned a strong work ethic from his parents. He worked his way through one of the best business schools in the country. Upon his graduation, he went to work for a large, successful company. For the next twenty years, Ben put in long hours. His prudent business mind helped to profit his company. *If I do the right thing, I will reap the right result*, he thought.

His belief about a predictable world was shattered, however, with one phone call from his boss. Later, he sat in my office, stunned by the fact that he had been laid off. It simply didn't make sense.

"I have done all the right things," Ben lamented, "How could they do this to me? *What did I do wrong?*" The truth was that the only thing Ben had done wrong was to believe that doing the right thing would always produce the right result—in this case, that he would be rewarded with long-term employment. Ben's belief set him up for great disillusionment.

Psychologists talk about the "illusion of invulnerability," which is our tendency to underestimate the likelihood of negative events and overestimate the likelihood of positive events. We take our own indestructibility for granted and assume the continuity of a safe existence. This naiveté makes the shock of suffering greater because our attitudes do not allow for the occurrence of adverse events in our lives. When a child dies, a large part of the parents' pain stems from the untimeliness of the loss. Parents naturally do not account for the fact that one of their children could die. Although Nathan Sours's close encounters with death revealed his physical fragility,

Dave and Teresa had been reassured when, during every close call, a miracle had occurred. That gave them the illusion that Nathan would always be okay. The unpredictability of an event shatters our illusion that we can control life. When that assumption is challenged, we feel helpless because we no longer know the right thing to do in order to control the outcome.

When our belief in an orderly and predictable world is crushed by a traumatic event, we often conclude that God cannot be trusted. Believing that the God who created perfect order is unreliable, we again attempt to control our own destinies in order to protect ourselves from life's tragedies. In our minds, or more accurately in our hearts, God is trustworthy only to the extent that things go in the way that we expect them.

I Deserve a Fair World

We have a belief that life is intrinsically fair and that consequently, people's decency, morality, and goodness essentially determine what happens to them. We perceive outcomes as either a reward or punishment.

This assumption—that the world must be fair and that we must be treated fairly—leads us to believe that people should get what they deserve and deserve what they get. This attitude enables us to minimize the role of randomness in our lives. If people get what they deserve, then suffering is the appropriate lot of those who are morally corrupt, but not right for decent people.

Think about the response to the verdict in the O. J. Simpson trial many years ago. Perhaps the words "It isn't fair" flowed from your lips or streamed through your mind. Many African Americans thought it was not fair that Simpson was charged with murdering his estranged wife and her friend. They argued that the courts were only seeking to convict a black man. Following the not guilty verdict, others said that it was not fair that a "guilty" man be deemed innocent and set free.

Because God is just, we have a sense of justice, which is appropriate when applied to the ways our judicial system operates, grades are earned, employees are paid, and pies are divided. The problem is not our sense of justice but instead our demand for mercy. Well-known researcher and social psychologist Melvin Lerner conducted a series of experiments on justice. In these studies, Dr. Lerner found that people want retribution when they have been wronged but mercy when they are the ones who have done something wrong.[11]

It's often through the lens of this self-centered notion of fairness that we view suffering and pain. Whether you have said it or not, consider this statement: "Good things should happen to good people and bad things should happen to bad people." Such a statement seems to have great merit. After all, that is the way things *should* be, but they are not.

At a conscious level, we know that our world is not fair and that we will be treated unfairly. Experience and Scripture both dispel the myth that this world is fair or even that it ought to be. The wise and wealthy Solomon bemoaned the emptiness in the world and acknowledged that bad things happen to good people and good things happen to bad people: "In this life, good people are often treated as though they were wicked, and wicked people are often treated as though they were good. This is so meaningless!"[12]

When we assume that our world is fair, our ability to tolerate and accept calamity is dramatically affected. We bristle when we experience unfairness, and we demand fair treatment. When we perceive injustice, we question whether God is truly just. Theologically, we may know that the notion of justice stems from God and that He is the epitome of fairness. Our doubts about God's justice are not rational but emotional.

The True Nature of Suffering

Modern Christianity has become quite comfortable with a theology of instant healing and recovery. We are quick to find passages to support these beliefs, but slow to consider that suffering can also be a tool of God.

At times, hindsight helps us see the good that results from our trials. But when we're tightly clenched in the grip of suffering, hearing that God has a purpose for our pain just adds salt to an already raw wound. The notion that suffering ultimately serves some better purpose seems cruel. Our painful feelings are too strong, making it nearly impossible to accept that idea in spite of what our theology might say. We would rather God simply leave us alone; we are content to forfeit the growth and blessings that might come out of our trials.

Valarie's childhood was devoid of most modern creature comforts.[13] Living in an economically depressed Arkansas county, Valarie's parents had little time to give individual attention to their seven children. Valarie was often left on her own or with a variety of relatives and acquaintances, some of whom sexually abused her. As often happens in such cases, Valarie carried these feelings and memories into adulthood, and in one way or another, almost every aspect of her adult life was overshadowed by them. She actually found purpose, meaning, and fulfillment in developing her role as a victim, and years of counseling helped her to firmly barricade herself within the safety of that position.

But Valarie was depressed, unhappy in her marriage, and ineffective as a parent. Though she expressed a desire to feel better, she seemed unable to move beyond her pain. As a victim of various forms of abuse, she was quick to discuss how unfair life had been to her. After much pressing, Valarie acknowledged that she believed God was unfair. If God was everywhere, how could He watch her be abused and do nothing? In her mind, God owed her. Asking Valarie to consider what God might want to accomplish through her suffering was simply adding insult to injury.

Valarie believed that God should deal fairly with people, particularly with her. She further expected God to always treat her graciously and kindly, as she understood these terms. Her belief that God must treat her well because she was a good person prevented her from seeing things any other way. According to Valarie, if God was operating at all, He was behaving in a way that didn't make sense to her. In fact, God had wronged her.

It is true that Valarie was abused and that her early years lacked nurturing, tenderness, and security. But these events had become the foundation upon which she built her life. In her unconscious commitment to protect her role as victim, she continued to sabotage the attempts of others to guide her to help and healing. Her friends saw her as someone to be cared for, a project rather than a person capable of a mutually supportive friendship.

In reality, being a victim relieved Valarie of accepting responsibility for her choices and actions. By maintaining this role she remained miserable and powerless to do anything else. Unfortunately, Valarie is not unique in her self-devotion. People seek counseling services because something is wrong in their lives that they want fixed. Often their spoken or unspoken goal is for their pain to go away. We all want to feel better, but some people are unwilling to do the difficult and uncomfortable work required to move beyond the pain.

Our inclination to pursue comfort by imposing order and fairness on a naturally random and unfair universe endorses our futile struggles to manipulate life to meet our selfish demands. Therefore, we tend to choose only black or white, right or wrong, good or bad.

Making Sense out of Nonsense

Most experts on attitude agree that the more that you know about a person, thing, or idea, the more stable your attitude will be. Likewise, the more strongly you feel about something, the more difficult it will be for someone to convince you to change your view.

Scientists speak about working within the confines of "accepted paradigms," which is nothing more than a framework or reliable theory. By way of paradigms, scientists theorize, test, and make modifications as necessary to their conceptualization of the problem. Unless some new discovery produces a mound of evidence that is so compelling that the old paradigm no longer holds true, scientists continue to incorporate new data into what they already know. This method is one reason that many scientists continue to use the evolution paradigm to explain the origin of the universe in the face of contrary evidence.

Our attitudes are built and reinforced by years of living. Originating in our earliest experiences, our views about the world, God, and ourselves are colored by the caregivers who attended to us, what they taught us, and how they lived before us.

Although our beliefs enable us to live each day, they go further in providing us with a feeling of relative invulnerability. When the great *Titanic* set sail on its fateful voyage, people believed that the ship was indestructible. Even when it became evident that the boat was sinking, the crew still failed to believe that it was vulnerable. This false illusion of invincibility set up the crew and passengers for tragic results. In like manner, our own illusions of security lead so many sufferers to say, "I can't believe this happened to me!" We know that bad things do happen, but in our guts we believe we are exempt.

Just as scientists process any new information through their accepted theories, we deal with new information by processing it through our own beliefs. Unless the evidence is so overwhelming that we cannot maintain our worldviews, we naturally resist changing what we believe.

Extreme crises profoundly challenge our worldviews and in fact shatter them: our typical framework for looking at the world and making sense of it cannot accommodate the event. The new puzzle piece doesn't fit neatly into our puzzle frame. Nothing seems to be as we once thought. Suddenly, presumed beliefs about others and ourselves are questionable at best or clearly mistaken. The comfort and complacency provided by our attitudes are seen as completely inadequate and painfully untrue. When we are no longer able to stretch our paradigms by distorting the new information so that it fits neatly into our views of life, we must entirely modify our theories of life to make sense of the trauma.

It's important to note that it is not wrong to have a mind-set that sees the world a particular way. All humans have a system to make sense of what they experience. The problem is that when we are confronted with a tragedy, the realization that our paradigms are not equipped to explain things disrupts our lives massively. Jarred out of our complacency, we face an additional problem. Not only have our worldviews been shattered, exposing how vulnerable we really are, but the disintegration of our presumptions has left us without a lens to navigate life.

The Questions of Suffering

As a toddler, my (John's) daughter, Katie, was very inquisitive. She asked questions about almost everything. All of Katie's questions began with the word "Why . . . ?" Unfortunately, the answers seldom satisfied her curiosity. Each answer led to another question. Eventually, we would end up on God's doorstep, saying, "Because God made it so!"

Within each of us is a desire for answers, a desire to understand this world and make sense of it. When we suffer, asking why is more a reflex than a conscious choice. The problem is that our questions often have no answers, at least no *apparent* answers.

"What did I do to deserve this?"

"How long will this pain continue?"

"Why didn't God stop this from happening to me?"

"Where do I go from here?"

"How can I make it through this?"

"What possible good can come from this mess?"

As natural as these questions are, they breed only deeper confusion. And yet we continue to ask. In fact, we often *demand* an explanation. But as we will see in the next chapter, God is not obligated to answer our questions. And even if God did provide answers, we probably would not accept them as justification. Confusion abounds when we are suffering. We require that God explain Himself in order to relieve our puzzlement.

As we've already seen, the questions that sufferers ask arise from the recognition that their circumstances do not readily fit their worldviews. They are shocked and bewildered when nothing seems to be as they thought. Suddenly, the beliefs they have taken for granted are unmasked as unreliable.

When confronted with our own fragility, we naturally pose questions. Such questions tend to fall into one of three categories, though sometimes we might pose all three at the same time.

Why me?

Because we are self-centered people, the worst kind of suffering is usually our own. It is one thing to learn about earthquakes, hurricanes, and tornadoes destroying the lives of other people. In fact, the more removed the tragedy is from us the easier it is to deal with. When our world is rocked, however, the pain is real and seems intolerable.

This reality was agonizingly shown to me (John) several years ago. At 5 a.m. on New Year's Eve 1997, a severe pain in my left side and back abruptly awakened me. I have never felt such intense, constant, and indescribable pain. My groans were so loud that dogs down the street started howling. My wife called the doctor, who suspected that my pain was caused by a kidney stone. He recommended that she either drive me to the emergency room or call for an ambulance. Believing I would get treated faster if taken to the hospital by ambulance, my wife called 911. After what seemed like an eternity, the paramedics arrived, took my vitals, and carted me off to the hospital. As I gasped for air and writhed in interminable pain, a nurse commented that this illness was a man's way of knowing how it feels to have a baby. After a two-and-a-half-hour wait, I was finally admitted to the hospital. The urologist believed that it would be best to retrieve my "baby" rather than wait for delivery. I wholeheartedly agreed.

My wife knew that I was bad off when I showed no interest in my annual tradition of watching football games. In addition, the timing of this illness meant that our special New Year's plans would be scrapped. While that was unfortunate, football and New Year's plans were of very little concern to my preoccupied mind. Suffering is like that. The things that once seemed so important to us have a way of becoming less significant in the light of pain, illness, or heartbreak.

Prior to my illness, I had known other people who had kidney stones. While I was sorry that they were not well, my day was not negatively affected by their news. The reality of my own pain, however, moved me from mildly concerned spectator to frontline warrior. Not only was my life interrupted, but I wondered why I had to go through it. Admittedly, I did develop a whole new empathy for people with kidney stones.

Why this?

As part of our bent for control, we contrive a world that assumes that while certain things may happen to us, others things will not. For example, we think that divorce is something that will never happen to us since we are so deeply committed to our marriages. In addition to our belief that marriage is sacred and divorce is not an option, we may regularly attend marriage retreats. Not only do enrichment activities help to prevent problems with our spouses from growing, they deepen our intimacy so that the risk of emotional distance, let alone divorce, becomes negligible.

We can possibly imagine that one of us might have an incapacitating illness or die, but divorce? Never! The former tragedies are things that none of us can control; therefore, it is easier to accept the possibility of their occurrences. Yet we all know of couples who seemed to share our beliefs and commitment to marriage but ended up divorced anyway. This reality is unsettling because we all want guarantees that our marriages will survive. We want to believe that divorce is within our ability to control and influence, but if the truth be known, the possibility exists for any marriage to go awry.

Divorce may or may not be included in your "why this?" category, but there are certainly many other possible events that could forcefully shock you. Whatever the random event might be, most, if not all of us, believe that certain things "could not happen to me."

Why now?

Not only do we misunderstand why certain things happen or why they happen to us, we also struggle with why things happen *when* they happen. A young woman from Utah was only a week away from her wedding. The excitement, as well as the stress, was at an all-time high. Both she and her fiancé were committed Christians, and they had decided to wait to enjoy physical intimacy until their wedding night. In the midst of making the final arrangements for the wedding, the bride-to-be started experiencing awful oral pain. Though she was terribly afraid of dentists, her family convinced her to go. Once there, she was told she needed to have a tooth pulled. The dentist and doctors are still not sure what happened, but during the tooth extraction, the young woman stopped breathing. They rushed her to the hospital, but she was pronounced dead upon arrival. Several days later, she was laid to rest in her wedding gown.

It seems unthinkable that God could allow someone to die at that time and in that way. We will never know why God allowed her to die, but in our finite minds God's timing appears misplaced. No matter how often the Bible speaks of God's goodness, faithfulness, generosity, and mercy, it will never be enough to quench our tendency to question them.

Because we believe that things ought to be one way and we never expect them to be different, we react adversely to crises. Such thinking fails to acknowledge what God's Word says about suffering. Too many Christians have beliefs that are not aligned with scriptural truth. It takes a traumatic experience to expose our actual attitudes. When our true beliefs are brought to the surface through calamity we can either strive to align them with Scripture or fight to maintain our view of life. As we will see throughout this book, God's Word helps us make sense of nonsense. If you can make sense of adversity—the emotional pain, the fear, the mental chaos, the faultfinding, the despair—you will move through the suffering without doubting your own sanity or ability to recover.

Suffering often operates according to certain principles, which we'll examine in the next chapter. When these principles are truly understood, they can dramatically influence our attitudes at the emotional level so that future hardships are perceived differently.

CHAPTER THREE

Suffering and the Hand of God

There is no human character more familiar with suffering than Job. Just the mention of his name invokes feelings of pity and incredible disbelief at all he endured. It boggles our minds that God could allow a godly man like Job to experience such dreadful pain.

The book of Job has never been a favorite of Christians. Many avoid the book because it seems so depressing. And frankly, we all probably believe that if such inexplicable things could happen to Job, we are just as vulnerable as he was.

It's Just a Bad Day!

Job, a devout follower of God, was wealthy beyond imagination. When the Bible introduces him, it starts with a description of his character. More important than his wealth, background, and credentials is the fact that he was a blameless and upright man, one who feared God and shunned evil.[1] Indeed, Job was so godly that he made ceremonial sacrifices for his children just in case they had sinned and failed to make their own sacrifices. The point of the Scriptures is simple: Job was a godly man.

With the quality of Job's character established, the stage is now set for what is the focus of the story. God peels away the curtain of heaven so that we can witness the celestial drama that is unfolding upon a heavenly stage. The story line is so incredible that it sounds like fiction. But this is no made-up story. It's an actual account of a conversation between two opponents, God and Satan. As their dialogue progresses, God brings up the person of Job in the manner befitting a proud parent. God is pleased with Job and wants to get Satan's take on his life. Satan, however, is not very impressed. He accuses God of apple-polishing Job. In fact, Satan basically accuses God of being naive. According to Satan's logic, the only reason that Job is righteous in character is because he has been so blessed. Satan doubts that anyone would continue to follow God when it is no longer in his or her best interest. But God knows better. So, in what seems to take on the feel of a bet, God turns Job over to Satan for testing.[2]

We can only imagine the devilish grin upon Satan's face as he leaves God to go on his mission of destruction. As a result of this uncanny encounter, Job loses his children, property, and wealth. And before he can find words for one tragedy, another servant arrives to inform him of an additional loss. In one short day, Job's life is literally turned upside down. But Job's faithfulness to God is never in question as he worships amidst his suffering and attributes no wrongdoing to God.

Subsequently, Satan returns to heaven and once again is given permission to bring suffering upon Job. Satan believes that Job has not lost enough of his comfort to turn from his faith in God. So this time, Satan robs Job of good health.[3]

Why? Why did God allow Job to endure such horrible misery simply to prove his faithfulness to the heavenly Father? My earthly father usually gave me the benefit of the doubt. Unless I misused it, I could use the car. However, that isn't what happened in Job's case. He had misused nothing. He was a righteous man, a good man. He was probably chairman of the deacons in his church, a Sunday school teacher, an active PTA member. He was clearly a man of integrity who loved his wife and children—yet Job's reward for living such an impeccable life was horrible suffering.

How does Job respond to this dreadful turn of fortune in his life? Even Job's wife tells him to curse God and die. But Job does not let his painful circumstances control him. He tells his wife that she is speaking foolishly. (Men, perhaps you should think twice before you quote that verse to your wives!) This time Job doesn't worship; he simply doesn't sin in his response. He tells her that if we take good from God's hand, we should also be willing to accept the bad. Only later does he begin to question God, and even then, he does so honorably and is vindicated in the end.

Compared to Job, very few of us measure up. During adversity and affliction, we rarely respond with a spirit of worship. Job's behavior makes it clear that, in spite of his circumstances, he regarded God as worthy of worship. Job also proved that he would accept both good and bad from the hand of God with an attitude of thanksgiving. And most importantly, Job continued to have blameless lips even when it no longer served his interest to be so faithful.

About fifteen years ago, I (John) developed a strong interest in tennis. In addition to learning how to play, I started watching tennis on television and quickly became a fan of Michael Chang, a formerly top-ranked player. His style was intriguing: he simply never gave up. Every point was given the same level of concentration and effort. Later, I discovered that Michael is a devout Christian. After each game, win or lose, Michael could be seen in his seat with his head bowed, praying. In postgame interviews, Michael typically made mention of God's will. No matter how he fared in his match, the results were left up to God, and his heart was set on worship.

Naturally, losing a tennis match pales in comparison to all that Job lost in one day, but the attitude displayed by both is similar. Michael, like Job, was willing to take good and bad from God's hand. I am sure that while he would have liked to be ranked number one as much as any competitor, his true preoccupation had always been God's purpose.

It is easy to receive blessings from God with a heart of thankfulness. It is another thing altogether to be grateful for affliction from God's hand. For us to accomplish this seemingly unnatural feat, we must have a belief system that accepts both blessings and calamities from the hand of God.

A Theology of Suffering

Many Christians have read the Bible and fashioned a personal theology that covers a collection of topics, including Creation, salvation, the person of Jesus Christ, and many more. While we believe that the Bible is without error, our theology is not inerrant. Our theology is a human attempt to bring clarity to topics or texts that are found in Scripture. It is our theoretical understanding, hopefully based upon a careful scrutiny and study of God's Word. Thus, when thinking about a theology of suffering, the main question is whether or not we have one that is as biblically accurate and coherent as possible. We must methodologically cull out the truths that are scattered throughout the pages of Scripture and form them into an encompassing truth.

Throughout the rest of this chapter, we will examine nine precepts of suffering. These precepts form the underlying truths that help make sense of suffering. We think they are biblically bound governing principles that give us a theology of suffering.

Precept #1: Everyone will suffer

God created man and woman with the capacity to transgress against their Creator. Hence, God programmed into His creation the possibility of suffering. Eventually, a world born by God's commanding word defied Him, and consequently creation lost its perfect destiny and no longer operates by God's perfect design.

After the Fall, the world changed its state of being. Relationships were dramatically altered; humankind's personality and physical life were corrupted. For Adam, the soil no longer yielded easily to cultivation. Now, he experienced futility in his labor. Eve experienced relational pain, both in her desire toward her husband and in giving birth.

Man's sin enslaved the earth. A creation that the sovereign God had declared good no less than seven times was now corrupted. The resulting fallenness would be one of the active forces in His new world.

But such suffering was not new. Prior to the Fall, Satan and his angels suffered the consequences of their rebellion. To strike back at God, Satan then plotted to destroy God's plan by prompting humanity to question and defy their Creator. The evil one devised a scheme to pass suffering onto the apple of God's eye—humanity.

The insightful words of C. S. Lewis cut to the heart of our post-Fall situation: "There is no neutral ground in the universe: every square inch, every split second, is claimed by God and counterclaimed by Satan."[4] As such, there is both good and evil in the world. God created all things good, but evil has disfigured what God created.

Since the first sin, fear and alienation have plagued us. Sadly, the resulting curse has affected everyone, the godly and ungodly alike. No one is exempt from pain; it is the common denominator for all of us. As members of the human race, we all experience suffering.

It is amazing how many good Christians have a worldly view of Christianity. We have allowed secular ideas to influence our theology. Some assume that God will reward good with good and bad with bad. Other Christians hold that being a Christian includes a life protection policy. This assumption was the thinking of Hannah, a woman I (John) counseled several years ago. Born of Jewish parents, Hannah experienced a great deal of rejection when she converted to Christianity. In spite of her family's reaction, however, she became a student of the Bible. Her devotion to Christ inspired her to excel in every aspect of her life.

Over time, however, her dedication to the things of God changed. Advancing in her career, raising two children, and maintaining a healthy marriage were more important to her life than serving Christ. Although God was still in her view of life, He was in her peripheral vision. Other pursuits consumed her time and interest. Her life revolved around the things of this world rather than the things of the Spirit. You probably would not fault her efforts. She was highly regarded in her profession and had two well-behaved, socially conscious children and a successful husband. Life was good. The blessings of God seemed evident in her life and family.

Unfortunately, her life would not remain so pleasant. Hannah's world collapsed when her husband of twenty years asked for a divorce. Soon, she was struggling to maintain a professional image, meet the demands of being a single parent, and put up a positive Christian front. Throughout the counseling process, I was unable to get Hannah to move beyond the question of why God would allow this suffering to happen to her. She was a good person—well respected, sincere, and diligent in her responsibilities. She thought the fact that she forsook her heritage and family's acceptance to become a Christian should have been enough to protect her from suffering. God owed her. Now, bitterness characterized her attitude. Since her beliefs about God were inconsistent with experiencing such pain, she abandoned her belief in God altogether. Sadly, she quit counseling, even more bitter than when she began.

The belief that a Christian will not or should not suffer is inconsistent with biblical teaching. As we've already seen, God allowed Job to experience seemingly unjustified misery. In the same way, many prophets and apostles were subjected to emotional and physical abuse, even death. And Jesus Himself, our Suffering Servant, endured substantial mistreatment. For the Christian, suffering is not an unusual experience; *everyone suffers*.

Precept #2: All suffering has meaning

Suffering is not accidental. Nor is it incidental. Suffering is not the result of randomness or chaos. It is allowed by God because suffering is purposeful. Thus, our responses to it are very important.

Personal trainers and athletic coaches are fond of asserting "No pain, no gain!" when you don't think you can lift another barbell or run another mile. In other words, there is no way to develop muscles without experiencing pain. We don't enjoy or take pleasure in the pain, but we do appreciate the results of the painful process. The same is true of suffering. It exercises our mental, emotional, spiritual, and theological muscles. In this vein, all suffering can make sense. Yet most of our struggles are due in part to our inability to make sense of difficult situations, trials, or adversities. That is, the real anguish of suffering is due to its perceived meaninglessness.

In the last chapter, we examined the "whys" of life. In our perceptions of the grand scheme of things, some experiences simply do not make sense. The famed Jewish physician Viktor Frankl was a prisoner in Auschwitz for two years during World War II. He spent most of his time in slave labor and near starvation. His parents, his brother, and his wife either died in the camps or were sent to the gas ovens. Except for his sister, his entire family perished. Frankl

himself suffered torture and innumerable indignities, never knowing from one moment to the next if his path would lead to the
ovens or if he would be among those spared to remove the bodies
or shovel out the ashes of others.

On top of that, Frankl was a physician who was repeatedly
called on to assist other suffering prisoners, thereby increasing the
level of his own pain. It is reported that Frankl asked his suffering
patients, "Why do you not commit suicide?" From their answers,
he found threads upon which to weave a pattern of meaning. In
his book *Man's Search for Meaning: An Introduction to Logotherapy*,
he describes how suffering and meaning go together. Although
Frankl believed that meaning could be found apart from Christ,
he accurately and perceptively wrote, "If there is a meaning in life
at all, then there must be a meaning in suffering. Suffering is an
ineradicable part of life, even as fate and death. Without suffering
and death human life cannot be complete."[5]

Corrie ten Boom also understood the value of suffering. From
the lice-infected bed of a concentration camp, Corrie penned, "We
are in God's training school and learning much."[6] Solomon, who
knew great pleasure, also learned that suffering is even better than
comfort. Whereas suffering instructs, pleasure and comfort teach us
little. We naturally prefer lavish comfort to deprivation and suffering, but in the long run, indulgence leaves us empty. [7]

Just imagine the pain of people like Viktor Frankl and Corrie
ten Boom, who suffered incredibly, time after time, in ways that
only their fellow prisoners of war could even begin to comprehend.
But their clear testimony is that meaning in life comes through
suffering—even of the most intense kinds. Moreover, they realized
that our lives are incomplete unless they include adversity!

Some things that happen to us are fairly easy to explain. We
can have a good sense of what God is doing or wants to do. Most
situations, however, are less clear. One of the major problems many
people, even Christians, have with Job's story is that the suffering he
had to endure seems so meaningless. His trials do not make sense.

Suffering is somehow easier to endure when we can make sense
of it—when we can make all the pieces fit neatly together. In fact,

many people are willing to face suffering if they can find meaning. For example, in order to obtain a desired outcome, athletes and pregnant women volunteer to suffer. During her second pregnancy, my (John's) wife was confined to bed for over four months. Though some of our friends envied Denise for being able to take it easy, the constant bed rest was hard on the entire family. In fact, Denise found it particularly difficult to survive those four months of total inactivity. She saw all the things that needed to be done but couldn't help. Her ability to play with and care for our three-year-old, Katie, was limited, which pained her greatly. Church was out, along with dates with her loving and humble husband! What might sound like a blessing to many overcommitted people was really an ordeal for my wife.

We knew that she was going to have a boy. The confinement had purpose: to protect the life and health of the baby growing within. Though some things were outside of her control, this one thing, this stillness, was something she could do to bring order to a frightening time. As she visualized the birth of our first son, Stephen, she found purpose and meaning in her pain—enough to carry her through the four months of confinement.

Following the birth of his second son, a psychologist confided to me (John) that he thought his wife had lost her mind. During both pregnancies, she had been hospitalized, almost died, and suffered long, arduous labors. After bringing their second miracle baby home, his wife told him that she wanted another child. Even with all his psychological training, my friend was dumbfounded that his wife was willing to once again subject herself to illness and possibly death.

Because God has a unique plan and purpose for each individual, no suffering is meaningless. To God, there are no puzzles with mismatched pieces. Suffering is one of the tools God uses to redirect our attention to what is really important because it mocks what we believe is important. We groan when we lose things such as comfort, order, and fairness—things we most depend upon. In struggling to understand our plight, we often demand that God explain Himself to us. We want God to make the pieces fit and then justify

Himself for making life miserable. If for no other reason, God uses suffering to get our attention. As C. S. Lewis noted, suffering is God's "megaphone to rouse a deaf world."[8]

God used the German concentration camps to shout into the lives of Frankl and Ten Boom. Later, God roused Lewis through the death of his wife. These great writers were veteran sufferers. And if Frankl is right, nothing else will make us grow. Perhaps Christians can even learn and grow simply by hearing about the pain borne by others. In this way, their pain can work to inoculate us, even as a flu shot prevents or lessens our suffering. Is it possible that pain can even increase the quality of our lives?

When we begin to understand that every painful ordeal has meaning and purpose, we can begin to see suffering for the precious jewel that it is.

Precept #3: Suffering comes from multiple sources

As you search the Bible to determine the answer to the question, "What causes suffering?" you may walk away with mixed answers. In the Old Testament, suffering resulted primarily from Israel's rebellion, though calamity sometimes had other causes. In the New Testament, people seemed to suffer more for their faith than for any other reason.

As we will see in section 2, God seeks to accomplish different purposes through suffering. Some are tied directly to the reasons that we suffer. Sometimes it is important to understand what might be causing you to suffer in order to know how you need to respond.

First, we encounter suffering because we live in a broken and fallen world. Philosophers refer to this as pain and suffering due to natural law. Because this world is not what God designed it to be, we will experience disease, disorder, disillusionment, and despair. A broken and fallen world produces disasters such as earthquakes, tornadoes, hurricanes, and other catastrophes. Sometimes these incidents are referred to as "acts of nature" or "acts of God." However, whether such incidents are sent by God to judge us, are the enduring consequences of Noah's flood, or are simply the result of a fallen world, the devastation they produce is much the same.

A broken and fallen world will not allow for exact justice or fairness. You cannot extract logic from an imperfect world. Following the fall of Adam and Eve, this fact was predicted in the Garden. God placed curses on everything, including the earth.[9] Solomon despaired that we live in a world that is broken and cannot be fixed.[10] The apostle Paul also acknowledged that all of creation has been groaning like a woman giving birth as it awaits the day when it will be redeemed.[11] All sorrow and sickness result from the Fall. Everyone will suffer.

Second, we encounter suffering because of supernatural causes. Job's suffering was the result of Satan's intervention. Both Satan and his demons can create great discomfort in the human life. The Bible clearly attributes some instances of muteness, blindness, epilepsy, insanity, and deafness to the work of Satan.[12] For instance, Luke presents the story of a woman who was ill for eighteen years. After healing her, Jesus states that Satan caused the woman's pain.[13] Because we are the image bearers of God, Satan seeks to destroy us by hurting, aggravating, and deceiving us. While Satan is certainly not the cause of every incidence of suffering, he does play more of a role than most of us are willing to admit.

During the Last Supper, Jesus shared some final words with His most intimate friends, the disciples. In His prayer to the Father, Christ asked that His people be protected from the evil one.[14] The word *evil* here can refer to an evil person or an evil thing. Jesus was not under the illusion that everyone would love those who love Him and follow His truth.

Although Satan's accusations may have led in some sense to Job's suffering, God allowed and permitted it. In fact, Scripture tells us that Satan sought permission from God to stretch out his hand against Job. God can allow suffering to come into our lives.[15] That is sometimes difficult to accept! The basic truth is that God permits and allows His children to suffer. Non-Christians, as well as many Christians, find it unthinkable that a loving God could permit—let alone cause—one of His children to experience pain. One psychologist, following the death of his spouse, said, "I've been a good Christian and have done what I can to serve God. Doesn't that amount to anything? I could never allow one of my children to be hurt; how can God watch me suffer and do nothing about it?" When we feel out of control, when life has treated us unfairly, we view God through a lens of victimization. The pillars that support our faith are shaken, splintered, and smashed. Ironically, the very weapon God has given us to persevere through suffering—faith—falls apart when we need it the most. No matter how we feel, the truth is that our supernatural God permits suffering. But that does not mean He is inattentive, indifferent, or callous about us. While the idea that God allows our troubles may make it seem that He is heartless, in reality it shows just how much He treasures us. God is not unfeeling about our human misery. On the contrary, He is actively present with us in it. The truth of the matter is that when we face tragedy, God knows that we hurt and cares that we hurt.

A second truth is found in Job's suffering. While God does allow and permit us to suffer, He places limitations. Essentially, God told Satan that He would allow Job to be tested and tried, but Satan had to refrain from taking his life. God never tempts us beyond what we are able to bear. He places limitations on the extent and severity of testing and, subsequently, protects us.[16]

Third, we encounter suffering because of other people's choices. Suffering may result from the choices and behavior of both Christians and non-Christians. In other words, sometimes we experience personal suffering through no fault of our own. In fact, the original poor choice of Adam and Eve has dramatically affected all of humanity. Later, Abel was murdered by Cain, Joseph was exiled because of his brothers' jealous rage, and Paul was tortured.[17] The cruelty these men suffered was not due to their own poor choices but the sinful choices of others.

We may be hurt either intentionally or unintentionally by other people. For most of us, the intentional wound is the worst. We simply believe that we do not deserve to be treated so poorly. But, whether harm is intended or not, the result is the same—pain. It doesn't matter whether a driver intentionally or unintentionally runs over you; broken bones are likely in either case. (Attorneys may see this metaphor differently.)

Sometimes you may be persecuted because of your desire to follow God. Paul remarked that people who desire to be godly *will* be persecuted.[18] Before his conversion, Paul was known as Saul, and he was a zealous persecutor of the church, making the lives of our early brothers and sisters miserable. Following his conversion, he became the target of others who sought to persecute the church. The role of unbelievers in the suffering of God's people can be seen from early in the Old Testament and throughout the history of mankind.

While Paul spoke of being a victim of religious persecution, there are other ways to be victimized. For example, criminals terrorize some people. Other people suffer from living with a raging alcoholic. Some children feel the pain of growing up in a single-parent home. We need only to recall the events of Hurricane Katrina, September 11, the Oklahoma City bombing, or the shootings at Columbine High School to see this truth. Consider the brutal acts of Ted Bundy and the faces of missing children on milk cartons to appreciate how extensively victimization occurs.

Our two families have been robbed more than once. My (John's) family was first robbed when we were in Florida during our first year of marriage. Though we did not have many possessions, the violation wreaked havoc in our lives. My (Gary's) experience happened in the driveway when our car was broken into and several valuables were stolen. In both cases, we experienced the feelings of any victim—fear, anger, grief, and confusion. Fortunately, neither of us allowed those acts to control us.

Perhaps more difficult to deal with is being hurt by other Christians. In particular, the pain is intensified when it's intentional. I (John) once had dinner with a minister who had experienced incredible mistreatment by his congregation. Certain members of the elder body had sought to remove the pastor by making life miserable for him and his family. In two years' time, this group of church leaders successfully ripped the passion from this man's heart and destroyed his children's faith. His wife plunged into a black hole of despair. She was hospitalized on three occasions for attempted suicide. When visiting the home of parishioners, he was told, "Go away, Pastor, you are not welcome here!" After years of continued abuse, this pastor and his family left the church.

Christ said the world will know that we are Christians by our love.[19] Sadly, we too often send a contrary message. One unbeliever rephrased Christ's comment, "You will know they are Christians by the way they fight and the way they hate." It is grievous that, in this person's mind at least, our legacy is no longer sacrificial love but unrelenting hate.

Even though pain and suffering are sometimes attributed to the sinful actions or choices of others, it is always God's intent to use them for our benefit.

Fourth, we encounter suffering because of the choices that we make. The vast majority of suffering that people experience is brought upon themselves. With this assertion, we are not "blaming the victim." Rather, years of experience in counseling and interacting with people in the church and community have taught us that we are our own worst enemies.

But accepting responsibility for pain is not easy. Flip Wilson, the 1970s television star, was known for saying, "The devil made me do it!" Even as we face the consequences of our own actions, all too often we point our finger at Satan, others, and even God, blaming Him for our pain. It is human nature not to take responsibility for our actions. But the truth is, the choice to defy God's will, defy common sense, or defy God's calling will inevitably lead to suffering.

Suffering due to defying God's will. In the Old Testament, God often described the sins of people like Jonah before pronouncing judgment on the Israelites. If the prophet had not disobeyed God's will, he would never have been swallowed by a fish.

Less dramatic is the story of Abraham, who chose not to believe God's promise that Sarah would give birth to his son and conspired to father a child his own way. Abraham slept with Sarah's servant, Hagar—a handmaiden from Egypt. Hagar gave birth to Ishmael. When the angel of the Lord visited Abraham years later, he reminded him that he and Sarah would have the promised son. Abraham begged for Ishmael to be that son. Like most fathers, he deeply loved his child. God had promised that Abraham's seed would be as innumerable as the sand and that the Messiah would be his descendant. Abraham desired this blessing for Ishmael. But it was not to be. Because of the choices that he made to defy God's will, Abraham had to experience the agony of losing a son when his wife demanded that Hagar and Ishmael be sent away.

Many people have felt the cold chill of reaping the consequences of their actions. For example, God's will is for sex to remain within the safety of a marital relationship. But when unfaithful marriage partners defy that original plan, they risk painful consequences: AIDS or sexually transmitted disease, broken families, damaged reputations. All of these circumstances are vivid reminders that we reap what we sow.[20]

Though most of us consider ourselves to be "good," our dark undersides are innately sinful. The theological centrality of our need for redemption because of our sinful nature runs through the Bible. Rather than humbly acknowledging our sins, however, we attribute many of our sinful choices to others.

When we allow the flesh to govern us rather than following the will of God, we make sinful choices. Since the fall of Adam and Eve, our nature has been self-centered and self-serving. Let's face it, we are obsessed with ourselves. Our preoccupation is totally inward. Although Paul's instruction tells us that believers are dead to the old nature,[21] those corpses have a way of repeatedly resurrecting themselves. Suffering is often the self-inflicted wound of disobeying God.

Suffering due to defying common sense. Suffering occurs not only because of the sinful choices we make, it also occurs because of choices that interfere with the laws of nature. If we get too close to a cliff and fall off, our choice interacts with the laws of gravity and we experience a broken bone or worse.

I (John) enjoy playing church softball. While I am not a great athlete, I do fairly well for a man in his forties. Unfortunately, I have a history of getting hurt in almost every game. The pain and suffering are not because playing softball is sinful. Rather, they stem from my foolish belief that I can still play safely.

Choices that result in suffering may or may not be senseless. In other words, we may or may not deserve the consequence or their severity. But either way, we must choose how we will respond.

Suffering due to obeying God's calling. Jesus experienced death, the ultimate in suffering, in order to do His Father's will. Christ did not want to taste the cup of death, but He chose to follow God's will even though He knew it would require suffering. There is a distinct difference between choosing suffering and choosing to follow God's calling, which may result in hardship. The former is a self-focused sign of masochism. The latter is a Spirit-focused sign of maturity.

Many American Christians typically view "suffering for Christ's sake" as a rejecting look, a lost relationship, a poor grade, or a legal dictate to remove a Christian symbol from public displays. While such things are hurtful and often unjust, they pale in comparison to the horrors other Christians have endured. Our American response to suffering is so self-focused: *How can you do this to me?* Too often, we lack the mature spiritual willingness to understand that God is truly involved in every aspect of our lives—even suffering. Because we view religious persecution as personal, we are not able to see that the evil one is really targeting Christ, not us.

While on a mission to persecute Christians, Saul experienced a supernatural encounter with the risen Jesus. Blinded by a brilliant light, he was asked a question that would drastically change the direction and course of his life: "Why are you persecuting Me?"[22] Saul realized that he was not only assaulting Christians but the Godhead as well. When God's children are abused, it is ultimately a slap in the face of Jesus.

Think of our brothers and sisters in countries such as Sudan. Because of their faith in Christ, these fellow believers are experiencing inhumane and brutal treatment. Many have been tortured, murdered, molested, jailed, sold into slavery, kidnapped, or raped. Their only crime, like that of the early apostles, is proclaiming the name of Christ.[23] As Oswald Chambers wrote, "God's way is always the way of suffering, the way of the 'long, long trail.'"[24]

Precept #4: There is no all-inclusive answer about suffering

There are no pat answers when it comes to pain and suffering. You can search the pages of Scripture, and you will not find one verse that completely and fully explains God's purpose for suffering. But we are people who want answers; in fact, we want easy answers. Some Christians attempt to explain suffering by attributing it to sin, lack of faith, or some other cause. They offer quick solutions, a microwave theology. "Just trust God," we are told. Oh, if it were only that simple! The beginning of understanding suffering is the acceptance that we will not always understand it. Theologians have spent untold hours studying the Bible's teaching about suffering. While no one particular verse completely explains why God allows suffering, the Bible does offer some insight.

Job knew enough about God to trust Him in those things he didn't know. And like Job, we must learn to cope with pain and decide to accept as sufficient the things that God has revealed to us, even when we don't have all the answers. God's will is that we respond to His work so that He can accomplish His plan in our lives and the lives of those around us.

Precept #5: God is not obligated to give us a reason

As I (John) have already mentioned, when I was in college, I experienced the loss of a significant relationship in my life. This loss produced great heartache that lingered for a long time. From the moment that it occurred, however, I knew exactly why God had allowed it to happen. As I reflect on that experience, I believe now, as then, that God was redirecting me back to Himself. Now, rather than feeling the loss, I feel a deep sense of gratitude that God intervened in my life. At times like that, it's fairly easy to see what God is doing in our lives through a difficulty or tragedy.

Other times, however, it may take years to understand what God was trying to accomplish through a past difficulty. Walt and Lynn Wilson were a typical young married couple with two small children. Walt was a rehabilitation counselor, and Lynn was a dental assistant. Both had grown up in church, but over time they drifted away from the Lord. "I was playing church, one foot in the world and one in the church," he said. After nine years of marriage, the bottom fell out. "We were shipwrecked with no hope of reconciliation." Despair prompted Walt to return to the church. Eventually, God began to work a slow but miraculous healing of their marriage. Through the support of the church and the help of a counselor, Lynn and Walt began to rebuild their relationship. In time, they became involved in leading a support group for divorced and separated people and conducting marital enrichment programs throughout the state. Twenty years later, after taking early retirement, Walt was called to serve as the family minister in the same church that brought healing to their marriage.

It took Walt about two decades to understand God's purpose for his suffering. "It was the hardest thing I ever went through, but if it took this terrible problem to turn me toward a serious and committed life to Christ, it was worth it. It changed my family, marriage, and life for the better!" Walt says today.

Sometimes we may never know why God allowed suffering in our lives. It may not be until we are in heaven that we learn from Christ Himself what He was doing through our ordeals.

The humbling reality is that God is not obligated to give us a reason. Biblical writers realized this truth. Solomon, the wisest man who ever lived, knew that his brilliance was not sufficient to comprehend God's ways.[25] The prophet Isaiah and the apostle Paul both remind us that we cannot tell God anything.[26]

Recently, as I (John) prepared to take my garbage to the curb, I found a host of maggots inching their way around some food scraps on the garage floor. As I stared in disgust, I thought of how we must look to God. While I (or Gary for that matter) am no expert on maggots, I suspect that there are some maggots smarter than others. Yet none have the intelligence, point of view, or experience of humans.

God's ways and thoughts do not compare to ours. We think that we are wise, but compared to the eternal God, we have no wisdom. Trying to understand God from our vantage point is impossible— finite beings can never understand an infinite Creator. Just like those maggots, we simply don't have a large enough frame of reference from which to make sense of our lives.

Here, however, is where the illustration breaks down. Whereas my plan for the maggots involved insect spray, God's plan is the exact opposite. He wants to grant us incredible love, grace, and mercy.

Precept #6: God knows our pain and is with us when we suffer

The First World War, which produced 40 million casualties, horrified people around the globe. Many soldiers died slow and agonizing deaths due to mustard gas and other poison gases, which hadn't been used in modern warfare before. The novelist H. G. Wells was angered by the carnage and wrote, "If I thought there was an omnipotent God who looked down on battles and deaths and all the waste and horror of this war—able to prevent these things— doing them to amuse Himself—I would spit in His empty face."[27] Because rewards and punishments, in the guise of happiness and discomfort, appear to be haphazardly distributed, many of us question either the goodness or the power of God.

Few of us would question God as H. G. Wells did in his novel. Yet if we were truly honest with ourselves, part of our confusion lies in not understanding what God's role is in our suffering. We simply do not understand how an all-powerful God could sit by and let us hurt. If God truly loved us, we believe He would protect us from problems, at least catastrophic ones.

Remember the old song that begins, "Nobody knows the trouble I've seen . . ."? During times of suffering, we typically believe that to be true. Nobody can possibly understand what we are going through; nobody can sense how hard we are struggling to stay afloat; nobody can fathom the depth of our fear and confusion. Nobody, not even God, can understand how badly we hurt. *If He did*, we reason, *He would do something about it.*

Fortunately, that song does not end on the word *seen*: "Nobody knows the trouble I've seen . . . nobody knows but Jesus." Jesus, God's only Son, knows the extent of our suffering. The shortest verse in the Bible, "Jesus wept," conveys the truth that God sheds tears.[28] Think about it: what is more incredible, a God who created everything or a God who weeps? He is not only aware of our suffering, He feels it. God is our fellow sufferer. Through His Son, Jesus Christ, He experienced suffering. No suffering has ever come to us that has not first passed through the heart and hand of God.

For most Christians, the fact that God is both present with us and knows our hurts provides at least some sense of comfort and assurance. But not everyone shares that belief. As a new counselor, I (John) met with a godly Christian woman who had been severely sexually abused as a child. As we examined her tormenting experiences, I commented that Christ did not leave her alone. He was with her the entire time. The lady's eyes became intense and her face stern as she remarked, "Then why didn't He stop it? Where was He when I was being abused?" As I sat speechless, I realized that I had exposed her anger toward God, but I had also cast God as the abuser. For her, knowing that God was present during her trials offered no solace. Instead, it confirmed her suspicion that God stood by and watched as she was abused. Clearly, He was indifferent to her suffering. My novice skills had created such a mess that I did not know what to do next. Unsure of how to respond, I asked God to help me know what to say next. I believe He gave me these words: "He was in the same place that He was when they crucified His Son."

In time, this woman understood that God does not intervene in every appalling thing that we do to each other. In fact, His willingness to allow us to make harmful and wrong choices is not evidence of His indifference but instead an example of His long-suffering and grace. Once she dealt with her feelings of betrayal and abandonment, this woman soon found that God's presence could calm her inner turmoil and heal her wounds.

While He doesn't always intervene, we do see God intervening throughout history in the lives of people at different times and in different ways. In the Old Testament God appeared to be actively involved. Whether in the drama of Noah's ark, Abraham and Lot's journeys, the bondage of Israel, the fight to gain the Promised Land, or the judgment of Israel, God took an active and direct role.

However, in the New Testament God made a transition. Although He was very involved in the lives of Mary and Joseph, the life of His Son Jesus, and in the development of the early church, He seems less involved than before. By the time of the Epistles, there is less mention of God directly intervening in people's lives as He did in the Old Testament. Just as in the Old Testament, suffering arrived via various avenues, but God's role in the New Testament was definitely different. When the time arrived for God to send a messenger to tell the people that He is actively involved, He punctuated His message with a baby.[29] That little Child was God's promise to move into the darkness of His children's lives and light an entirely darkened world. God had a purpose and would achieve it through an eternally designed plan.

Although the children of Israel thought that God had forgotten them, God reassured Moses that He knew His people were suffering.[30] And in the same way, God knows our plights and predicaments. He not only knows what is happening in our lives, God also understands our pain. According to the psalmist, He even counts our tears.[31]

Because He experienced what suffering is through Jesus, God knows the extent of suffering.[32] Through Jesus Christ, God took on the same body as ours, fully identifying with humanity. He saw and felt what the world was like through our eyes. In becoming like us, He felt rejection and incredible suffering. The prophet Isaiah, foretelling the agony of Christ, spoke of the sorrow that Christ would experience.[33] Jesus Christ knew suffering, temptation, and infirmities; He did not fit into the mold of this world.[34] At the end of His life, He endured incredible pain from the beatings and crucifixion. It was through Calvary that God succumbed to pain. Think about it—if God is responsible for suffering, He was at least willing to take His own medicine. Many religions have gods, but only one has a God who cared enough to become a man and to die.

Precept #7: God is always at work
Imagine how it would have been to live during the four hundred years between the Old and New Testaments when God was silent.

How lonely the children of Israel must have been during those dark days. Their lives were governed by a foreign power, both politically and religiously. What was God up to during those years? Why had He stopped speaking to them as He had done previously?

Our experiences seem to parallel that of Israel's. At times, it seems as if God is silent. Because of our limited understanding, we think that He has become distracted. Or maybe He has too many irons in the fire to really watch over us. It is during these times that the pain of suffering seems greatest. God's presence during suffering is like a backstage worker in a drama—active, involved, and working to fulfill the ultimate thrust of the play, although usually hidden from the audience's view. But He is just as involved as ever.

Perhaps you feel as if God is silent. Be assured, He is up to something; He is faithful to His Word. He has a specific plan for you and a timetable to accomplish His great work in your life.

Precept #8: God can redeem suffering

I have always found it intriguing that in the book of Job, God responded to Job's declaration of his own righteousness by pointing Job back to Creation and to the very character of God Himself.[35] The Creator asks Job, "Where were you . . . ?" The Lord declares that He created and sustains the universe. No one can duplicate God's acts of splendor, wisdom, and power. The all-powerful, all-knowing, and eternal God stands against the meager, ignorant, and mortal man, Job. Just as Job was unable to contend with God, we are incapable of doing so as well.

Nevertheless, God is still the Creator and Redeemer. There is no random event in God's world. God's original plan has been marred by sin, but all is not lost. Evangelist Ron Dunn has said that we gained more in the Cross than we lost in the Fall.[36] Suffering, along with all evil, was completely defeated at Calvary. Therefore, even suffering can have a redemptive purpose. Even in the midst of his own confusion and pain, Job contended that he knew his Redeemer lived.[37]

Since God created the world with structure and order, even suffering operates according to a set of rules and principles. Just as

God governs us by His wise Word, so He also governs suffering in our lives. The Bible does not romanticize life. It provides a realistic picture of the human predicament and invites us with the hope of redemption. The day is coming when Christ will reign and destroy the greatest enemy, death.[38] Christians will be ushered into the New Jerusalem, where suffering does not exist.

But we live today between the Garden of Eden and the new Jerusalem. When you are hurting, redemption seems a long way off. As Christians, we need to realize that nothing, including suffering, is beyond the scope of redemption. Since suffering is a prominent topic in the Bible, we need to fashion an accurate theology of it to better understand God's purposes and promises. Such a biblical notion of suffering will help us avoid glib answers to such a complex problem.

Precept #9: There is an end to all suffering for the believer

As I (John) pecked out the preceding words on my laptop, I initially stopped this precept after the word *suffering*. But as I prepared to elaborate on this point, I realized that statement was wrong. There is not an end to *all* suffering. There is an end only to all suffering endured by the believer. The Bible states very clearly that those who don't believe will perish and suffer eternal damnation. The apostle John conveyed a glimpse of what will happen to the unbeliever. Near the end of his vision, John saw people whose names were not written in the Book of Life being cast into hell. For those without Christ, earth will be the only "heaven" they know. Believers, however, will experience something quite different; they will know the eternal comfort of God.[39]

Perhaps you have never had an opportunity to turn your life over to Jesus Christ and ask Him to forgive your sin. Now can be that time. Confess your sins to God and ask Him to be the Lord of your life, in light of His death and resurrection on your behalf.[40] Then you, too, can have the guarantee of where you will spend eternity and know that your suffering will eventually end.

For Christians, a time will come when every tear will be wiped away from our eyes. As the hymn writer says, "What a day that will be, when my Jesus I shall see, and I look upon His face, the One who saved me by His grace. When He takes me by the hand and leads me through the Promised Land, what a day, what a glorious day that will be."[41]

CONCLUSION OF SECTION ONE

The famed and fabled story of Chicken Little captures the essence of this section. We all recall reading about that fateful day when Chicken Little was hit on the head by an acorn while walking through the woods. Concluding that the sky was falling and terrified at the consequences, Chicken Little hurriedly headed off to the palace to inform the king. On his journey, he met up with other animals along the way and warned them of the impending danger. Concerned by the news, they joined Chicken Little on his quest to the palace. Although various versions of the story exist, the fable's main message is that jumping to the wrong conclusion is disastrous.

Our natural tendency is to make assumptions about what happens around us. When adversity hits, we attempt to make sense of it. We explain adversity by attributing either direct or indirect causes. In psychology, this process is referred to as "attribution theory," which explains the way we attempt to predict and control our lives. Research indicates that we rationalize our own behavior in terms of situational factors, while we explain the behavior of other people according to their intentions and dispositions. People assume that they have more control of their lives than they actually have.[1] We hold tenaciously to this assumption, because if it is not true, then random events can happen to us. That is one reason the very belief in control is a strong predictor of physical and mental health. But when the illusion that we can control life is destroyed, we are likely to fall apart spiritually, psychologically, and physically. Like Chicken Little, we have arrived at the wrong conclusion.

Therefore, whether we attribute our suffering to our poor choices, the insensitivity of others, or supernatural forces, the bottom line is that we *have to trust* that God is good, trustworthy, and just. Suffering is not so much a problem to be solved as it is an opportunity to trust in God's ability to capitalize on our pain for greater purposes. Of course, our finite minds cannot or will not grasp the complexity of suffering. Many people find themselves in a crucible of choice. Some wobble back and forth between what they perceive to be the only options to explain suffering. Perhaps they think that God is either good and loving (so their suffering is from another source) or He is not good and loving (so He is responsible for the pain). The first perspective does not permit God to allow us to suffer in any way, because to do so would negate His goodness and love. The second view implies that suffering cannot come from anyone or anything else except God Himself. Yet the Bible is clear that while God is both good and loving, He does permit His loved ones to suffer. We will never fully understand the matter. In the next section, we'll take a look at some of the reasons God may allow us to suffer.

THE PURPOSES OF SUFFERING

Philosopher and atheist Friedrich Nietzsche said that his problem was not the suffering but the desire to ask, "Why the suffering?"[1] We all long for answers to the immense suffering that we see. The answers, however, are often elusive and hidden.

Although God's Word gives insight into His ways, He did not intend for us to comprehend everything, especially when it comes to His ways of dealing with the world.[2] Yet within our hearts we have a craving to be "in the know." Call it curiosity or interest, but even when something does not concern us, we desire to understand why things happen as they do. Adam and Eve illustrated this truth when they ate from the only tree that was restricted. The prohibition consumed their attention.

Philosophers, theologians, and others have long discussed the problems of evil, pain, and suffering. This has been called the most serious challenge to religious belief. The approach that is generally taken is to point out that evil, pain, and suffering are justified if, by allowing them, God either allows a greater good or curtails an even greater evil. What sort of good, for example, could possibly offset such pain and suffering? In recent decades, probably the most attention has been placed on the value of free will.[3] The freedom of God's creatures is a vast subject, far beyond our purposes here. It encompasses topics like the ability people have to harm others. Further, we often overlook the repeated biblical teaching that Satan and his demons are also able to afflict human beings by the use of their own free will. The results of such actions are usually referred to as moral evil.

While most of us would presumably want to get rid of our personal suffering, whatever the source, we probably would not trade our freedom in order to achieve this. I (Gary) often ask audiences a question: "How many of you would push a button that, if activated, would cause all your pain and suffering to cease?" Of course, many people raise their hands. We all want to end personal suffering. But then I ask them, "Would you still push it if, at that very same moment, all your freedom would also end? In other words, is your freedom a fair trade for your suffering?" Intriguingly, very few people—either believers or unbelievers—indicate that they are willing to push the button!

Why are we unwilling to lose our freedom, even if doing so would eliminate all suffering? Could it be that we actually like our freedom more than we dislike our suffering? If so, then is it possible that God could have made the same decision on our behalf when He created us? Perhaps this is one of the "greater goods" that helps to justify evil and suffering.

In addition to free will, another good is natural law. Jesus said that God sent His common graces on the earth by allowing the sun to shine and the rain to fall on the just as well as the unjust.[4] Everyone may benefit from God's creation. But the sun that provides heat can also burn. The water that sustains life can also drown. The gravity that keeps us grounded can wreak havoc with tensions in the earth's crust, leading to earthquakes and other natural disasters. In short, the same natural laws that nurture life can also cause pain and suffering.

The obvious question here is, what's wrong with God's creation? Shouldn't God have created a better world than the one in which we live?

While free will and natural law are excellent explanations for some of the pain and suffering in the world, in this book we will concentrate specifically on a third reason—what is often called soul-making.[5] This approach recognizes that suffering develops our character and helps (or even forces) us to grow in ways that we would never achieve apart from the hardships that we face. This is what the apostle Paul had in mind when he explained that God comforts us in our struggles so that we can comfort others during theirs. Paul explains further that our model is Jesus Christ Himself, whose sufferings serve as our pattern to develop patience and endurance in our lives.[6] Jesus was tempted in every way that we are, though He never sinned.[7] And rather incredibly, as we've already seen, the Son of God even learned obedience from His suffering.[8] What does this indicate about Him serving as our model?

James tells us that various trials in our lives should promote virtues like perseverance and maturity.[9] Since Jesus learned obedience through His own suffering, should we think that we are exempt from the same lessons? Do we know more than Jesus, or are we more mature than He was, so that we should be immune from suffering? With this in mind, this book concentrates chiefly on the idea that God uses suffering in his work as a Soul Maker. Suffering promotes personal growth and development, and in this section, we'll look at fifteen specific ways God can use pain to achieve growth and victory in our lives.

God's Word provides information that satisfies our hunger for knowledge and understanding. Too often, however, it seems to stimulate a greater hunger. In other words, the Bible sometimes fosters more questions than answers. This ambiguity is particularly true when considering why God allows suffering. Yet perhaps the answer to this question is best understood by considering the character of God. As strange as it may seem, God loves us so deeply that He uses suffering to accomplish something positive in our lives. No matter how dark our world becomes, no matter how helpless we feel, and no matter how confused we might be, we can know that God is always at work. The prophet Isaiah penned God's role this way:

> I create the light and make the darkness. I send good
> times and bad times. I, the LORD, am the one who does
> these things. Open up, O heavens, and pour out your
> righteousness. Let the earth open wide so salvation and
> righteousness can sprout up together.   ISAIAH 45:7-8, NLT

Even though God may not have revealed all the reasons why we suffer, this passage makes it clear that sometimes pain is necessary in order for salvation and righteousness to grow.

No one knew more about comfort and convenience than King Solomon. Ironically, he learned an important truth about life— sorrow is better than wealth because it leads to wisdom.[10] Through suffering, Solomon found that real treasure was not in those things he possessed, but in what he could grow to be.

Charles Haddon Spurgeon said it this way: "The Lord's mercy often rides to the door of our heart upon the black horse of affliction."[11] Truly, there is rich value in suffering.

Understanding God's Purposes

In this section we will examine fifteen biblical purposes for suffering categorized into four directions. Of course, we must remember that God may also be trying to accomplish something other than these fifteen purposes. It is foolish and even dangerous to pretend that we have a complete answer as to why God allows suffering. Regardless of the aim of suffering, however, we can rest assured that God has a definite plan in His divine mind! We can also learn how to respond to suffering so that we not only please God, we grow from the ordeal.

As you reflect upon the biblical reasons for suffering, you'll notice that a pattern emerges. The fifteen purposes seem to indicate that God's intention is to move the sufferer in one or more of four different directions: inward, forward, outward, and upward.

Sometimes suffering turns us inward, opening the doors and windows of our souls so that God can accomplish an inner work. Suffering purifies us, removes our self-sufficiency and pride, tests our faithfulness to God, and when necessary, disciplines us. We see this when God tested Job's faithfulness and removed the arrogance deep within Job's heart.

God can also use suffering to move us forward. Through suffering we develop, grow, and mature because our sense of normalcy is shaken. Suffering disturbs our lives, taking us from our comfort zones into new, wild frontiers. God knows that we need a refreshed faith and outlook on life to thrive. Suffering often allows God's forward work as He matures us, shapes us into the image of Christ, and produces within us a personalized faith. In the last chapter of Job, Job said he had known of God by what he had heard, but now he truly knew God—a personalized faith had been produced in his life.

Inward and forward directions of suffering change *us*. But God also uses suffering to change others, an outward direction. When we suffer, the lives of others are typically touched through our pain. Consider how many people have been positively impacted by Job's suffering. Where would our lives be without the transforming power from the suffering of Christ? The Bible seems to convey that our suffering can bring others to Christ, build a strong and caring church, and provide encouragement and comfort to others when they experience adversity.

Suffering also has an upward direction. In the final analysis, everything in life brings us back to God. Suffering points us toward heaven and to the very person of God Himself. Through suffering, we are able to see God's character. God can also use difficulty to prepare us for blessings, give us dying grace, reward us, and ultimately be glorified through us. Job encountered a God whose character is good, generous, and loving, and his life was rewarded twofold through his suffering.

Our Western minds like to think logically. We love formulas and straightforward action steps. But God does not adhere to Western thinking. Thus, we should not think that God is only working in one direction through our suffering. Any time we experience suffering, God may be moving us in more than one direction, sometimes even all four directions at once. Yet, clearly no human can know the mind of the Lord. Whatever goals He has for you as you walk the path of pain are part of His divine plan, which He will make known to you at His discretion.

Thoughts on Soul-Making

Before we explore the fifteen purposes and four directions of suffering, we want to provide several important cautions about these purposes. First, knowing "why" does not eliminate the pain. Many years ago, I (John) developed plantar fasciitis, which is a chronic inflammation of the tissue along the bottom of the foot that connects the heel bone to the toes. It is a common yet painful problem in people who exercise a lot or who are overweight. When I tried to walk on my foot in the morning, the pain was unbearable.

Since I'm both overweight and a regular exerciser, I knew why my foot hurt, but that didn't change the fact that I still had to cope with the recurring pain. We may know why we are going through a particular crisis, but that does not in and of itself get rid of the sting of pain.

Second, the Bible speaks comparatively little about the "why" of our suffering. Philosophers and theologians read between the lines, and while there are some broad areas of agreement, some differences also emerge. But God chooses to deal deeply with the "how" of suffering. As in the story of Job, many would say that the way we respond to difficulty is more important than why it is occurring. God's direction tends to be future oriented, moving us forward and upward through our pain.

Finally, even after reading about these fifteen reasons for suffering, you might never know why you are going through your trial. Therefore, do not become consumed with searching for the specific reason. More will be said about this in section 3.

As we begin our study of soul-making, our hope is that you will begin to understand the amazing way God uses suffering to give His children a higher quality of life. Through soul-making, new characteristics and abilities develop within the sufferer. These may include Christlikeness, humility, an ability to minister to others, a stronger and more personalized faith, and even heavenly rewards. Together, we will explore the many ways in which trials and difficulty can actually make believers more mature, even increasing our appreciation for life.

INWARD DIRECTION

The Bible teaches us that God uses suffering to help us look into our hearts and lives. The following four chapters discuss ways in which suffering moves us inward.

CHAPTER FOUR

God Desires a Purified Faith

One cold day in the mountains of Oregon, a hiker came upon a logging site. While walking through the area, he noticed a lumberjack working on the river. As he made his way toward the worker, he observed the man jabbing a sharp hook into logs that floated down the mountain stream. Some logs he let pass, others he hooked and separated into a different area. The hiker, perhaps curious or lonely for conversation, decided to inquire about the logger's work. Without taking his eyes from the floating logs, the man replied, "These may all look alike to you, but I can recognize that a few of them are quite different. The ones I let pass are from trees that grew in a valley, protected from the storms. Their grain is rather coarse. The ones I have hooked came from high in the mountains. From the time they were small, they were beaten by strong winds. This toughens the trees and gives them a fine grain. We save them for choice work because they are too good to be used for ordinary lumber."[1]

Just as the wind and storms toughen trees to make fine lumber, suffering works to toughen us, thereby refining the quality and grain of our faith.

God Values Faith

The book of 1 Peter was written to Jewish believers who were facing merciless persecution. One can only imagine their thoughts as they reminisced about what life had been like when they were practicing Jews. At one time they had been under Roman rule, but there was no persecution from their own people. Now, although Rome still ruled, they were experiencing cruel persecution from fellow Jews: slander, suspicion, violence, and hatred. Since they had no idea who could turn on them, fear was a significant element. If Jesus Christ was truly who He said He was, it seemed impossible that He would sanction His followers to experience such appalling persecution.

Their response to suffering was probably not any different from ours today. As Americans we cannot comprehend persecution, but Christians in other countries can readily identify with these early believers.

Rather than responding to their suffering with despair and disillusionment, or even promising that it would end soon, Peter tried to encourage his readers to develop a proper response to suffering. To help them come to grips with their experiences, he attempted to foster a divine perspective on their suffering. He told them to rejoice because adversity tests the genuineness of faith. Peter's attitude was one of joy because he knew that Jesus' resurrection secured heaven for believers.[2] In other words, the Resurrection provides the foundation for our ability to cope with trials. Peter added that this heavenly hope cannot be taken from us or otherwise lessened.

As a student at Liberty University in Lynchburg, Virginia, I (John) often heard Pastor Jerry Falwell say that a man's wealth or education does not determine his greatness; rather, a man's greatness is determined by how much it takes to discourage him.

Likewise, the apostle Paul knew the inward faith-building benefits of trials. Having endured tremendous suffering while serving the Lord, Paul realized that the end result of pain would be soul-making perseverance.[3]

A Life of Faith

God also allows suffering and testing to purify and increase our faith. Although Christians toss around the word *faith* with great frequency, many would be hard-pressed to define it. In essence, faith is a commitment to abandon all reliance on our own efforts. It is a complete trust and dependence on God that assumes He will be true to His word. Faith involves appropriating the promises of

God with unwavering assurance. It is not so much the absence of doubt as it is experiencing uncertainty in such a way that we come to know and depend on God more deeply. Therefore, the process of increasing our faith is often contrary to what seems right, just, and purposeful. Corrie ten Boom said, "Faith brings us on highways that make our reasoning dizzy."[4]

In describing the accident that caused her to become a quadriplegic, Joni Eareckson Tada reported that she believed her injury was God's way of refining her faith so that it would not be based on her emotions but rather on God's character and nature.[5]

We also see this when Jesus and His disciples were crossing the Sea of Galilee and a great storm occurred. The disciples, many of whom were experienced fishermen, quickly began to fret and despair. Panicked, they woke Jesus, who dusted the sleep from His eyes while they clamored to Him about the storm. In response, Jesus simply rose to His feet, stretched out His soon-to-be pierced hands, and calmed the storm. The bewildered disciples were speechless, but Jesus had something to say. Rather than simply returning to His nap, Jesus rebuked them for their lack of faith. How I wish I could have seen the faces of the disciples at that point. Admittedly, my face would not have been any different. They were astonished by this Man's ability to eradicate a storm with His words. In spite of seeing Him do amazing things before, they lacked confidence in Him. Every difficulty seemed to shake whatever faith they had.

The Blessings of Trials on Faith

The storms of this world tend to drench our minds and our spirits. The trials and tragedies we experience reveal our true "god," and crises have a way of exposing who or what we depend upon for life. A well-known adage says it well: "There are no atheists in foxholes." Certainly, in the midst of life's storms, we *should* cry out to God. But God expects His followers to trust Him, to have confidence in His will and plan for their lives, even in the storms. Failure to trust God in the alarming moments of life is evidence of a weak faith.

Sometimes God deals with self-reliant thinking by challenging it with something that requires us to rely on Him. Mac Cauley, a minister of a small, conservative church, learned this when his world was turned upside down in a matter of seconds.[6] On a dark, foggy, and rainy evening, he and his family approached a red light on their drive home from the store. Before his vehicle came to a complete stop, the light turned green and Mac accelerated to the posted speed limit. Suddenly, he saw the face of a man directly in front of his car. Before he could react, the vehicle struck the man, throwing him against the windshield and then fifty feet through the air. After stopping and running to the man's side, Mac realized that the man was dead. Shocked and numb, he returned to his family. As a minister, he worked to preserve life. Now he had killed a man. He knew it had been an unavoidable accident. But facts failed to remove the stark reality that this man was dead. The next hours, days, and months were difficult. At times, Mac felt so desperate that he truly did not want to breathe another breath.

Eventually, the victim's family asked Mac to speak by telephone with the bereaved father of the victim. The conversation went well. The family held no contempt for him and had no desire to sue. But talking with the father made the young man he'd struck even more real. No longer was he simply a stranger, but a person with a history and a family who loved him. Once again, Mac found himself in the depths of another depression.

Throughout the ordeal, however, Mac never doubted the sovereignty of God. He knew that God was all-powerful. He knew that God had allowed this accident for some unknown reason. He tenaciously clung to the promise in Romans 8:28, that God could redeem suffering. And today he believes that his adversity strengthened his dependency on Christ. Mac does not believe God wanted him to kill the man, but he sees the ways that God used that tragedy. He had lived his life pursuing the will of God, but his suffering made him even more reliant on Christ.

Someone has said that Christians are like teabags; they are not much good until they have gone through hot water. Sometimes God places us in circumstances that make it impossible to trust in our own resources, in the latest medical advances, or in the people around us. God may allow us to experience things that leave us no option but to pray and place our faith in Him. In so doing, God is using the painful experiences to purify our faith.

Faith comes as the result of hearing God's Word.[7] Our faith is further shaped by our own experiences and by observing God at work in the lives of others. The Bible gives countless examples of faith, including Hebrews 11, which is a record of normal, everyday people who trusted God. Even though on occasion many of these people failed to believe God, their lives were characterized by faith rather than doubt. God counted them as men and women of faith because of their obedience. They were faithful, though they were tortured, mocked, scourged, imprisoned, dismembered, and forced to live as outcasts.[8] Their faith was evident as they trusted God to reward them for their endurance of hardships.

I (Gary) will never forget the night my phone rang and I picked it up to hear my friend Ken's voice. I knew instantly that something was seriously wrong. Ken explained that his wife and two of their three children had just been diagnosed with the same disease, one of the best-known killers in America. And there was no cure. What were they to do? Having served his church well over the years, this Texas pastor calmly asked me why God would allow this to happen to his wife and children.

Over the course of the next several weeks, it became obvious that other issues were involved as well. On top of the horrible physical problems, Ken's wife was reacting against the Lord and no longer wanted to participate in their ministry. This emotional element exacted an even heavier toll, adding to their already heavy burdens.

We continued to talk regularly, and as we did, Ken began to understand that there was a marked difference between what had happened to them and how they had processed that information. While there was no cure for the disease, the worst pain was being caused by the emotional aftermath. Quietly but forcefully, I pointed out to Ken a number of biblical truths. God had *not* broken His promises to them. Moreover, other believers *had* suffered even worse. After all, did Jesus' loving Father remove Him from the cross during His horrendous, prolonged torture? And isn't Jesus our example? Throughout the ages, Christians have grown in the process of such sufferings. Further, a wonderful eternity, full of heavenly rewards, awaits faithful believers.

As they began repeatedly reminding themselves and each other about these truths, Ken's family began to experience real change very quickly. Not only did they grow spiritually, but they also began to acquire information on how to cope with the dreaded disease. Today, they continue to minister together with peace of mind. While they cannot substantially change the physical sickness, they have learned how *not* to heap emotional hurt onto the situation.

You might ask why faith needs to grow and why it is so important that God would allow His children to experience perilous circumstances in order to purify their faith. We will not deepen our trust in God unless we are forced to do so. No prudent person would choose suffering in order to become a person of faith. Yet God knows that faith is important because it gives us a greater perspective on life and eternity. God desires His children to have a genuine and purified faith, a belief that God is good no matter what we experience. Faith allows us to enjoy God's riches in spite of our pain or turmoil, to have a calm assurance and joy, and to know that God has everything under control.

Dependence upon the Provider, Not the Provision

The prophet Elijah's ministry offers an intriguing story of the way God's provisions always point us back to the Provider. Perhaps Elijah is the Old Testament's best example of boldness. Before God used him to mightily defeat the prophets of Baal, He prepared Elijah by showing him His own sovereignty and character. Prior to telling Elijah of the coming drought, God miraculously sent him food by ravens as Elijah hid near the Brook Cherith. Then the provisions stopped and the brook dried up. Imagine Elijah's confusion. But his training was not finished.[9]

God told Elijah to go to the home of a widow who would provide for him. Now Elijah must have been really confused. Widows were usually unable to care for themselves, let alone a stranger. Though God's plan seemed irrational, Elijah decided to obey Him and went to the widow's home. When he arrived, he discovered a woman whose outlook was as bleak as her financial state. The widow's savings and her hope had long expired. Her cupboards were bare. The only thing that she had left was one meal's worth of flour and a few drops of oil. Seemingly unmoved by her meager means, Elijah requested dinner. Although the widow had received instructions from God to feed His prophet, she wearily confessed that the handful of food she had would barely provide her and her son with a final meal before they died of starvation. By human standards it would seem that this widow had a right to feel discouraged; after all, she had nothing left. The prophet told the anxious widow that God would make the bin of flour and jar of oil last until the drought ended, but first she must demonstrate her trust by providing dinner for him. Elijah was not insensitive to her plight, but he had learned that provision comes from the Lord. The widow took a step of faith and did as he said. True to God's Word, the flour and oil were never used up. God multiplied the provisions because the widow had placed her faith in the Lord. Imagine the widow telling her son to gather all their old jugs to hold the blessings of God. Her former hopelessness had been rooted in the belief that her situation was hopeless. She had focused on what she did not have, rather than on what she did have.

Through His provision, God taught Elijah *and* the widow that in His hands little is much. The widow and her son may never have come to trust God's ability to meet life's darkest circumstances unless they had been on the brink of death. It is through our difficulties that we too come to understand God's presence and power over despair.

Later, God even allowed Elijah to raise the widow's son from the dead. This depressed and discouraged woman learned that even when we think all hope is gone, God continues to demonstrate His faithfulness. And the prophet Elijah was once again reminded of God's power to control substance, sustenance, and the inevitability of death.

Understanding God's power and character, the prophet was then prepared to take on King Ahab and his wife, Jezebel. He challenged the prophets of Baal to a contest on Mount Carmel, mocked them continually, and then, to win the contest, called down fire from heaven. With the victory in hand, he led an immediate attack on these so-called prophets in which they were all killed.

Queen Jezebel did not take kindly to her priests and prophets being killed and promised to do the same to Elijah. Though God had provided miraculously for him in the past, this evil queen's words were more than he could handle, and he was filled with terror. Afraid for his life, downcast and in despair, Elijah fled into the wilderness where the God who had proven that He is the miracle provider met Elijah. Once again God provided for Elijah's needs, even in this situation, continuing to teach Elijah about His character.[10]

It's easy to criticize Elijah until we realize that we are just like him. It is easier to depend upon our own resources rather than on the One who provides them. Most of us rely upon what God does for us rather than upon God Himself. We judge His character, especially His goodness, by the things that He gives us. But only indulgent parents give gifts in hopes of being seen as a good parent. Wise parents know that indulgence produces indulgent children.

God, the perfect Parent, knows that we need to trust Him, not His answers or provisions. When we become focused upon the things that God has given us, He may choose to remove those distractions so that we can see Him more clearly and redirect our attachment from the things of this world to God Himself. Although God may provide a brook of comfort, He may also allow it to dry up to see whether we depend upon the brook or upon Him.

Suffering reveals the insufficiency of our own resources. The apostle Paul saw that suffering kept him from trusting in himself.[11] His tendency had been to depend on his own resources, but suffering changed that bent. Affliction forces us to rethink the direction of our lives and to consider our priorities, values, dreams, pleasures, and what we depend upon for strength. Suffering redirects our attention to spiritual realities rather than earthly realities.

Summary

Like Job's faith, our trust in God is to be based on what we know to be true about God and His character. After all, our dependency and confidence in an object are only as sound as the object to which we have committed ourselves. When it comes to God and His character, we have good reason to place our trust in Him, even in the midst of suffering. The truth of God's character is that He who holds the future also holds the present. He is the same yesterday, today, and forever.[12]

CHAPTER FIVE

God Desires a Humble Heart

Bill was a formidable, self-made man who had climbed high on the ladder of success. Although Bill never considered himself to be a harsh man, he prided himself on being direct and decisive with others. A demanding work schedule and a strong commitment to achievement left little room for other things in Bill's life. He had a devoted Christian wife and two academically bright and well-mannered teenage children. But rather than being people with whom he shared his life, his family was little more than a trophy of his accomplishments. His schedule reflected the importance and success that characterized him. Bill had made a profession of faith as a young high school student when his idealism and time were plentiful, but that was such a long time ago. Spirituality was now crowded out by things that demanded immediate attention. Since God was not plainly demanding Bill's involvement, he gave God only the time and energy he had left over. Sadly, he had very little left.

One evening, following a late night at work, Bill was in a minor car accident. Over the course of several months, Bill's behavior began to change. His wife and children noticed it first, and soon his coworkers began to complain about his hot temper. Nothing pleased him. He would lash out at others for the most trivial reasons. Though he had never been a gentle man, he had never been as cold or harsh as he was now acting. In time, Bill noticed that he lacked the energy to maintain his hectic schedule. He was forgetful, unable to concentrate, and felt a growing sense of malaise. Finally, at his wife's urging, he saw his doctor.

One doctor's appointment led to another, each leading to more tests. Late one Friday afternoon the doctor informed Bill and his wife that the tests revealed a traumatic brain injury. Surgery was needed at once. Since the outcome was uncertain, the physician urged Bill to settle his affairs prior to surgery.

Bill was unable to sleep, eat, or concentrate over the weekend. After what seemed like an eternity, the day of his surgery finally arrived. Throughout the long, tedious surgery, his church family provided support to his wife and children and continued to pray for Bill.

Eventually, the surgeon came into the room to inform his wife that they were able to repair the damaged area and the surgery was a success. They said that following his recovery, Bill would soon be back to normal. Bill, however, said that he would never be back to normal because during that miserably long weekend, he had returned his life to God's control. He would never again be the old Bill.

The difference in Bill was evident to all. No longer did his job come first. He became active in church and more committed to his wife and family. It would seem that God allowed pain and suffering in Bill's life in order to challenge his pride and dependence upon himself.

The Blessing of the Thorn

Paul learned that God uses suffering as a means of eliminating pride. Even though Paul wanted his thorn in the flesh to be removed, he knew it had value.[1] God had revealed Himself to the apostle Paul in a wonderful experience. But with this special blessing, he received a painful reminder not to see himself as more blessed than others. Paul believed that his agony was a gift from God to redirect his focus and to keep him humble.

Due to our forceful flesh, we readily exchange a focus on God for a focus on what we believe is important. We have become more concerned with knowing ourselves than with knowing God. Paul's thorn in the flesh taught him that God detests self-absorption. Since our lives are littered with distractions to an intimate relationship with Christ, God may need to introduce suffering in order to redirect our attention back to Himself. Like the church of Ephesus, many Christians have lost their first love for God.[2] Jesus Christ has been displaced as the central figure in their hearts and lives.

When I (John) first begin counseling patients, I ask them to identify their most important goal for therapy. Typically, there is little difference in the priorities of believers and nonbelievers. More than anything else, they simply want to feel better. No client has ever asked me to help him take up his cross daily. No one sets as her goal to become more like Christ. As we saw earlier, our deep-seated beliefs are revealed through times of suffering. Adversity has a way of revealing what is most important to us. There is nothing wrong with wanting to be rid of a problem. Yet when our primary motive is self-improvement, we fail to see how suffering can help us know Christ more deeply. Given our attitude of wanting control, predictability, and fairness, we experience the same emotional turmoil as the unredeemed. When our dependence is upon Christ rather than on how we feel, we find that *His grace is enough*. The apostle Paul knew that he should brag only about the Cross of Christ, never himself. Only when our self-pride is crushed are we broken and humbled so that we must rely on God rather than ourselves.

Not only does suffering remove self-absorption, it also allows the power of God to be displayed in our lives.[3] Paul was able to see God's power and grace manifested through him because his times of suffering were not joyless. He found a deep sense of joy in giving God the glory, even in the midst of affliction. Just as the power of God rested upon the Ark of the Covenant, the *shekinah* glory that Paul experienced during his suffering was witness to God's presence in his life.

I (Gary) can still remember the day that Randy arrived in my office. Randy was a brash young man who was an excellent university student as well as an exceptionally gifted athlete. And Randy knew he was special. But he also had experienced a pretty rough life. Suffering physical abuse as a child, Randy still bore the scars on his face. Rejected by his parents, he had entered military service and now sought other ways to gain attention. A young Christian, he wanted above all else to be absolutely sure of his salvation.

At first, Randy promised to be an eager learner. He studied the theory behind several of the assignments that I gave him. But he steadfastly refused to attempt any application to his own situation. After many visits, Randy decided not to pursue our discussions. The results were a bit demoralizing for me—why wouldn't a person who had suffered so much take advantage of substantial pain relief?

Years later, I was speaking in a California church and discovered that Randy was in the audience. Not only was Randy married and doing very well as an engineer, he had gone back to the lessons that we had discussed so many years earlier. I was thrilled to learn that Randy had gained victory over his lack of assurance and now taught classes in his own church on how to think and live biblically! Thus, many more students had benefited and gained victory over their own pain. Somewhere along the way, Randy had shed his pride. God had replaced it with a humility that was itself very inviting.

It is easier to act spiritual when all is going well. When our families are healthy, friendships are warm and comfortable, and the bills are paid, we tend to take our blessings for granted and regard them as benefits of our own hard work rather than God's provision. Like Bill, when life is good we think that all we have was gained by our own power, that we are in control. But one phone call, one doctor's visit, or one unexpected turn can knock the props out from under us. Our self-assurance is gone and we find ourselves like children, small and helpless. We are unable to make things work on our own power, and we must be dependent upon God.

Like Bill, we can learn never to take things for granted. We can begin to see each day and each circumstance as a gift from God. In essence, we can learn gratitude. As we confess our weakness to God, He releases His power in us. Our weakness is exchanged for His divine strength.

Pain and heartache are God's prompting to turn our focus on

Christ. By learning that our resources are insufficient for life, we learn that, without Him, we are nothing. As we realize our total dependence on Jesus Christ for every good and perfect gift, our suffering might even lead to a genuine sense of humility.

Summary

Pride and self-sufficiency are recognized by groups like Alcoholics Anonymous as character flaws that harm relationships. A biblical view of pride is that it not only affects our relationships, it also distances us from Christ. In other words, pride is not just a character flaw but sin. Through the spotlight of suffering, the pride that lurks in the shadows of our souls is illuminated. By being confronted with the reality of our hearts, we, like Bill, can allow God to remake our souls for His glory.

CHAPTER SIX

God Desires to Test
Our Faithfulness

Shortly after my (John's) family moved from South Carolina to Virginia, my wife sent me to the store for cleaning supplies. On my shopping list were sponges. The variety of sponges available and the price variation amazed me. Not being led of God to choose a particular sponge and having failed to consult *Consumer Reports*, I chose a man-size sponge. In spite of its magnitude, the only way to know if I had made a smart choice was to see how it performed on a tough job.

God's Sponge Test

Like sponges, Christian faith is tested on the tough jobs. You may have been a Christian for ten, twenty, or thirty years, yet the true test of what you have genuinely absorbed over those years is found when you are gripped by adversity. Even though the sponge I purchased had the look of quality, it actually failed to live up to its size when we used it on a big spill. Sadly, many of us also fail to make the grade in manifesting a deep faith when we are put to the test.

As we've seen, there is no better example of a person being put to the test than Job. From an observer's point of view, Job was a man of righteousness, a true worshiper of God. His character was unquestionable; his reputation was impeccable. Even God highly valued Job's lifestyle. As if that weren't enough, Job lived the good life. He was prosperous, financially independent, and the head of a large, loving family. Job was faithful to God and his family; by everyone's standards he was undeniably a blessed man.

Even though Job's devotion to God appeared first-rate, it would not go without inspection. Of course, if anyone could handle tragedy, it had to be Job. He had everything going for him. No matter how tightly adversity would squeeze Job, godliness would surely pour out of him.

But who could have imagined such a turn of events. "Job! Job! You have lost your livestock, animals, and camels." Following that message, another employee burst into his office, saying, "Your shepherds and servants have been killed!" Then, worst of all, came this message: "Job! All of your children have just been killed." The shock must have been enormous! Job's world was literally shattered in five minutes.

Days later he would stand beside the graves of his ten children, not long after also burying a number of employees. He was both financially and emotionally broken. Imagine Job's neighbors as they dutifully attended the funerals. They must have been confused; how could such an apparently godly man experience this magnitude of calamity? But picture their confusion when they did not find a bitter or despondent man. Of course they could see Job's grief, but his face did not show a hardened man. At least at the outset, Job's tragedies only brought forth his deep faith in God.

Job was more committed to what was happening inside of him than what was happening around him. He knew that he could not control life, only himself. We want to believe that the enemy is adversity, but Job realized that the real enemy was not what had happened to him. God wants us to see that the real enemy lies within our hearts. Remember that God told the Israelites that He led them through the wilderness for forty years to determine what was in their hearts.[1]

The real truths of Scripture cannot be completely grasped in a classroom setting. They are only discovered and fully understood in the laboratory of life.[2] You see, from God's point of view, suffering is applied theology. In the crucible of life, we display those things in which we deeply believe. In other words, suffering doesn't create our theology, it reveals it. When suffering challenges our attitudes, we tend to act out what we truly believe. When squeezed by hardships, the apostle Paul pleaded with God for deliverance. The Lord responded, "My grace is sufficient for you, for My strength is made perfect in weakness."[3] Paul then responded to his distress by boasting more joyfully about his weakness, so that Christ's power would rest on him. Paul realized that when he was weak, he really was strong.

But God can also use the classroom of suffering for His "schooling" process. Over the years, many of our students have gone on to further graduate work. Some have struggled with more than their studies—they have wandered from the faith. As C. S. Lewis observed, religious doubts usually derive, not from intellectual challenges, but from peer pressure, sin, or bad news.[4]

Heather was one such student. While doing doctoral studies in philosophy at a major university, she experienced the mighty sway of peer pressure. She found it difficult to hear her arguments challenged and her conservative positions ridiculed. The comments wore her down, and her first move was to walk a distance away from her Christian background. Realizing that she had flunked what may have been a test from God, Heather again reviewed the case for Christianity. As she reaffirmed her beliefs, she resolved to never again allow simple sneers to cause her to question her faith.

The Final Exam

The story of Abraham and his promised son, Isaac, is a good example of faith under fire. Without any explanation, God instructed Abraham to offer Isaac as a sacrifice.[5] Since sacrifices generally don't get up from the altar, Abraham knew that God was asking him to give up his beloved son. But this was not the first time that he had been asked to sacrifice something he loved.

The New Testament characterizes Abraham as a man of faith; however, on many occasions he lacked the faith to follow God's instructions. For example, at God's direction he left his homeland.[6] But instead of settling where God told him to, he ran to Egypt to avoid a famine. Eventually, doubting God's protection, he told Pharaoh that his wife, Sarai, was his sister.[7] Later in life, he devised a plan to help God because he mistrusted God's ability to provide a promised heir.[8] In fact, when God told Abraham he would have a son, he fell down on the ground in laughter.

But by the time God asked Abraham to sacrifice his promised son, Isaac, Abraham did so without any noticeable debate. As we've already seen, Abraham's previous trials had taught him—the hard way—that God could be trusted. So when God told him to offer his son as a burnt offering, he willingly obeyed without hesitation. Abraham tied Isaac to the altar and raised his knife to plunge it into his son's heart. At the very last moment, a heavenly voice interrupted, telling him not to harm Isaac. There at the altar of sacrifice, God explained that the purpose of Abraham's ordeal was to prove his faithfulness.[9]

God's testing is effective because it cuts through the surface issues to reveal the heart of the matter. In the heat of the moment, Abraham's sinful responses to famine, Pharaoh's jealousy, and God's promises brought logical, painful consequences. However, his ultimate challenge came out of the blue. In his wildest imagination, Abraham could never have anticipated what lay ahead. His heart for God was put to the test, not by his perceived circumstances, but by having to wrestle with his deepest vulnerability. Often the most difficult trials are not those due to willful rebellion but those designed to test the mettle of our faith and commitment. Abraham was able to demonstrate his heart-held theology because he learned that God could be trusted.

The great Christian Missionary Alliance preacher and writer from the mid-1900s, A. W. Tozer, said that all great Christians have been wounded.[10] In fact, Tozer believed that God could not use someone greatly until He had hurt that person deeply.

Summary

Have you ever purchased a product that did not work properly once you got it home? Even though most companies invest heavily in quality assurance, missing parts and defects do occur. A "try before you buy" policy would certainly benefit many of us.

God's inward work of making the soul through suffering not only exposes our weak and sinful sides, but also what is good and godly. Perhaps your pain and affliction is God's way of testing your quality and your faith. Ask yourself if you are all that you pretend to be. Give thought to what it takes for you to crack under pressure. Like Abraham, you may have to fail and fail and fail before finally acing the final exam.

CHAPTER SEVEN

God Desires
Well-Behaved Children

"If you disobey," I (John) said to my son years ago, "you will lose your cassette player."

"No!" he cried. "Please don't take my tape player! That's my favorite toy! You can have anything else. You can even spank me!"

Spanking, time-out, and *grounding*—when I was a child, such words were enough to make me shudder. Whether they have been treated appropriately or regularly exposed to maltreatment and abuse, all children have an aversion to discipline. It is never an enjoyable experience.

Just as we received discipline from our parents, we also receive discipline from our Father God. Unlike the imperfect judgment of earthly caregivers, however, God's discipline is perfect. And because of our sinful choices, God may even allow suffering as a form of discipline.[1] The fundamental principle of obedience is that we will reap what we sow, and our actions are never without consequence.[2]

Consider Miriam, who was stricken with leprosy after challenging the God-given authority of her brother Moses.[3] And David, who suffered the death of his son following an adulterous affair.[4] And Ananias and Sapphira, who were killed by God for lying, cheating, and hypocrisy.[5] There is often a clear link between sinful choices and the suffering that follows.

God Dares to Discipline

As human parents responsible for the training of our children, we know the need and value of sound, effective discipline. But seldom would we dare to discipline someone else's child unless we've been given permission to do so. In the same way, God disciplines only His own children. So if you are experiencing God's hand of discipline, there is good news: you can be sure that you are His child.

At times God may delay His discipline, giving us the opportunity to return to Him on our own. But if we continue in our sin, God may need to bring the sting of pain into our lives in order to get our attention.[6]

Our challenge as God's children is to learn not to despise His discipline, but to see the pain and affliction as a good thing. Suffering is an opportunity to learn the ways of our Father. Such an attitude is impossible without a passionate desire to serve God.

Three different words are used in the Bible to describe the way God deals with us: *chasten*, *rebuke*, and *scourge*.[7] The word *chasten* (*paideo*) describes God's goal to train and instruct rather than punish us. The word *rebuke* (*elegcho*) means to convict, to refute, or to reprove; in particular, it describes a conviction that results from having a wrong exposed. God will use suffering to cause us to see our wrongs and repent. The third word, *scourge* (*mastigoo*), was used to describe Jewish beatings.[8] This word is used in a metaphorical sense to reveal that we have transgressed God's law and need to be punished. God sometimes uses the actions of other people to accomplish this purpose.

Just as parents want their children to become healthy and mature adults, God also wants well-behaved children who will mature into spiritually stable and healthy adults.

While God's primary way of dealing with His children is unconditional, nurturing love,[9] when a spiritual spanking is needed, God *will* discipline us. His goal is not to harm us, but to bring about repentance.

Godly Limit Setting

Most family experts recommend that parents set limits. God seems to agree, providing clear boundaries and telling us the consequences for stepping over the line. As humans, we may tend to be overly strict or overly permissive in our parenting. But our heavenly Father is always balanced and just in His parenting, tempering justice with mercy and always working for our good.

The Old Testament provides many examples of God's children experiencing the consequences of their choices. In Leviticus, for example, continued disobedience resulted in persecution and plagues.[10] We might assume that such stern lessons would cause the people of Israel to look long and hard at their choices, but the Old Testament is filled with stories of the continuing rebellion of God's people. In the book of Judges, we see a cycle that begins with the people serving the Lord. After some time, however, the people forsake the Lord, and God raises up an enemy to discipline them. In pain, the people then cry out to God for help. God hears the cries of His repentant children and, with great compassion, delivers them.[11] For a time, the people serve the Lord, but then the cycle begins again.

Perhaps that cycle sounds familiar to you. So often, we are walking intimately with God but for some reason turn aside to do our own thing. After a period of time, God uses adversity to discipline us. We recognize the hand of the Lord on our backsides and cry out to Him. Thankfully, God, who is rich in grace and mercy, has already raised up the Deliverer, Jesus Christ, and through Him we are restored to a right relationship. And so the cycle goes.

The point is clear: our disobedience hurts God and He will not tolerate it forever. Following the great repentance of Nineveh, the prophet Jonah whined a prayer to the Lord, acknowledging His gracious and merciful heart.[12] The pouting prophet knew that God did not want to punish Nineveh but would grant to them His mercy and grace. God abounds in compassion both to the repentant and the unrepentant. God will, however, use whatever is necessary to get our attention and turn our hearts toward Him.

Why God Disciplines Us

In Hebrews 12:5-11 we find five specific reasons why God may choose to discipline His children. The first two reasons are primarily aimed at reorienting our wrong behaviors, whereas the last three are targeted to positively motivate us. God disciplines us:

- to teach us obedience
- to bring about confession and repentance
- to demonstrate His love
- to help us know Him in a personal way
- to make us holy

God disciplines us to teach us obedience

Sometimes suffering is God's way of taking us to obedience school. In other words, God seeks children who are mindful of Him, and suffering has a way of helping us to become obedient. As we saw in chapter 1, even Christ learned submission to the Father through suffering.

When the prophet Samuel learned that King Saul had sinned, he rebuked the defiant king on God's behalf. Unmoved by Samuel's reproof, Saul continued to justify his actions by insisting that his disobedience was a way of making an offering to God. But the unrelenting prophet explained that God valued obedience more than worship.[13]

God's discipline is an invitation for us to return to His ways and character. As parents we can appreciate our heavenly Father's desire to raise dutiful children. We want our children to respect authority, to adhere to our heartfelt convictions and values, and to learn to choose right. God longs for the same character from us.

It seems a stretch to think that suffering and pain can help us learn God's laws. But apparently King David found this to be true. Perhaps he was thinking about his sin with Bathsheba and the subsequent misery that befell his house when he admitted that through his affliction he had learned God's statutes.[14]

God disciplines us to bring about confession and repentance

When my (John's) family was ready for a pet, we decided to adopt a retired greyhound. The adoption agency told us that greyhounds hunt by sight, not smell. Therefore, when they see something interesting, they will take off after it. (And, boy, can they take off!) For safety's sake, the agency required "adoptive parents" to enclose their backyard. This sounded like a relatively simple task since our front yard was already lined by a split-rail fence. All we had to do was stretch a fence line from the house to the existing fence and then cover it with wire.

Though we had never put up a fence, we tackled the job. We eyed the spot on both sides of the house that seemed to make a straight line, and off we went. That was the day we discovered that our yard was a shallow disguise for an acre of rock. So we made logical choices. When we hit rock, we would move a few inches to the left or right and dig again. When we were finished, the fence looked like a radio wave! That evening, as I rested my sore muscles, I saw a home improvement show on how to put up a fence. (What timing!) A day late, I learned that to lay a straight fence, you have to figure a three-by-four-by-five triangle with the house and the end of the fence line.

God intends for us to use His Word the way builders use the three-by-four-by-five triangle: to keep us straight. The book of Amos was written during a time of economic prosperity in Israel. Everything was going well for the people, except that they had drastically strayed from God's Word. (The problem with getting offtrack is that we often do not realize how far and how quickly from the truth we have strayed.) Though the people maintained a form of religion, worship had become only a perfunctory ritual. Amos, a farmer-turned-preacher, was called by God to warn the people of God's impending judgment. In a vision, Amos saw a plumb line from which the people had departed as they lived by their own standards. The newly anointed prophet urged the people to repent and realign with God's standards.

The Greek word for *repentance* is one of the better known Greek words. It is the word *metanoia*, which means "to perceive afterward," "to go in another direction," or "to change one's mind." Repenting, therefore, occurs when we become unsatisfied with the direction in which we are heading and determine to change course. Consider the Prodigal Son, who was no longer satisfied being at home on the farm. Borrowing from his future, the young man took his inheritance to find the good life. And that he did! Perhaps he mused to himself, *Life can't get any better!* But the laughs did not last long; when the money disappeared, so did the pleasure. Broken by prolonged hardship, the prodigal returned to his father and repented.[15]

Misery is a good teacher since it presses us to do something to change our predicament. That is one reason why painful experiences are valuable to God. They compel us to stop, consider our circumstances, and change our ways.[16] Fortunately, God is rich in mercy and grace. The Prodigal Son knew that he had sinned, but he failed to recognize the grace and mercy of his father. God wants close fellowship with His children, so He will do whatever is necessary to bring us back to Himself. He knows that we are committing spiritual suicide, destroying our testimonies, and missing out on His blessings.

The book of Habakkuk deals with the wickedness of Judah. As the book opens, we find the prophet asking God how long He will allow their sinful ways to continue without discipline. When God tells Habakkuk that He plans to use the brutal Babylonians as His rod of judgment against Judah,[17] the prophet can't understand why God would use such an evil and corrupt nation to punish His people. But God is willing to take whatever action or means is necessary in order for His children to accept His ways, confess their sins, and repent. And when the Lord directs the world to be silent before Him,[18] Habakkuk comes to know and acknowledge the glory, power, and holiness of God, finally affirming his trust in God's salvation.

God disciplines us to demonstrate His love

Do you remember your parents telling you that the spanking you were about to receive was "going to hurt me more than it is going to hurt you"? I (John) always had a hard time understanding such sentiment. If it did hurt them, it certainly did not hurt them in the same place it hurt me! But now as a parent myself, I have a better idea of what my mom and dad meant. Although I do not tell my children that their punishment hurts me more than them, I do tell them that I would prefer never to discipline them. I do not like being the bad guy. Yet I'm willing to accept that responsibility because I want the best for my children. Parents understand that sometimes discipline brings sadness both to their children and to themselves. However, they know that the lesson learned will outlast the unhappiness and discomfort of the moment. Even research shows that children who are not disciplined do not feel loved by their parents.

The author of Hebrews tells us that God disciplines those He loves.[19] We may sometimes feel like telling God not to love us so much, but in truth, His discipline is not just for wayward children, but for the best of us as well. We all made mistakes as children; and we will make many more mistakes as spiritual children. We will do the wrong thing, say the wrong thing, or go in the wrong direction. But God knows that when we are spinning our spiritual wheels our prayer lives are hindered and we are hampered in our ability to minister and serve. Like any parent, when God recognizes that His children are playing near a cliff or strolling through traffic, He seeks to draw us to safety. Through discipline, God reaches out to bring us back into balance and in line with His character.

God disciplines us to help us know Him in a personal way

Hebrews 12:5-8 teaches us that those who are not disciplined by God are not part of God's family. In fact, the writer chooses some very strong language to convey this point. The King James Version captures the intensity of this thought when it uses the word *bastard* to describe those people who go without discipline. God chastens *every* son; not a single child is exempt from His lovingly administered discipline. Only those individuals whom God receives through faith in Jesus Christ are God's children. Many people may profess to be in God's family, but the lack of discipline by God's loving hand indicates that they are not His rightful children. Discipline affirms that we are God's legitimate sons and daughters.

God disciplines us to make us holy

Parents desire to rear their children so they will become solid citizens. Christian parents strive for more—raising children who love, honor, fear, and serve the Lord. Godly parents want children who will be citizens befitting a heavenly Kingdom. God's ultimate aim at parenting us is much the same.[20]

As we'll see in the next chapter, one of the blessings that emerges out of suffering is sharing in God's holiness. God longs for us, His children, to be holy as He is holy![21] The passage makes clear that our holiness is not measured by the way others live. We are not to compare our lives to those around us, but rather, we are to use God's own holiness as our reference point. Holiness doesn't mean having holy behavior. Instead, a holy man or woman is a person whose inner being reflects God's character. Holiness is revealed from the inside out. Our heavenly Father seeks children whose characters reflect His. And as we've already seen, God is willing and able to use whatever it takes to generate holiness in our lives, even if it means putting us through various ordeals.

Summary

A story is told of two artists who were putting the finishing touches on a church ceiling. One of the artists was older and a master of his craft. The other artist was his young but very talented apprentice. After working tirelessly all day on the painting, the young artist stepped back on the scaffolding to admire their work. Captured by the beauty of the painting, the young man didn't realize that he was standing dangerously close to the edge of the high platform. The master artist knew that his pupil would plunge to his death if he stepped back any farther. Fearing he would frighten his student by a warning cry, the master quickly grabbed one of the paint buckets and deliberately splashed paint across their masterpiece. Stunned by the master artist's apparent insanity, the young artist lurched forward screaming, "What have you done? Why did you do that?"

Upon hearing the reason, the young artist's anger and confusion melted into tears of joy and thankfulness.[22]

God sometimes uses suffering to protect us from ourselves, especially from disastrous choices that could destroy our testimonies, our families, and ourselves. Moreover, God grieves when we sin because it means that He also loses out on fellowshipping with us.

In love, He may even need to pick up a can of paint and splash it across the sinful masterpiece we are creating in our lives. Suffering redirects our eyes to our wrongful inner passions so that we might correct them and mature into godly adult children.

FORWARD DIRECTION

God seeks to grow us through suffering. The next three chapters will look at ways in which suffering helps us develop spiritually.

CHAPTER EIGHT

God Desires to Mature Us

For about sixteen years, I (John) have been a member of a fitness center. Typically, I jog for a cardiovascular workout and use the weight machines for strength training. It can be very intimidating to work out with many of the other members, who all look like young Arnold Schwarzeneggers. Over time, however, I have come to know some of these muscle-bound behemoths fairly well, and recently I asked one of them what I needed to do to improve my overall fitness. He told me that many people use the weight machines incorrectly, and that if I wanted to build muscle, I needed to do multiple sets and sufficient repetitions so that the last several repetitions required significant strain. So far, this sounded fun, so I asked him to continue. He told me that in order to increase muscle size, I first must break the muscle down and then build it up. "No pain, no gain," he told me.

God often uses suffering in the same way. In order to build His strength into us, He must first tear down our natural strength. Of course, this runs contrary to our natural philosophy of "No pain, more sane!" We wish to do the minimum amount of repetitions and sets possible. But God desires us to be spiritually fit.

Developing Patience and Maturity

My (John's) muscles' response to the prescribed torture was to become bigger and stronger. A similar process is what James, Jesus' half brother, meant when he encouraged the persecuted Christians who were scattered throughout various regions:

> My brethren, count it all joy when you fall into various trials,
> knowing that the testing of your faith produces patience.
> But let patience have its perfect work, that you may be
> perfect and complete, lacking nothing.   JAMES 1:2-4

No matter how much internal resolve we might muster, facing James's blunt challenge seems implausible. Harvesting the benefits of suffering is daunting enough without trying to find joy in it as well.

Several keys words in the Greek can help us better understand suffering. The word *know* (*ginōskō*) refers to experiential knowledge. James told his persecuted friends that in the midst of troubles there is something they could know with certainty. Most of us are so baffled by suffering, particularly what appears to be unjustified suffering, that we don't even know what we believe anymore. But James assured his readers that they could have absolute confidence in the fact that patience always results from tested faith. The word *patience* originates from the word *endure* (*hupomenō*), which means the ability to live underneath something. In times of adversity, God typically doesn't deliver us from the problem. Instead, in order for us to experience His grace and strength, we sometimes must remain under the problem so that patience can make us perfect. The word *perfect* does not mean faultless; it means complete and fully mature.

Consider Jesus, who suffered in order to enter the fulfillment of His maturity and mission and learn obedience.[1] The following words of Scripture are amazing in relaying this truth:

> Although he [Jesus Christ] was a son, he learned obedience
> from what he suffered and, once made perfect, he became
> the source of eternal salvation for all who obey him and
> was designated by God to be high priest in the order of
> Melchizedek.   HEBREWS 5:8-10, NIV

The word *obedience* means to follow someone who has greater authority. Jesus chose to remain under His Father's authority, even when it required pain and suffering. Jesus' response to His Father's will *perfected,* or matured, Him. It might be difficult to think of Jesus as needing to mature in some sense, but that is what we are told.

Much of Christ's suffering came from bearing the disgrace and shame of the Cross. We, too, are called to lose ourselves and take up His cross. Sometimes this involves suffering, but in the end, we know it's worth the price because through our pain, we can become the disciples of God we have been called to be.

It's human nature to want to avoid suffering. We often seek to minimize pain even if it means that others will suffer. As Victor Hugo said, "Adversity makes men, and prosperity makes monsters."[2] When I (John) am lifting weights, I don't always notice any changes in muscle development. However, with time and consistent training, it becomes obvious that the muscles have strengthened. The same thing happens to our spiritual muscles when God uses problems and suffering to stretch us for growth.

James suggests a second benefit of trials—they help us to grow so we will *lack nothing*—or we might say, so we will become "entire." The word *entire* means to be in balance. Whether it is a ceiling fan, vehicle tires, a checkbook, or scales, balance is critical. My (John's) muscle-bulging friend suggested that in addition to changes in my strength-training program I should vary my aerobic workout to include activities other than jogging. Apparently, runners build their hamstrings more quickly than they do their quadriceps. This imbalance can lead to knee problems since the muscles behind the legs are weaker than the muscles in front of the legs.

God wants us to have every area of our lives in balance. To help us mature spiritually, God knows just what buttons to push, just what trials to bring, and just what crises to put into our lives. As we are spiritually toned by suffering, the character of Jesus Christ is bred into our lives, and we become more spiritually balanced. Paul recognized that spiritual maturity resulted from problems, and Peter also spoke of God using suffering to make us spiritually mature.[3]

Summary

The cocoon of the emperor moth is flask shaped. In order for the perfect insect to appear, it must force its way through the neck of the cocoon after hours of intense struggle. Once, someone witnessed this insect's labor and out of pity snipped the cocoon's confining threads to make the insect's exit easier. Soon the moth emerged, but it had a swollen body and small, shriveled wings. Because this man had unwittingly eased the moth's struggle, its wings never developed. It spent its brief life crawling instead of flying through the air on rainbow wings. The man, in his kindness, did not understand that the moth *needed* the struggle in order to force fluid from its body into the wings so that flight would be possible.[4]

In the same way, we would not develop the emotional and spiritual maturity we need if God removed all the struggles from our lives. Suffering is not meant to be fun or easy. Without discomfort in our lives, we would never develop a life of righteousness. No suffering or pain is needless. It all works to mature our souls and build inner beauty. May God use your struggles and trials to propel you forward so that you will develop fully and completely in Christ.

CHAPTER NINE

God Desires for Us to Be Christlike

Imagine yourself as a lump of coal, relaxing comfortably in a cool, dark mine. Suddenly, a large, sharp object jabs into your side. The pain is excruciating! You are torn away from your comfortable home and shoveled into a wheelbarrow with other pieces of coal. Your life has been turned totally upside down. But things are about to get worse.

You will be forced to endure incredibly hot temperatures that will exert great pressure on you. If you could talk to the men handling you, you would scream, yell, argue, plead, and perhaps even kick them in order to avoid this fate. If the men listened to you, a huge weight would be taken from your shoulders. But while it is true that you would avoid a very painful experience, you would also miss your transformation into a diamond.

Synthetic diamonds, the strongest, most beautiful jewels in the world, are not born; they are made. They are the result of extremely high temperatures and pressure applied to carbon. Even if we knew that in the end we would become priceless diamonds, most of us would still refuse to undergo that process. It might help you to know that the word *diamond* is a derivative of the Greek word *adamas*, which means "unconquerable."

Suffering has a way of honing our character like nothing else. As a young girl, Helen Keller became very sick. Although she recovered from her illness, she would never again be able to see or hear. Isolated from the voices and images of everyone she loved, Helen became overwhelmed by her life of darkness and filled with rage—life was surely over.

But Helen's parents hired a gifted teacher, Annie Sullivan, who taught her to communicate by reading words written on her hands. Eventually, Helen was even able to attend college and write her autobiography, *The Story of My Life*.[1] She became a world-famous speaker, and her story inspired many because of the great obstacles that she had overcome. Truly, Helen Keller knew of suffering, but rather than being embittered by her loss, she learned to recognize suffering's character-building effects. She once said, "Character cannot be developed in ease and quiet. Only through experiences of trial and suffering can the soul be strengthened, vision cleared, ambition inspired and success achieved." Even though she was both blind and deaf, Helen Keller could honestly say she was grateful: "The struggle of life is one of our greatest blessings. It makes us patient, sensitive, and Godlike."[2]

God wants to transform rough, sullen, and sin-shaped people into grateful, joyous, and holy men and women of godly character. Yes, God loves and accepts us unconditionally. But because He loves us so much, He wants to make us the very best that we can be. He calls us to the highest standard: to be perfect like Him.[3] His love requires that we become spiritually transformed.

God's Transformation Process

Perhaps one of the verses most often quoted—and misquoted— in times of trials is Romans 8:28-29:

> And we know that all things work together for good
> to those who love God, to those who are the called
> according to His purpose. For whom He foreknew, He also
> predestined to be conformed to the image of His Son, that
> He might be the firstborn among many brethren.

The passage's promise carries a condition: all things work out for our betterment *if* we love God and *if* we are called according to His purpose. This promise is not given to the unsaved; it is only for those who belong to God.

God's sovereign purpose is that our pain and suffering be transformed from bad to good. Our Redeemer specializes in making huge profit from what seems like obvious loss. In God's economy, bad often possesses the power to accomplish God's ultimate good. In this famed passage to the Romans, Paul defines *good* as being "conformed to the image of His Son." We are the chosen people of God, called to prepare the world for the returning King. To accomplish this mission, we must become like Him. The work of conformity changes not only the outward demeanor but the inward character as well.

In speaking about people with disabilities, Howard A. Rusk of the Institute of Physical Medicine and Rehabilitation wrote, "You don't get fine china by putting clay in the sun. You have to put the clay through the white heat of the kiln if you want to make porcelain. Heat breaks some pieces. Life breaks some people. Disability breaks some people. But once the clay goes through the white-hot fire and comes out whole, it can never be clay again; once a person overcomes a disability . . . he has a depth of spirit you and I know little about."[4]

If this process is true for those who don't know God, imagine how much more Christians can benefit from trials because of the transforming nature of a Christ. Consider the apostles Peter and John, who were arrested for preaching the gospel of Jesus Christ in the Temple. This injustice provided an opportunity for Peter to preach to the Jewish ruling council, the Sanhedrin. They experienced more than a message that day; they experienced the very power of God. Peter and John's response to suffering was so radical that it unnerved even their unbelieving audience.[5]

Brussels is well-known for its fine lace shops. A man visited one of these shops with his wife, and while she was shopping, he spoke with the shop owner about the lace-making process. The owner led him back to a small room that was used for the production of their finest, most delicate lace patterns. To his amazement, he saw that the room was completely dark except for a narrow stream of light from one very small window that fell directly upon an artisan and his work. The owner explained that the most delicate and expensive lace is made when the worker is completely in the dark with only his pattern in the light. Similarly, God uses the darkness that accompanies problems as a means of transforming us into His pattern—Christ's image.[6]

God's Transforming Purpose

When followers of Christ were first called Christians, it was not a compliment. Just as Plato's followers were called Platonists, those who bound themselves to Christ were credited with His name. The believers in Antioch were known for leaving all to follow Christ. Their critics mocked their lifestyles by referring to them as "Christians." The label didn't dismay them; in fact, they couldn't have chosen a better name for themselves. So the name took. Perhaps the name was even part of a divinely conceived plan, and God's intention was for His followers to be given His name because they were to be like Him. Even though we know that becoming like Christ is accomplished by God's work in our lives, it runs counter to our self-serving human nature. The following poem clearly depicts the difference between our natural self-orientation and a Christlike orientation.

> For He was a man of sorrows and familiar with suffering;
>   I prefer to be familiar with comfort.
> He was a man despised and rejected; I prefer to be honored
>   and accepted.
> He took up your infirmities, disabilities, and sickness;
>   I prefer health, strength, and wholeness.
> He was pierced, crushed, and oppressed; I prefer no injuries,
>   no smashing, or injustices.[7]

There is no escaping the fact that as we go through the process of becoming like Christ, we will experience hardships. Our responses to those painful experiences will indicate our progress toward that goal. The Bible says that being corrected may not be welcomed, but if we learn to be obedient through it we will live in peace.[8]

Summary

You've likely had the experience of traveling downhill and being passed by heavy trucks as their speed and weight propelled them past you. At times it seemed as if they would run you off the road! Their ability to intimidate you was short-lived, however, when they attempted to climb the next hill. The ease with which they had traveled down the road was lost; momentum subsided and these beasts of the road slowed to a crawl. To maintain their normal speed, the drivers must be able to accelerate in order to compensate for the steep incline. Without the speed and momentum to carry them up the next hill, the weight of the trucks negates having the pedal to the metal.

Sometimes Christians experience similar acceleration and deceleration patterns. When traveling down level roads, they maintain their acceleration, feeling particularly empowered in their commitment to grow in Christ. Maintaining speed and forward momentum is no problem as long as the conditions around them are favorable. Like the heavy trucks, however, when they encounter the steep ordeals of life, forward momentum sometimes diminishes. Then they either crawl or stall! They are fair-weather Christians. Such people believe that their momentum is dictated by road conditions, not their ability to increase their speed. They view suffering as a logical justification for their dark attitude. After all, how can one move forward in their spiritual life when things are so difficult?

Consider the early church. Common sense says that the persecution the early church endured should have minimized its growth. Not so. Nothing—not arrests, not beatings, not imprisonments, not threats—seemed to deter these followers of Christ. Instead these challenges accelerated the growth of both the early believers and the church as a whole.

To become like our Lord, we must move forward in the good times and the bad. In the process of sculpting the image of Christ into our lives, our souls are remade into the image of the One who created them. The apostle Paul graphically described it this way: "My dear children, for whom I am again in the pains of childbirth until Christ is formed in you . . ."[9]

How does Christ become formed in us? It is not by accident. Becoming Christlike must be intentional, though it may not necessarily be actively pursued. God may use difficult circumstances, even suffering, to push us in that direction. Suffering is not always virtuous, but what it produces is. When suffering has performed its work in turning our characters of coal into the character of diamonds, we will more naturally do what Jesus does. When we ask, "What would Jesus do?" the answer will be clear and decisive. We desire to grow our souls so that we will aspire to make choices, think thoughts, and feel feelings that are in harmony with a Christ-centered life regardless of the road conditions.

CHAPTER TEN

God Desires for Us to Have a Personalized Faith

When the movie *Titanic* was released, it broke box office records. The multimillion dollar movie follows a fictional couple through the reality of that maritime tragedy. While the movie contains many moving scenes, my (John's) favorite occurs toward the end as the many passengers frantically try to get into the few lifeboats. In an attempt to assuage the panic of the passengers, the band plays music on deck. In the final moments before the ship is totally submerged, the bandleader thanks his friends for the privilege of playing with them over the years. As the band members begin to disperse, the leader takes his violin and begins to play "Nearer, My God, to Thee." Hearing their leader playing the hymn, the band solemnly returns to accompany him. Tears streamed down my face as I watched the movie and felt the sorrow of the moment. There was not a more fitting song in those final minutes. Tragically, many of the passengers were approaching an eternity without God.

As it did for the bandleader, grave adversity often prompts us to assess our relationship with God and eternity. God's purpose is to draw us into a more personalized faith relationship. Oswald Chambers poignantly professed, "Why shouldn't we go through heartbreaks? Through these doorways God is opening up ways of fellowship with His Son. . . . He comes with the grip of the pierced hand of His Son, and says—'Enter into fellowship with Me; arise and shine.'"[1]

God's passion is for His children. He longs for us and wants us to long for Him. Engulfed in the pit of anguish and depression, the psalmist longed to draw closer to God because he realized that only God's character could help him.[2] And through adversity, he experienced a deep longing for God.

The Fight of the Century

Because Job's initial response to his affliction was humility and worship, many Christians presume that Job never swayed in his attitude. But chronic suffering takes a toll. Consider Job's comments and accusations in the aftermath of his suffering:

- "I desire to speak to the Almighty and to argue my case with God." (13:3, NIV)
- "I will surely defend my ways to his face." (13:15, NIV)
- "Can anyone bring charges against me?" (13:19, NIV)
- "[I] know that God has wronged me and drawn his net around me. Though I cry, 'I've been wronged!' I get no response; though I call for help, there is no justice." (19:6-7, NIV)
- "Let God weigh me in honest scales and he will know that I am blameless." (31:6, NIV)

The man who had initially not charged God with wrongdoing changed his opinion. Job demanded his day in court before God, and he got what he asked for: God showed up.

In the concluding chapters of Job's biography, we find Job silenced by the cross-examination of God. In chapters 38 to 41, Job and God were engaged in a battle of words over God's justice and goodness. Every time Job thought he had God on the ropes, God landed a powerful blow to Job's argument. In the end, God's opposition sapped the fight from Job, and the struggle was soon over. At one time, Job had stood before the Creator of the universe a prideful man. Finally humbled, however, Job was unable and unwilling to get up from the mat. But humility does not equal defeat.

God hadn't declared the depths of His power and greatness in an attempt to defeat Job, but to give him a special understanding of Himself. Though God knocked Job down, He did not knock him out. And as he lay stretched out before God, Job exclaims that though he had heard about God from others, he has now seen Him with his own eyes.[3] For the first time, Job understood the ultimate prize, an enriched and personal relationship with a generous, loving, and lavishing God.

Prior to his trials and travails, Job thought he knew God, but he had only known *about* Him. Like many of us, Job held traditional assumptions about what God was like, how God should act, and what God could do. He had probably heard about God's goodness, grace, mercy, and sovereignty from the testimonies of others. After his own battle with the Almighty, however, Job had a more personal knowledge of God, as well as a changed life. Suffering had opened an opportunity to experience God in a way that Job would never have chosen, yet he could now say something like, "God, I have experienced you in a deep and personal way. I no longer have secondhand knowledge of you but firsthand experience."[4]

Many believers have a traditional understanding of God. We go to church, where we learn about the Lord's nature and hear messages and testimonies about His power, love, and justice. Such instruction is good and necessary in developing us as believers. But it is only as we battle with God that we are brought from a head knowledge to an experiential knowledge. Then, like Job, we can testify to what God has done personally for us.

Drawing near to God through Prayer

The great English preacher Charles Haddon Spurgeon once said, "The best style of prayer is that which cannot be called anything else but a cry."[5] Sometimes our hardships are so great and our futures so bleak that we are driven to our knees. There we can do little else but cry out to God, but it is from that position that we draw near to God and learn to rely upon Him in the most personal way.[6]

When the pain is greater than our ability to tolerate it, we find ourselves much more willing to pray. No longer does prayer seem like drudgery or an obligation. Instead, in pain, we fall on our faces before the Lord, pleading and begging for His help. When our needs weigh heavily upon us, our prayer lives reflect a personal sense of urgency, and we come to understand that prayer is more than an activity. It is a relationship with the Creator of the universe.

Therefore, prayer goes beyond simply asking God for help. It becomes a means of seeking communion with God so that we can experience His power and presence to sustain us. When Moses was on Mount Sinai receiving the Ten Commandments, God informed him that the people of Israel were committing grievous sins. God told Moses that because of their rebellion, He would destroy Israel, but Moses prayed desperately for their deliverance.[7] And because of his prayer of intercession, God agreed not to harm His people.

Perhaps the children of Israel never knew that the warrior efforts of their leader protected them from God's hand of discipline. Clearly, the people benefited from Moses' prayer. What might be less obvious is that Moses benefited more than anyone from battling with God. Being informed of God's plan to punish His people, Moses knew that he was the only one who could intercede. But imagine being in Moses' sandals. How could one man possibly get the Lord Almighty to change His mind? Confronted with the fear of what would happen to him and the people, Moses fell to his knees and did what only a desperate person can do: he pleaded for mercy. Though the people did not come to a more personalized faith through that ordeal, Moses did. His spiritual understanding of God's power and grace improved through hours of fervent prayer.

In desperate times, knowing what to say and how to pray can elude us. We may want to pray, but like Moses, we do not have a clue about how to move the heart of God. In thinking about our struggle to know how to pray in times of suffering, I (John) was reminded of a story. A mother was working in the kitchen preparing an evening meal when she saw her little boy sitting in a corner of the room saying, "ABCDEFG."

"What are you doing?" she asked.

"Mom, you told me I should pray, but I don't know how. So I gave God the alphabet and asked Him to make a good prayer out of it."

This anecdote illustrates an important point about our suffering. Like the boy, there are times when life's difficulties make it nearly impossible for us to pray. There are simply no words to describe the longings of our hearts. Or maybe we've been hurt, perhaps are even angry with God, and we don't want anything to do with prayer because that means having to deal with Him. In such times, being told to pray to God is about as inviting as being forced to interact with someone we're fighting with. The last person on earth we want to be around is the one we blame for our problems. The fact is, we'll do just about anything to avoid the discomfort of being around that person. We know that if we speak, our words will be polluted by hurt and self-defensiveness, creating even more distance between us.

Just as communication is the lifeblood of a relationship, prayer feeds our spiritual lives. Most people blame a lack of communication for relational problems, but in reality, it is simply the by-product of a much deeper issue. Communication is only a vehicle we use to share what is inside our hearts with someone else. The vehicle is not the real problem; it's what's inside us that's the problem. When a relationship is in trouble, those involved often become impassioned in their communication: "I can't live without you," "Just give me one more chance," "I'll change," "I'll do anything to make things right." In the same way, when we face troubled times in our lives, our passions flow out toward God. Whatever we're feeling—desperation, anger, fear, or shame—is reflected in our communication with the Lord.

During times of tragedy or distress, our willingness to pray does not always become greater, however. We cannot wait until we feel like praying; we must pray whether we feel like it or not. God wants us to communicate with Him. Since He knows our hearts, He knows what we are thinking and feeling anyway. Our words will not surprise Him. We simply need to be real before God. Regardless of what we have to say, God longs for us to open up to Him in prayer.

It is through prayer that we find God.[8] It is through prayer that we harness the power and sustaining grace to face any trial.

Christianity's uniqueness is found in this truth. We believe in a personal God who desires to have a relationship with us. Moses captured this truth in the following words:

> What other nation is so great as to have their gods near
> them the way the LORD our God is near us whenever we
> pray to him?   DEUTERONOMY 4:7, NIV

A dear friend of ours went through many months of dark depression. She simply could not find an end to her gloom. Like the little boy praying the alphabet, she knew that the Holy Spirit promised to intercede on her behalf, but she wondered if He had forgotten about her. Then one day, her pastor explained that when we can't pray, not only does the Holy Spirit say to the heavenly Father what we are not able to say, He also burdens the hearts of other Christians to intercede for us as well. The Comforter comforts by understanding our hearts' cries, giving them words, and then speaking the passion of our hearts to the heavenly Father.[9] This woman was broken by the reality of God's love for us, and in particular His love for her, and this realization was a key factor in her recovery.

I (Gary) still remember the day Lynn came into my office, took a seat, and spoke rather caustically: "I'm going through severe problems that are beginning to affect my marriage and family, as well as my business. I've read your two books on Christian struggles, and I need some help. But if we're going to talk, I want to have something understood from the very beginning. Don't say that my problem starts with me, and don't just tell me to go pray or read the Bible. I've tried these things ever since becoming a believer and they simply don't work."

Wow! What an introduction and challenge! Talk about rolling out of the wrong side of the bed! But Lynn was right—she needed someone with whom she could talk, and once we worked past her initial barriers, the conversation started to flow more easily. Over the next few months, I met weekly with Lynn, concentrating on the problems that had caused her so much pain. In spite of her initial proclamation, Lynn began to see that her own perception of her struggles was indeed the chief culprit in her suffering. She began to dispute her false views, and after less than two months, she was doing wonderfully.

Soon, Lynn made a personal discovery—having worked again through her faith, she realized both that it was real and that it had been there all the time. She simply had to learn how to appropriate the truths that God had long before set forth. Years later, she called me and declared that not only had her faith survived the rocky times, but that God had become more real than she had imagined. She had been liberated!

These experiences are not unique. Many of us struggle to pray at times. Any attempts at prayer seem futile and unproductive. Yet God longs for us to pray, even when forming words seems more than we can manage. As we struggle with the loss of a desire to pray, seeking His face in whatever way we can, we begin the journey of drawing near to Christ.

When we are suffering, prayer may seem impossible. But no matter how we feel, we need to set aside familiar patterns and get down to business. As we do so, we become drawn into a deeper fellowship and personal intimacy with God. Prayer teaches us that we cannot depend on ourselves, that we need God's strength. God reaffirms the promise that His power is made perfect in our weaknesses.[10] In light of your suffering, consider the following promises found in this familiar hymn:

What a friend we have in Jesus . . . all our sins and griefs to bear!
What a privilege to carry everything to God in prayer!
O what peace we often forfeit,
O what needless pain we bear,
All because we do not carry everything to God in prayer.[11]

Corrie ten Boom sang those words from solitary confinement in the Ravensbrück prison camp. Finishing the verse, she heard the voice of another woman in an adjoining cell reply, "O what peace we often forfeit, O what needless pain we bear, all because we do not carry everything to God in prayer." It was the voice of a woman who had just watched as their Nazi captors shot and killed her husband.[12]

Summary

Even in the midst of incredible torment, we can find rest in the warm, comforting presence of our Savior. If the trials of a concentration camp were not enough to hinder Corrie ten Boom's Christian walk, what does that say about our own suffering? In actuality, God uses trials of different sizes and shapes to remake our souls. Suffering moves us forward by drawing us into a more personalized faith through prayer.

OUTWARD DIRECTION

The Scriptures reveal to us that God uses suffering as a means of redirecting our eyes toward others. Our passion is no longer aimed at making our lives more comfortable but at helping other people. The next three chapters will examine how suffering enables us to comfort others.

CHAPTER ELEVEN

God Desires to Build His Kingdom

A story has been told about a missionary whose wife and child died of disease while they were ministering overseas. The family had been striving with little success to introduce a primitive tribe to Christ. Following the death of his family, the missionary began to see a great work of God happening in the lives of the people. Pleased but confused about this turn of events, the missionary questioned one of the tribe's leaders about the reason for their change of heart. The leaders told him that following the death of the missionary's wife and child, the people observed him very carefully. They watched him walk quietly to the grave, exhibiting a sense of hope and confidence. The leader said, "We don't understand your religion, but we like the way you bury your dead."

Truly, our walks speak louder than our talk. Yet when we experience deep tragedy or affliction, it is often so hard to exhibit hope, joy, and peace.

Paul Walked His Talk

The apostle Paul did not write the book of Philippians, known as the "book of joy," while he was on vacation. The book would have been so easy to write if he had been sitting alongside a sparkling pool or dangling his feet in a hot tub. But Paul penned these words from a very different venue.

On Paul's second missionary journey, he and Silas ministered in the city of Philippi, located in the Roman province of Macedonia.

While there, they were beaten and imprisoned. It was following his third missionary journey that Paul was taken to Rome and put in prison. Most commentators believe that Philippians was written from a Roman prison cell. It is that setting that forms the backdrop to this book of joy. Ironic as it might sound, it was while he was incarcerated that Paul found greater purpose in his own suffering.

> But I want you to know, brethren, that the things
> which happened to me have actually turned out for the
> furtherance of the gospel, so that it has become evident to
> the whole palace guard, and to all the rest, that my chains
> are in Christ; and most of the brethren in the Lord, having
> become confident by my chains, are much more bold to
> speak the word without fear.   PHILIPPIANS 1:12-14

Sometimes suffering opens up a door to win people to Christ. In fact, from a prison in Philippi, Paul and Silas introduced the jailer and his entire family to the Lord.[1] Paul saw times of tribulation as opportunities to share his faith. He may have been imprisoned, but he used his incarceration as a means of evangelism. In the original language, the word *furtherance* is a military term. It refers to those soldiers who went ahead to prepare the way for the advancing army, ensuring safe and easy passage. These men would cut away all the underbrush, clear all the obstructions out of the path, and if necessary, build bridges so that the army could advance. In this passage, Paul was saying that his imprisonment was accomplishing the same kind of work as these soldiers—it was clearing out the debris and building bridges so that the gospel of Christ could progress. His suffering did not prevent the gospel from going forth, but actually promoted it. Though the authorities had intended to hinder the gospel by persecuting the early church, their actions had the opposite effect on believers.

Paul recognized that his trial would advance the gospel and also help him reach government officials who typically would not have an opportunity to see a Christian in action. He commented that his incarceration was known throughout the whole palace.[2] Because of this benefit, he was willing and able to bear any trial.

Adoniram Judson, the renowned missionary to Burma, endured untold hardships in his attempts to reach the lost. For seven years he suffered hunger and deprivation. During that time he was thrown into Ava Prison and for seventeen months was subjected to the most horrific mistreatment. In fact, for the rest of his life he bore the marks of the chains and shackles on his arms and legs. Upon release from prison, he asked for permission to enter another province to continue his ministry. After hearing Mr. Judson's request, the godless ruler indignantly denied it, saying, "My people are not fools enough to listen to anything a missionary might say, but I fear they might be impressed by your scars and turn to your religion."[3]

In the same way, Daniel's three friends, Shadrach, Meshach, and Abednego, illustrated the power of a testimony formed in the face of a fiery trial.[4] King Nebuchadnezzar commanded all the people of the land to bow down and worship his statue, threatening to throw anyone who refused into a furnace.

The three Israelites, however, stood firm in their conviction that God alone is worthy of worship. It was not their desire to be seated in the smoking section, but if forced to dine at a table in that section, they knew it was of little consequence. They understood that God could rescue them from the furnace and determined that even if He chose not to, they would remain loyal to Him.

When he realized that Shadrach, Meshach, and Abednego had defied his orders, the king ordered that they be thrown into a furnace that had been heated seven times hotter than usual. But when the king checked on the three Israelites, he was astonished to see four men in the furnace, and exclaimed that the fourth looked like the "Son of God."

Wouldn't it have been interesting to know what those four men were talking about? Perhaps Shadrach started singing a chorus, "Give me oil in my lamp, keep it burning, burning, burning. . . ." Our imaginations will have to fill in the details. But since they were fellowshipping with the presence of Jesus Christ, it's probably safe to assume they weren't in any hurry to get out.

Nebuchadnezzar's life was transformed when he saw the way these three men faced their ordeal. He proclaimed that their God was the one and true God and decreed that anyone who spoke against the God of Shadrach, Meshach, and Abednego would be put to death.

When we get a promotion, when the bills are being paid, when the children are behaving, and when we have good health, our neighbors and friends see us as being no different than them. If in the midst of adversity and suffering, however, they can see that there is a difference in the way we cope, they conclude that something—or Someone—is making this difference in our lives. When we endure suffering in a way that demonstrates our eternal hope, God is magnified and people see that there is no other god like ours! As they see our joy and hope in spite of the worst of circumstances, they may even be compelled to say, "I want what they've got!" It is through our scars and hope-filled lives that people can come to accept the Savior.

Years ago, I (Gary) knew a couple who had recently lost a son in a horrible car crash. Their son had been among the many thousands of innocent victims whose lives are lost or changed forever by an intoxicated driver. Even while this husband and wife were in the middle of their own grief recovery, struggling with the rawness of their own pain and suffering, they started a ministry to others. They used their child's photo as the means of drawing attention to the problem of drunk driving, and today, they have distributed more than fifty thousand pieces of literature! While they don't believe that God caused this situation in order to promote the work of His ministry, they know He has certainly blessed their message. You might be thinking, *But why must it fall on me and my family? Aren't there other ways God can accomplish His purpose?* As we saw in chapter 3, this kind of thinking is the result of an attitude that demands comfort, fairness, and predictability. Since we are self-serving, anything that is not to our liking will evoke negative emotions, passions, and behaviors. God's call is to redirect this attitude so that it begins to accommodate His will. Think about what it took to redeem us. If there were any other way to accomplish our salvation without requiring Jesus to die, God would have done so. But Jesus had to sacrifice comfort and fairness to bring us eternal life. Though committed to God's will, even in His final moments He asked God to let the cup pass from Him.[5]

Often, it is only through our pain and suffering that people see the grace, hope, and joy we have in knowing Jesus Christ. Remember as you go through suffering that God may be opening a door of opportunity through which you might share your faith.

Paul recognized that his suffering not only opened a door to witness to unbelievers but also gave him a chance to be an example to fellow believers.[6] His outlook was much different than ours often is.

One of the well-known early church fathers, Polycarp, lived just after the apostle Paul. Polycarp made significant contributions to the early church. In prayer, he believed he had a vision in which he was martyred for his faith. His vision did not alter his message or ministry. Eventually, Polycarp would be confronted with an opportunity to either fulfill or void his vision.

As an elderly man of eighty-six, Polycarp was summoned by governmental authorities. They required him to call Caesar "Lord Caesar," but Polycarp said there was only one Lord and it was not Caesar. The officials told him that he could spare his own life simply by saying those words, but Polycarp held his ground. He contended that he had served God his entire life and that God had never let him down. How then could he possibly blaspheme the One who had saved him? At first, the authorities threatened to unleash wild beasts on him, and Polycarp told them to go ahead and do so. Figuring that the sting of fire might better capture Polycarp's attention, they threatened to burn him at the stake. Polycarp's response? Such fire only lasts a short period of time and then it burns out, but the fire of hell burns forever. Again, he told them to do with him whatever they wanted.

History tells us that Polycarp was burned at the stake, but his body was not all that caught fire. His testimony so ignited the early church that the gospel spread like wildfire.[7] It takes a selfless attitude to view suffering as an opportunity to benefit another individual. Yet when we use our suffering to reach out to others, we benefit as well. Despair will never become our companion when our eyes are securely focused on Christ.

Summary

The furtherance of the gospel was the heart's passion of Paul's life. Suffering not only provided an opportunity to advance the gospel but also to advance his soul. Americans cannot appreciate how suffering and winning others to Christ are connected like those in countries closed to the gospel. I (John) have made several trips with a mission organization to Romania. While there I met pastors and lay leaders who understood what Paul was speaking about through personal experience.

Before Romania came out from behind the iron curtain, believers in Christ had to worship and share their faith in secret. The gospel was not publicly promoted, yet the church continued to grow. Pastors and believers were beaten and thrown into prison for doing nothing more than telling people about Christ. I felt so unworthy to be teaching these men and women anything. Following one of the seminars I was leading for these godly heroes of the faith, I was dining with a pastor and his wife. Though his English was broken, the pastor shared about the suffering he endured for being a preacher of the gospel. I was astonished at what being a Christian was like under Communist rule. But the pastor smiled as he shared story after story of people being saved through his suffering. The conversation ended on a most unusual note. When freedom was brought to the Romanian people, he said that while he rejoiced in the opportunities such freedom would bring, he feared that the Romanian church would become complacent and soft without the constant threat of persecution. The pastor knew that the lack of persecution could actually be a negative rather than a positive for the church. Over the years, the pastor has seen many good things result from the country's newfound freedom. At the same time, his fears have been realized as well. Many in the church have lost their fervor.

Suffering has an outward impact on others. Through hardships, our souls are revived as we watch others come to Christ by seeing the hope and joy in our lives amidst the pain.

CHAPTER TWELVE

God Desires a Strong and Caring Church

During World War II, the German government sought to find the best method of torture for extracting information from prisoners. They conducted numerous experiments and eventually concluded that solitary confinement was the most effective option. After only a few days alone, most captives told all that they knew.[1] Clearly, we were created with the need for relationship. At no time is this need greater than when we are experiencing suffering. As this German torture technique proved, we need other people to emotionally support us through tough times in order to persevere.

During periods of testing and suffering, it's important to turn to other committed Christians for support and encouragement. Without it, we are easy prey for temptation, despair, and abandonment of faith. Sometimes God allows us to go through suffering so that we can learn and experience the loving care of God's people, the church.

God calls the church "the body of Christ." This description portrays Christians as a unified group of people whose lives are intricately woven together. The Holy Spirit indwells each Christian and is, through Christ's body, an extension of His presence on earth. Though each individual makes a unique contribution to the body, we all work together to fulfill Christ's mission for the church in the world.[2]

Unfortunately, many church folks act as if they have no problems. Rather than honestly and genuinely revealing personal struggles, we assume we can open up only *after* we have navigated the rough waters. Our testimonies tend to be stories of recovery and triumph rather than honest admissions of current pain and struggle. The fear of looking like a "poor excuse for a Christian" compels many hurting people to go into hiding. Because they fear being criticized, some people even stop attending church.

One of my (John's) recovering alcoholic friends once told me that the great thing about Alcoholics Anonymous (AA) is that it "reaches out without reaching down." Of course, there are times when judgment is necessary, but judgment alone is not sufficient. People long to be loved and accepted. Without unfailing love, it is difficult to truly hear truth. Quite honestly, most of us do a poor job in relaying truth to hurting people. Consequently and sadly, some Christians end up being undeservingly judged or treated harshly by other Christians when they need love the most.

I (John) once overheard a conversation between two women about another church member whose husband had left her after the tragic death of their son. The two women wondered what this woman had done to "cause" her husband to leave.

Eventually one of those women faced similar problems and, because of her skewed perspective on suffering, struggled to determine what she had done to drive her husband into the arms of another woman. Whenever we can attribute irresponsibility to someone else's behavior, we convince ourselves that as long as we are responsible we can avoid such adversity. We thus fabricate a view that life must be orderly, controllable, and manageable. As a result, sufferers live in isolation. True feelings are hidden from others so that no one suspects how deep the pain and struggle are. The isolation reinforces the lack of Christian unity and validates the soul shame. Unfortunately, it also makes sufferers easy prey for those promising comfort from a source other than God.

Suffering Illuminates the Value of the Body of Christ

The human body is designed so that wounds generally can heal spontaneously with remarkably little medical interference. A thorough analysis of the body's response to injury is beyond the scope of this book. Yet it is important to know that when someone is hurt, a physician depends heavily on the body's own ability to repair any damage. For instance, when your finger is cut, the whole body is affected, including loss of blood and fluid, pain, and the release of cellular products into the bloodstream. In response to the injury, the body depends upon a highly dynamic, integrated series of cellular, physiological, and biochemical events, exclusive to itself. In fact, medical scientists are unable to reproduce the entire process of wound healing in a laboratory setting. Many physiological adaptations are at work to fight off foreign material or bacteria, remove any cellular debris and injured tissue fragments, and redirect blood flow. As the body goes through various phases of the healing process, the individual begins to notice increased strength, vigor, and appetite. All of these are signs that healing is taking place within the body.

The biblical design for the body of Christ is much like the physical body. Just as the body seeks to heal an injured member, so the body of Christ should minister to other members who need healing. As Christians, we are to promote restoration, which also means that we are to protect the wounded from the additional pain of insensitive words and thoughtless actions.

Callous comments have no place in the body of Christ. They break the heart of God and violate His command to love, encourage, and care for one another. Because we share the same Father, we are to feel the affliction of others and respond in ways that promote healing.[3]

This truth was evidenced in the early church. People who may have been strangers prior to conversion went to great lengths to demonstrate love and concern for each other. Believers provided mutual support by sharing their resources with those in need.[4] In the same way, we accurately reflect the love of Christ when we embrace and actively support our fellow believers.

I (Gary) first met Chris when he was a graduate student. Chris was also a gifted musician—one of those rare students who had so distinguished himself from his classmates that he was constantly being sought out, not only locally, but around the country. Very few people knew that Chris had been diagnosed years before with a very serious personality disorder. Although he had been treated by a physician, he decided on his own to discontinue the treatments.

Chris first contacted me to ask if I could speak with him about his personal assurance of his salvation. His lack of assurance was taking a tremendous toll, affecting both him and his ministry. Not being a trained physician, psychologist, or counselor myself, I referred him to a Christian psychologist. Chris faithfully kept his appointments and placed himself back under his physician's care. After learning to recognize the signs of his illness and to change his thoughts as well as his actions, Chris made great strides. With the full support of his physician, he later received permission to stop their visits. Through it all, Chris turned his personal struggle and victory into an avenue to help others who are hurting similarly. Today he is a nationally recognized musician, frequently performing in churches and giving his testimony. Whenever we talk, I always ask Chris how he is doing. Over the years, he has remained a wonderful example, not only of how suffering can be treated, but also how the body of Christ can benefit from the lessons we learn.

The Ministry of the Body

Many church members ask how they can help someone who is going through the valley of suffering. As members of Christ's body, we are the physical representation of Christ to others. You can minister to others who are going through a time of suffering in the following ways:

Pray for hurting members

One of the more humorous stories in the New Testament depicts the church responding to suffering through prayer. Following James's execution, King Herod arrested Peter and threw him into prison. Herod was so angry with Peter that he had him guarded by four squads of soldiers. These circumstances motivated the Jerusalem church to pray continually for Peter's release. Even as they were diligently praying for Peter's freedom, he was miraculously released from prison and arrived at their door. When the servant told them that Peter was standing at the door, their response was, "You are beside yourself!" To put it in present day terms, "Honey, get a grip!" While believers debated whether or not God had answered their prayers, Peter had to keep knocking until someone finally let him in. When the door was opened and they saw Peter standing there, "they were astonished."[5]

When our brothers and sisters in Christ hurt, Christians should pray—fervently. Do you remember the story of Nathan in chapter 1? Prior to Nathan's surgery, members of his church gathered throughout the week to pray. When we pray for others, we are saying that we will intercede to the Father on their behalf. In essence, we dedicate our time and energy to them through prayer.

Encourage hurting members

Many recovering alcoholics say that the key to recovery is spending time with others. Interestingly, this camaraderie is one of the reasons many go to bars, and it is one of the very things used to sell alcoholic beverages. The reason such advertising is successful is that it caters to a critical human need—namely, the need to belong and feel accepted.

People are less interested in being part of a "friendly church" than in having genuine friendships within the church. Friendships require spending time and getting involved in people's lives. The writer of Hebrews framed this point as follows:

> And let us consider one another in order to stir up love
> and good works, not forsaking the assembling of ourselves
> together, as is the manner of some, but exhorting one
> another, and so much the more as you see the Day
> approaching.   HEBREWS 10:24-25

The word for *stir up* above is the same Greek word as the word for *provoke*, which is used in Ephesians 6 where fathers are told not to provoke their children to wrath. In other words, Christians are to provoke one other to love and do helpful things.

Affliction often provides fertile ground for establishing friendships. By reaching out with helpful hands, empathetic ears, and willing feet, we can provide practical help to those who are hurting.

This type of help is what Paul had in mind when he spoke of bearing the burdens of others.[6]

Help hurting members

In the days and months following Nathan Sours's death, Dave and Teresa's church family provided practical support. The grass was mowed, meals were prepared and delivered, and cards and calls poured in for almost a year.

Solomon recognized the value of friendship at times like this when he said, "A friend loves at all times, and a brother is born for adversity."[7] Literally, the passage means that a brother is born for "a time of adversity." True friends prove themselves by helping in whatever way possible. During such times, genuine love is revealed. Truly, they will know we are Christians by the way that we act out our love.[8]

It is our pain, not our blessings, that touches people. This is another reason God allows us to suffer. Through suffering, His people are drawn together to respond to the needs of a hurting member. If you are deeply hurting, knowing that your pain could benefit others might offer little solace. While God may not specifically orchestrate a trial for this purpose, it is His desire for the church to be bolstered by the suffering of others.

Summary

If you ever watch football games on TV, you have likely seen an injured player or two. Sometimes someone is hurt so severely that he can't even move. At times like this, the crowd falls silent, and even the opposing team becomes somber as the medical responders come out onto the field. When the problem is very severe, the players sometimes arrange themselves in small groups to pray right there on the field for their injured colleague.

The Christian life is not a spectator sport. We actively participate with one another on the field of play. When a fellow player is wounded, it's up to us to spring into action in whatever way we are led or are able. Pain and suffering often have healthy effects upon the sufferer and others alike. As the body of Christ, when we are aware of others who are hurting, we are to respond to the wound with love, comfort, encouragement, and support. In this way, the benefits found in pain move outward into the lives around the sufferer, validating our need for each other.

CHAPTER THIRTEEN

God Desires to Minister through Us

Tom and Maria Whiteman were high school sweethearts.[1] In addition to their love, they also shared a commitment to serve the Lord through the local church. They attended Bible college together and were married during their senior year. After a romantic honeymoon and graduation, they packed their few possessions and moved back to their home state where Tom became the youth pastor of a conservative church. It was a storybook beginning for a young Christian couple, deeply in love. But Tom and Maria did not live happily ever after.

After four years of marriage and ministry, Maria told Tom that she was no longer happy in their marriage and that she no longer loved him. She confessed that for the past six months she had been involved in another relationship. Tom's shock was complete; he had been blindsided. Perhaps he should have seen the warning signs, but he didn't. "It was like a bad dream, listening to my wife's explanations and reasoning. I kept thinking, *This can't be happening. She must have had a bad day.* Tom had never considered that his marriage might fail. He had grown up in a Christian home, committed his life to the Lord, attended Bible school, become a minister, and maintained a regular devotional life. "I had a formula all worked out: As long as I committed my life to God and put Him first, He would bless me. God would surely protect me from anything serious," said Tom. Sadly, when put to the test, his formula for life failed. His beliefs about an orderly and predictable world were shattered.

Now Tom was alone. Not only had he lost his wife but, as a divorced man, he was no longer eligible to serve as a minister in his church. Confusion, fear, and hopelessness characterized Tom's life. "My ambitions were dashed. I had no future. I was convinced God could no longer use me." As he endured the harsh comments of those who blamed him for failing as the head of his home, feelings of loneliness and denial gave way to anger. Perhaps the most addictive and intoxicating of emotions, anger gives a euphoric burst of power and energy. Like unspent fuel, anger can keep feeding on itself, shielding a brittle self-image from potentially damaging revelations.

Guilt and gnawing shame mounted beneath the shallow veneer of anger. For Tom, there was no escape from the gut-wrenching questions that penetrated his flimsy defense. "What have you been doing wrong? What secret sins do you have in your life?" Wounded by those to whom he had turned for comfort, Tom left the fellowship of the church. "If this was Christianity, I wanted nothing to do with it," he said.

After about a year, Tom decided to come out of his spiritual desert and give the church another try. He searched for a church that would be less judgmental and more open-minded than his former church. Tom found one that offered a divorce recovery program. He joined, hoping that people in this congregation would treat him differently. He was pleased to learn that although these believers treated him more lovingly, they did not compromise on biblical doctrine.

With the help of the divorce recovery group and other Christians, Tom began to move through his grief. He realized that God could still use him to minister in ways he had not yet explored.

Tom returned to school and earned a master's degree in counseling and a doctorate in psychology. He began to minister to others who had suffered the pain of separation and divorce. Along with several other people who had experienced divorce, Tom founded Fresh Start Seminars. Today, there are Fresh Start offices throughout the United States, England, and Australia. This ministry provides hope and healing to broken people all over the world. Tom learned that God could use his personal tragedy to witness to others. "He took the worst thing that ever happened to me and used it for His Kingdom," he said.

Godly Comfort

In 2 Corinthians 1:3-6, we find a wonderful promise: there is no trouble that we go through in which the comfort of God is not available to us. The word *comfort* comes from the Greek word *paraklesis*, which means "to encourage or console." It has the idea of sighing with another—walking along with the person who is suffering and sharing God's love through support and encouragement.

The perfect manifestation of God's comfort is the Holy Spirit, the constant presence of God in a believer's life. While a friend may lighten a burden for a time, God's Spirit journeys with the Christian through the trial, understanding the pain and communicating the unwavering love of the Father.

In this second letter to the Corinthian church, Paul spoke of the "sufferings of Christ," which he endured in obedience to the Father's plan. In fact, Paul noted that God comforts us in all tribulation.[2] The present tense of the verb assures us that the God of all things is willing to comfort us continually and constantly throughout the duration of the trial.

But notice, too, that God provides comfort in *all* our troubles. Even when our miseries are the result of our own poor choices, God offers Himself as our Comforter. When our disobedience and selfishness bring about suffering, healing can begin only with confession and repentance. At that point, we begin to know God's comfort.

A Ministry View

When problems are plentiful in our lives, the comfort of God abounds even more.[3] Paul further explained that suffering teaches us *about* God's comfort. Without experiencing trials, it would be impossible to personally know how God can minister to a broken heart. One of God's expectations, however, is that we not become preoccupied with ourselves during times of suffering. He desires that we share His comfort with others who are also in need, giving out of the resources that have been provided to us. The passage says consolation is given "that we may be able to comfort those who are in any trouble, with the comfort with which we ourselves are comforted by God."[4] Paul had suffered much, and consequently had experienced the comfort of God. He then was able to share that solace with the Corinthian believers. Such action reminds us that those who are continually experiencing the comfort of God are well suited to minister to others in need of support. C. S. Lewis knew of this truth when he wrote, "Think of me as a fellow-patient in the same hospital who, having been admitted a little earlier cd. [could] give some advice."[5]

Paul emphasizes that we need not have experienced the same problem in order to be helpful to a person in need. Because we ourselves have experienced the ministry of God's comfort, we can comfort those in *any* trouble. Author and evangelist Ron Dunn poetically describes this ministry by saying, "Sometimes the tears we shed water the flowers in other people's gardens."[6]

One day I (Gary) received a disheartening call from Jason, a middle-aged, philosophically minded evangelist who desired some advice. This servant of God was deeply troubled by the problem of suffering, so much so that he was beginning to question his own salvation. Jason had graduated from a prominent Midwestern seminary and had published a couple of very helpful books. He wished to keep up his nationwide ministry, but his struggle over the issue of suffering was beginning to affect his ability to preach and teach. He confided that he even felt somewhat suicidal.

I recommended that Jason contact a Christian counselor in his area. Through that contact, Jason learned that he was creating most of his own struggles. He was a quick study and made rapid progress. His questions were answered, and most importantly, Jason was able to come to grips with his own emotional issues. After completing a university doctorate while pastoring a church, Jason realized his lifelong dream of teaching. For several years now, he has been a seminary apologetics professor. With God's help, Jason moved from being suicidal and desperately wanting to leave the ministry to equipping others to pastor and teach. As in the New Testament days, God still changes lives and uses our struggles to help others.

By providing comfort to God's children, Paul himself was blessed and able to avoid self-pity. He realized that finding God's comfort in the midst of adversity allowed him to minister to others more effectively.[7] Mac Cauley, whose story we read in chapter 4, discovered that his car accident actually helped him to develop a keener sensitivity to hurting people. "Throughout my ministry, I was always sensitive to depressed and hurting people, but now I have a whole new appreciation and different understanding for those who are hurting," he says. Mac Cauley is a better shepherd because he experienced the profound comfort of God during his own time of suffering.

In an interview regarding his role in the movie *Tootsie*, Dustin Hoffman described the experience of being disguised as a woman. One of the makeup artists told him that it was impossible to make him look like a pretty woman. Hoffman says that he went home that night and cried as he recalled how many women he had rejected in his past. Regardless of how smart, kind, or talented they were, he had rejected them solely on the basis of their physical appearance. Because he had now been judged on appearance alone, Dustin Hoffman could now be more empathetic toward these women.

Similarly, suffering allows us to identify with others and provides us an opportunity to testify about God's comfort to a broken soul. Someone has said that encouragement is like peanut butter; the more you spread it around, the more it sticks to things. As Christians, we need to spread our experience and comfort to others so they may come to know the God of all comfort.

Like Tom Whiteman, we may find that God will take the greatest pain and suffering of our lives and use it as a springboard for ministry to others. Of course, this doesn't mean that each of us will develop an internationally known and respected Christian ministry. However, it does mean that through our difficulties, God has equipped us to share His hope and comfort in our own particular corner of the world.

Summary

Think back to the story I (John) told earlier about losing my fiancée. When she broke up with me, I was studying and preparing to
become a missionary. In the aftermath of the loss, however, I started
taking psychology classes in order to better understand my hurt.
Through the painful sting of rejection, God redirected my career
pursuits from missions to counseling. Prior to this loss, I could
not figure out why anyone would want to see a counselor. But as
I wandered in my own desert of loneliness and abandonment, I
learned the value of the helping relationship.

Today, nearly thirty years later, I have had the opportunity to
share that story with countless clients who have experienced similar
losses. My suffering taught me the value of obedience, depending
upon God, helping others, and becoming more like Christ. The
messages hidden beneath my clients' pain have been different and
unique to them. But they've been encouraged by hearing how my
own suffering has been redeemed. The opportunity that God has
given me to comfort others through my own loss demonstrates that
God does not waste His comfort. He has redirected my suffering
outward to other people who are hurting in one way or another.

UPWARD
DIRECTION

The Bible reveals to us that God uses
suffering to move our eyes heavenward.
The next five chapters explore ways in which
suffering gives us an upward focus.

CHAPTER FOURTEEN

God Desires That We See His True Character

Belinda, an attractive thirty-eight-year-old woman, cried her way through my (John's) first counseling session with her. Her dress and mannerisms proved that she was trying hard to present an image of someone who had it all together. However, her recent hospital admission for severe depression revealed a different story. It took several sessions to get Belinda to share her experience. Obviously, trust was not something that came easily to her, so establishing rapport was a painstaking process. But eventually the walls were let down enough for me to see inside.

Belinda grew up in the Midwest and attended a very conservative Bible-believing church. She was active in her youth group as well as other church activities. By all standards she was a model child. Like most teenage girls, she dreamed of meeting the right person to marry. Until then, however, she vowed to keep herself pure.

A youth pastor joined the staff at Belinda's church and quickly got to know this young lady through her willingness to serve in any way that she could. Perhaps he recognized her need for affirmation, because before long he was sexually abusing her as often as he could get her alone. In addition, he was also abusing several other girls in the church. Belinda's innocence was shattered. No longer could she see "godly men" as trustworthy.

After several years of the abuse, one girl finally told her parents, and the minister's sin was exposed. The elders and staff members decided it was best to keep the ordeal quiet since they thought nothing good could come from having "a man of God" and a

Christ-centered church in the middle of such a horrible contro-versy. Not only would the church's reputation be tarnished, they reasoned, it would also cause great upheaval within the church. In order to avoid a scandal, the minister was asked to resign. Unbeliev-ably, he was offered a favorable recommendation. Belinda's parents told their daughter not to speak about the "episode," and for years, this child of God had nowhere to go with her inner pain. Because Belinda saw herself as "spoiled goods," her self-esteem plummeted. She felt terrible, blaming herself for allowing the abuse to happen and for letting it continue for so long. She truly believed there was something wrong with her.

She married after graduating from college, but her sex life never lived up to her expectations. In fact, she tried to avoid intimacy at all costs. Sex left her feeling dirty. Her confused and hurt husband withdrew, leaving Belinda to battle feelings of abandonment and rejection all over again. *Who could blame him?* she thought. *I am not worthy of such a good man.*

Spiritually, Belinda did not fare much better. She was active in the children's department of her church, served as chairperson for the benevolence committee, and worked tirelessly in the drama ministry. She was even involved in a local crisis pregnancy cen-ter. Everyone considered Belinda to be a godly Christian wife and a wonderful lady. But no one sensed the growing emotional and spiritual unrest in her soul.

Belinda viewed God as someone to be appeased. Of course she believed in grace, but she had a hard time applying that grace to her own life. Her spiritual journey was little more than repeated attempts to gain God's approval. No matter how much Belinda tried to feel peace in her relationship with God, His approval always seemed beyond her reach. Her resolute efforts only left Belinda lonely, fearful, tired, and depressed. Like a field officer, she mar-shaled her forces in an effort to reclaim a sense of control in her life, but in spite of her resurgent resolve, she could not withstand the powerful assault of her internal turmoil.

Combat fatigue eventually resulted in an inability to fight any longer, and unable to overcome her overwhelming feelings of shame and despair, Belinda surrendered to her emotions. She experienced a debilitating depression that necessitated a prolonged hospitalization. Belinda, like so many other sexual abuse survivors, felt incredible inner pain. She could see no redeeming value in her experiences.

Through counseling, however, Belinda began to realize how many battle scars she bore. Some were the result of her past wounds, but others had been caused by her own ineffective tactics to control the pain. As her sense of safety increased, she began to lower the walls that she had erected to hide her pain and protect her already depleted reserves. Energy she once had used to avoid her feelings was now channeled into therapy, and eventually Belinda was able to move through the issues of trust, fear, control, abandonment, and acceptance. Her marriage improved beyond her imagination. The shame and fear that once paralyzed her was replaced with comfort and enjoyment. Belinda now speaks to groups on sexual abuse and counsels with other women who have experienced sexual trauma.

Most importantly, Belinda came to see God in a different way. No longer is she bitter at God for allowing the sexual abuse to occur. She is finally able to worship God deeply.

Like Belinda, Tom Whiteman also came to know God in a whole new way when his belief in a predictable God was shattered. No longer did he see God as just black-and-white but now in shades of gray. Once Tom realized that he could not anticipate what God was doing or going to do, God did not seem as judgmental as Tom once thought Him to be.

What was true for both Belinda and Tom in the twentieth century was also true for Job thousands of years ago. Following his discourse with God, Job was left practically speechless. His arguments had proved agonizingly insufficient. His attitude was exposed as arrogant.[1] He realized that God alone is in the position to decide what is best for any of His children.

Job responded to God on this issue one last time. In the final chapter of the book, we find Job with a new outlook on life, as he realized that God can do everything. His mind had been opened to see his ignorance before the Almighty God, and he finally understood that his terrible experience had allowed him to see God in a bigger way.[2] He realized that nothing is too difficult for God. Humbled by the hand and words of God, Job exclaimed that he now had a fresh grasp of the power of God. His burning question of "Why me?" was never answered. Rather, God changed Job's preoccupation from explanation to worship. His new understanding of the vastness of God settled Job's confusion and eliminated his demand for answers. Sovereignty was no longer just a theological concept to Job but a first-hand reality because God had used suffering to enlarge Job's capacity to know Him. Job once saw God as oppositional, but he learned to see sovereignty in a fresh way.[3] Knowing that he had an all-powerful and glorious God, Job could now live in triumphant confidence.

Thousands of years after the penning of Job's words, the prophet Jeremiah found himself in the king's prison for preaching God's message. As God tested Jeremiah's faith, the weeping prophet declared that there was nothing too hard for the Lord.[4] In response to his prayer, the Lord told Jeremiah that he was correct; nothing was too hard for Him.[5] Just as suffering had changed Job's under-standing of sovereignty, Jeremiah's heartache unclouded his percep-tion of God's nature.

We are similarly encouraged today by those who have walked through deep waters with God and have emerged, not only rela-tively unscathed, but as brightly shining individuals whose relation-ship with God has clearly matured. I (Gary) met one such saint during a speaking engagement at a Midwestern college. Charles was seriously handicapped and found it quite difficult just to walk. On top of that, he had also been recently diagnosed with a severe emotional disorder that required constant medication. To further complicate his situation, a rare blood condition plagued him from time to time. Combined with repeated mistreatment and neglect as a child, Charles lived constantly with pain of various sorts. One bout with illness brought him to the threshold of death. Many would wonder about the fairness of someone suffering from such severe physical and emotional hurts.

Charles often struggled with nagging doubts regarding his salva-tion. Sometimes this would erupt into anger at God, as he lashed out at Him for his myriad of problems and blamed God for not intervening or taking them away. As we talked, Charles and I developed what has become a long-term friendship. I helped him identify his errant thoughts and substitute God's promises in their place. It took some time, but over a few years, Charles achieved very significant victories over his religious doubts. Later, he used similar techniques to make major strides in dealing with his emotional condition, as well as with the wounds of his past. While his disability and blood disease remain incurable, Charles today has grown to such an extent that he has been able to bless others in their struggles. Having completed his college degree, Charles now works with people with disabilities and has also published several items in apologetics, his chosen field of research. Incredibly, in spite of a serious speech impediment, Charles now teaches an adult study group!

Above all, it was his personal, detailed study of God's attributes that changed Charles's attitude. In fact, he has never gotten over this look at God's character. He often tells me he cannot wait to go to be with his Jesus, who has transformed his daily existence in ways that would seem impossible to everyone who knows him and his handicaps. He constantly works on applying these truths to his life. God's grace and mercy have triumphed, infusing Charles with a joyful attitude that has become obvious to those whom he meets and with whom he works.

To be honest, when we suffer, we typically see it as an attack, and the God who allowed it as the enemy. We're quick to point a finger at some person or some circumstance. Ultimately, we have a deep sense that God could have prevented us from experiencing the calamity if He had really wanted to. No responsible parent would let his or her child proceed into harm's way without doing everything to stop it. God seems too irresponsible, if not downright cruel and callous, to be trusted. The pain is compounded by the sense that God has wronged us.

I (John) had been counseling a forty-year-old widow named Olivia, whose pain was immense. Her husband had been killed by a drunken driver, and Olivia's joyless and gloomy existence cast a shadow on all who saw her. Though I did not believe it was warranted, her family wanted her in the hospital. She was grieving deeply, but her grief was compounded by a pessimistic and melancholic personality.

From the onset of therapy, Olivia recognized that she was angry at God. She couldn't pray, have devotions, or sing in church. In fact, it was a struggle for her even to go to church. After about seven months of counseling, I told her that she had the right to be angry at God. After all, God had cheated her out of a future with her husband. She did not deserve that kind of treatment from a God who was supposed to be loving. At first she agreed with me. Then I went a step further, continuing to "shake my fist" at God, so to speak, in an attempt to help her see the irrationality of her perspective. Finally, I hit on a key phrase. "God has wronged you," I said. "He has wronged you, and He had no right to do so!" It was as if the floodgates of her soul opened, and she began to weep uncontrollably. Though she had said similar things in many of our previous counseling sessions, this time it was different. Through her tears she kept saying, "No, no! God didn't wrong me. God can't wrong anybody." Her anger and resentment toward God began to melt. And though her grief did not disappear, her faith was rekindled.

In contrast to most of us, Betsie ten Boom's unwavering faith gave her a greater appreciation of the wonderful inexplicability and sovereignty of God. Before her arrest, Betsie stoutly affirmed, "But if God has shown us bad times ahead, it's enough for me that He knows about them. That's why He sometimes shows us things, you know—to tell us that this too is in His hands."[6] Betsie was able to see every evil and jarring plight as an opportunity to praise God and share the good news of Christ.

When Betsie and her sister, Corrie, were placed in the filthy conditions of Barracks 28, Betsie found comfort in 1 Thessalonians 5:15-18. Reading from a Bible that had been safely concealed from the prison guards, she told Corrie that regardless of their circumstances, they were to praise God. She even thanked God for the fleas since the guards avoided entering the barracks because of them. Betsie's unflinching assent of God's personal involvement in her suffering encouraged Corrie to rethink her own understanding of God's character. And on her deathbed, overcome by the awesomeness of God, Betsie envisioned the remarkable opportunity their imprisonment offered: "We must tell [people] that there is no pit so deep that He is not deeper still. They will listen to us, Corrie, because we have been here."[7] Despite the horror of a concentration camp, the Ten Booms were able to see the glory of God. Just like Job, Corrie and Betsie learned that God was the God of their worst situation, even Ravensbrück.

Two thousand years earlier, on a peaceful evening, Jesus and the disciples were sailing on the Sea of Galilee. Suddenly a violent squall rose, frightening even the most experienced fishermen on board. As the little boat filled with water, perhaps Peter manned the sail and James took over bailing. No doubt the scene was one of chaos and anxiety. As the water rose, so did the panic of the crew, who feared they might run aground or die.

Oh, and by the way, Jesus was asleep. In desperation the disciples woke Jesus to tell Him that they were about to meet their Maker. Jesus rubbed the sleep from His eyes and told the sea to be still. In stunned silence, the disciples wondered just who this guy was that He could calm a storm. As the boat quietly bounced in the lake, Jesus didn't say, "Now do you guys feel better? How about letting me get back to sleep!" Rather, He scolded them for their lack of faith. The disciples, overwhelmed by the magnitude of the miracle, may have missed the lesson on faith, but they couldn't help but feel deep awe toward the man who would become their Savior.[8]

When we experience the storms of this life, we, too, are prone to fear. We clamor, act impulsively, or slump into despair and depression. But Jesus is in control, waiting to demonstrate that He has power over the storm. We will never know of God's power over the tempest unless we go through the storm and experience His capacity to calm it. Because Jesus was and is the Creator God, He is able to speak to His creation and bring peace and restoration.

Summary

Throughout the divorce process, Tom Whiteman learned that God has compassion for those who hurt. If God lavishes mercy on the wounded, we should certainly do the same. Since Tom no longer saw God as judgmental, he surrendered his own judgmental attitude. Yes, sin is sin and should never be condoned, but sinners need a Redeemer, and our Redeemer saves by loving.

When we, like Job, see God for who He is, we can stop blaming Him for our pain and suffering. We learn to accept both good and bad from the hand of the Lord.[9] We come to know God's power when we see Him move in an impossible situation and meet our personal need. Possibly St. Augustine had this in mind when he exclaimed, "In my deepest wound I saw your glory, and it dazzled me."

CHAPTER FIFTEEN

God Desires to Prepare Us for a Blessing

The story of Job reveals another purpose in suffering. By the end of the book, we realize that Job's steadfastness in suffering was not only meaningful but also recognized by the heavenly Father as worthy of reward. Job declared early in his biography that he would bless the Lord no matter what happened to him.[1] And because of this faithfulness, he was able to receive blessings from the Lord—more than what had been taken from him, in fact.[2] Job had experienced loss, but he also understood what it meant to obtain grace.

Indeed, God blessed Job by giving him twice as many things as he had had before his adversity began. He was given double the number of livestock, sheep, camels, and donkeys. Though his seven sons and three daughters had all been killed, he and his wife had seven more sons and three more daughters. Finally, Job lived another 140 years and was allowed to see his descendants for four generations. In the long run, Job's suffering was short lived when compared to the years he was given to enjoy his family, wealth, and health.

Once again, life looked promising for Job. But his new life was the result of a changed heart. Because of his ordeal, he had discovered that God is more than a concept or an impersonal being, and that nothing in his life had occurred outside of God's watchful eye. With a humbled heart, Job realized that God could be trusted. And because of Job's changed attitude, God knew that He could trust Job with a double portion of blessing.

Imagine the gossip that must have surrounded Job. After all, people of his day believed that suffering was punishment for wrong-doing. Perhaps they considered him a first-class hypocrite during his suffering. In the end, however, God silenced Job's critics. The blessings that Job received communicated to his accusers that he was a just and upright man. But it wasn't Job's goodness that earned him a reward, it was his broken and contrite heart that brought about the blessings of God.

Of course, it is very difficult to know what God has planned for our futures. Often it is even tough to make sense of our present struggles. About twenty years ago, I (Gary) got to know one of my philosophy students pretty well. Al seemed to have a very promising future, but a short while after I met him, he was diagnosed with cancer and quickly underwent surgery. Al's future was put on hold, as the next few weeks and months included further tests, treatments, more tests, and more treatments.

Al knew he needed to pull his life back together. He just wasn't sure the best way to do that. Should he finish his studies even though he couldn't be sure that he would live long enough to graduate? Should he do something else while he waited for his treatments to be finished? Living his life from day to day, Al decided to go back to school and finish his bachelor's degree. Every three months, he had to travel to a hospital for more specialized tests to ascertain whether or not the cancer had returned. Once he received his degree, he went straight to graduate school and finished his master's degree. Then he completed his Ph.D. and a lengthy residency.

Today, Al is a well-known Christian psychologist. He has a private practice, is an adjunct professor at a prestigious Texas university, and so far has written four books and many journal articles. He is constantly in demand as a speaker. Moreover, he married his college sweetheart and thoroughly enjoys their three children. Incidentally, three of his books address various issues of pain and suffering.

When Al was on his back in more than one hospital, God could very well have been preparing him for a future blessing. One thing is for sure—his struggles definitely prepared him to be a blessing to others!

How often we miss the blessings of God because we have chosen to pursue our own way. The blessings we receive may not necessarily be like those of Job. Yet suffering can prepare us to receive greater blessings. Consider Joseph, who told his brothers that while their hateful actions had been meant to harm him, God had used them to accomplish good.[3] We can now see how God redeemed Joseph's trials to bring incredible blessings to the nation of Israel. In the film *Star Trek: Wrath of the Khan*, Mr. Spock sacrifices himself to save the *Enterprise*. As he's dying, he exchanges a few words with Captain Kirk:

> *Spock*: The needs of the many outweigh . . .
> *Kirk*: . . . the needs of the few.
> *Spock*: Or the one.[4]

Joseph's trials were unfair and unjust if the few, or in this case the one, is more important than the many. But Joseph was not greater than the nation of Israel. As God's child, Joseph knew that God could use him in whatever way He deemed appropriate to attain a greater good. Joseph's ability to accept that truth gave him not only the power to endure but also the ability to forgive his offenders.

Summary

The book of Job has always intrigued both of us. However, when we arrive at the later part of Job 42, it is easy to simply skip over it. After an initial reading of the epilogue, some may even think that God is restoring Job's losses twofold in order to apologize. Perhaps it looks like it is a convenient way for God to bless Job by saying, "I'm really sorry for putting you through such misery." Of course, God doesn't do wrong, nor does He need to apologize.

But if we dig into this passage more deeply, we may finally realize the richness of those concluding verses. Job's epilogue is a vivid illustration of Solomon's words: "The end of a thing is better than its beginning."[5] Job's life was full prior to his suffering, but he emerged a "new and improved" Job. Suffering had personalized and purified his faith, tested his faithfulness, matured him, and prepared him for a greater blessing than he could ever have imagined. His enhanced financial portfolio likely paled in comparison with the new sense of life he now experienced. Though his wealth increased greatly, the changes in his life loomed even larger. Job learned that there is a God above and beyond the suffering, a God who is incredibly grand, gracious, good, and generous. Knowing a God like that was Job's true reward. The blessings of God were not a payoff; they were only the manifestation of how our outrageous and extraordinary God operates.

The character of God compels Him to be a generous lover. He deliriously desires to bless His children. His blessings are never to be seen as indulgent. No. At the same time, our God knows that an ungrateful heart is ill prepared for His unimaginable blessings. Unless He prepares our hearts and remakes our souls through the sting of suffering, we might selfishly bask in His blessings without any sense of humility or gratitude. Those who have either never faced serious suffering or who have reacted to their pain in less than constructive ways may find it difficult to get past Job's actual circumstances. But when we meet people like Charles (introduced in chapter 14) who are so marvelously transformed as a result of their suffering, we get a small glimpse of what wonders God works through those who are willing to grow.

CHAPTER SIXTEEN

God Desires to Give Believers Dying Grace

The subject of death and dying touches everyone at one time or another. A group of researchers found out that even preschoolers have ideas about what it means to die. One young boy named Jimmy shared his view of death: "When you die, they bury you in the ground and your soul goes to heaven, but your body can't go to heaven because it is too crowded up there already." Judy said, "Only the good people go to heaven. The other people go where it's hot all the time like in Florida." John responded by saying, "Maybe I'll die someday, but I hope I don't die on my birthday because it's no fun to celebrate your birthday if you're dead." Marsha offered another perspective on death. "When you die, you don't have to do homework in heaven, unless your teacher is there too."[1]

We will all die someday, but only God knows how and when. Thinking about one's own death is not pleasant for many people, but for the believer, it should not be the cause of fear. Through death, we walk into the presence of God.

The Meaning of Life according to Paul

The apostle Paul seemed to always know how to make the best of a bad situation. He viewed his imprisonment as a means to advance the gospel, sharing his story with those who might not have otherwise heard it. When jealousy and envy created a competitive environment in the church, Paul simply rejoiced in the fact that the Good News was being preached.

Paul was able to use bad circumstances for good because he was preoccupied with honoring Christ. He was willing to esteem Christ, even in death, which he thought was better than earthly life.[2] Through his life, he desired that Christ would be magnified—brought into sharp focus. Not only did Paul want to glorify Christ through his words and deeds, but even in his own body. This concept might be what Paul meant when he told the Roman church to present their bodies as living sacrifices.[3]

Like Paul, we should be devoted to honoring and magnifying Christ. In the face of suffering or adversity, this is possible only as we die to ourselves, take up our crosses, and follow Him.[4] But what does it mean to take up our cross and follow Christ? For readers in Paul's day, the cross was a symbol of death, a painful death, a death that robbed the cross bearer of dignity. Paul used the analogy to exhort Christians to consider the things we desire from this world as dead. Taking up our crosses means viewing those internal desires of our hearts as having no value, as if they could—or more accurately *should*—be thrown away. We must yield the demands of our hearts and allow God to have the right of way. In other words, we are to view our desires for comfort, financial security, good health, status—things that are not bad in and of themselves—as buried and gone.

What do you desire most in life? Very few Christians would earnestly hunger to glorify Christ through their lives if doing so meant torment. As we have already seen, though it pains even the most devoted believer to admit, our central passions are for ease, comfort, predictability, and fairness.

But Paul gave us the conditions by which this goal can be accomplished: ". . . whether by life or by death."[5] We've all heard the saying that the only things that are certain in life are death and taxes. Technology has helped us to postpone death but not eliminate it. We can hope for tax relief, but as long as we live under government officials, we will have taxes. Needless to say, we cannot do much about either. Paul recognized that the logical conclusion of his imprisonment might be death. And as he considered the definite possibility of his life coming to a violent end, the apostle was able to recognize God's hand even in death. Paul wanted Christ to be magnified in his life no matter what the cost. His heartfelt passion was not that Caesar would spare his life but that Christ would be honored. How Paul responded to his suffering or how he faced death would not deter his determination to exalt Christ. Paul knew that he served a God who could control life and death; after all, He had raised Jesus Christ from the grave.

Often, God gives His saints what we might call "dying grace." While my (Gary's) wife, Debbie, was dying of cancer, she reported that God had spoken directly to her, imparting a very personal message. She had never before made a claim like this, but it was clear that God had given her a special peace about her impending death. She told me that she was not afraid to die, and that although she loved her family dearly, she did not even feel any emotional pain when she thought of being separated from us. In the days and weeks leading up to her death, Debbie spent many mornings sitting in a chair with her arms upraised as she listened to Christian music through her earphones. To the family, these reactions were unmistakable signs that God had blessed her during a very difficult time.[6]

Unless the Rapture occurs first, Christians eventually will leave this world through death. Although when and how we go is up to God, the work and person of the risen Jesus Christ ensures our eternal life in heaven. Paul understood this when he radically claimed that dying and being with Christ is much better than living.[7] Moreover, almost as if to make sure we understood what he was saying, Paul added that he even *preferred* to die and go be with Jesus Christ, since this was *far better* than earthly living.[8] While such words may sound pious to some, the implications of the statement are profound. Paul was not being trite in his letter to the Philippians. Deep within his soul he realized that death was not something to be feared but was a doorway to come into God's glory. Paul knew that heaven is being in the presence of Christ, and he understood that death was simply a passing into a wonderful new world—to a home prepared for us by Christ Himself.

Paul was totally consumed with living and serving Jesus Christ. He was one with Christ, and even death could not break that union. In this way, Christ was brought into sharp focus in Paul's life. What was true for Paul can also be true for us. Death is the ultimate healing. It is an end to all misery and discomfort, but not the end of living. The Bible promises that we will be glorified with new bodies.[9] God's way of bringing us to heaven, however, may be through the doorway of pain and suffering.

Summary

William Nagenda, an African evangelist, understood the hope of heaven. He said, "My life is like a ball bouncing on the floor. Sometimes the devil gives me a blow downwards, but at the deepest spot Jesus is there, and He gives me a blow upwards so that I come up higher than I was before. One day the devil will give William a blow downwards so strong that he will go all the way to the valley of the shadow of death. There Jesus will give William a blow upwards so strong that he will come into heaven. The devil will say, 'Where is William? I don't see him anymore!'"

Some may see death as a step backward. In fact, our human tendency is to pray that a loved one will live. But Paul reminds us that suffering may actually be God's way of bringing a Christian home to heaven. He wants us to understand that death is not a step backward but a step upward. This fact may be hard to accept, but God's ways are not our ways, nor are His thoughts our thoughts.[10] Truly, God's purposes are greater than our own concerns and needs.

CHAPTER SEVENTEEN

God Desires to Reward Those Who Endure

In addressing the problem of pain, C. S. Lewis keenly observed, "A book on suffering which says nothing of heaven, is leaving out almost the whole of one side of the account. Scripture and tradition habitually put the joys of heaven into the scale against the sufferings of earth, and no solution of the problem of pain which does not do so can be called a Christian one."[1] It is this hope of heaven that is the prime ingredient in a theology of suffering.

The biblical writer James knew that heaven played a significant role in helping people find meaning in suffering. His book is addressed to Christians who were suffering due to their faith. In order to direct their eyes from the sorrows of this world to the joys of heaven, James wrote, "Blessed is the man who endures temptation; for when he has been approved, he will receive the crown of life which the Lord has promised to those who love Him."[2]

Heaven and an eternity with God truly are rewards for those who suffer. But this reward has a condition: we must endure. As we saw in chapter 8, the word *endure* (*hupomenō*) comes from the word *patience* which means "to live or abide underneath a problem."[3] Patience doesn't mean living without anxiety but rather enduring adverse circumstances without letting them sour our attitudes.

In a world of instant gratification, we typically expect God to respond immediately when we pray. Some Christians even preach spiritual formulas that, when properly applied, guarantee quick and effortless results. When these formulas work, we feel great. Things have gone our way, and the notion that God can be manipulated is reinforced. But when the formulas don't work, and that is often the case, we may either be bitter toward God for not giving in to our demands or experience incredible guilt, thinking that we are not worthy to gain His favor.

Paul assures us that earthly suffering cannot compare with the glory that we shall one day experience.[4] This passion for heaven helps to explain how Paul could characterize his immense hardships as "light affliction." In spite of such adversity, he was able to see this life of suffering not as a sprint but as a marathon. He realized that the ultimate reward awaited him if he remained steadfast and faithful to the task of following Christ.

During graduate school, I (John) and one of my friends decided that we needed a break from our studies and made plans to go to Kings Dominion amusement park. The big day finally arrived, bringing with it record high temperatures. But that didn't stop us. With the foolish arrogance of youth, we decided to brave the heat and headed to the park.

Eager to be the first in line for the park's new roller coaster, we arrived early. Unfortunately, so did a thousand other people. We grabbed a map and huddled to devise our strategy. With a confident battle cry we sprinted through the park, pushing through hedges and hurdling small children, always being sure to offer a hurried "excuse me" along the way. Near the back of the park, the gray-green skeleton of the snaking coaster consumed the skyline. Victory was in sight! Judging the goal to be a mile away, we paused to catch our breath. Instead, our breath was taken away when we saw a sign that stated, "The line for the Anaconda starts here." Even worse was the realization that we had to backtrack three hundred feet to find the end of the line. Still, in spite of the heat, we took our places for the three-hour wait. I thought we would never make it. By the time we got to the roller coaster, we were sick from the heat and soaked with sweat. But at long last, we climbed into the coaster and strapped ourselves securely into the seat. Then off we went! And for the next forty-five seconds we experienced the ride of a lifetime!

Why would anyone endure such a long, tortuous wait for such a short ride? Simply because we knew that once on the ride we would experience exhilaration. As enlivening and thrilling as a ride on a roller coaster can be, heaven is far, far better.

Living in this world is like standing in that line. Sometimes it's uncomfortable, chaotic, and trying. Some days seem as if they will never end. Yet we continue to struggle on, day by day. We can endure this world of pain and suffering because we know there is a glorious and wonderful ride beyond comprehension waiting for us on the other side. The trials of this world are nothing compared to the ride ahead. Our suffering is to be endured only momentarily, but the crown of life will be worn forever.

Too often we try to make living in the world the ride itself. But lines are only a means to an end. Of course there's nothing wrong with making the wait as comfortable as possible. In fact, some people have the capacity to turn waiting into a party. They bring sleeping bags, chairs, and countless other things to entertain themselves while waiting to purchase concert tickets or to see their teams play. But without the ultimate payoff of purchasing that ticket or seeing the game, the waiting is futile. Reasonable comforts are understandable. But when we focus more on worldly comfort than on heaven, the situations that seem out of our control become nearly intolerable.

Viktor Frankl wrote, "The prisoner who had lost faith in the future—his future—was doomed. With his loss of belief in the future, he also lost his spiritual hold; he let himself decline and became subject to mental and physical decay."[5] God wants us to live for what is on the other side. As we strive to gain God's perspective, we will learn to see beyond our present circumstances and focus on what is in store for us in the life to come. As Christians, we need to live "top-down," pursuing God's eternal Kingdom above all else. In dozens of New Testament texts, we are told to live in the present with an eye to the future. When we apply the truths of heaven to our earthly issues and problems, suffering takes on a whole new meaning. The great heroes of the faith, whose credentials are recorded in Hebrews 11, considered the future promises as present realities, thereby transforming their adversities into hope.

There is no greater understanding of suffering than to live with a future hope.[6] The hope of heaven allows our present sufferings to be covered in the peace that God provides for those who are at rest in His sovereignty, promises, and faithfulness. God has the power to transform suffering into a glorious expectation for the faithful Christian. And when we reach heaven, not only will we receive rewards, but the immediate presence of God as well.

I (Gary) met Jennifer when she stopped by my office to ask for help choosing a research paper topic. Because of her tremendous leadership abilities, Jennifer had served in several influential capacities. For example, one summer she had led a team of students into an impoverished area of the country to feed and provide shelter for the needy. She had earned a reputation as a very caring person who truly loved others, as well as someone who was willing to spend her own time and energy in helping to make real changes in people's lives.

In spite of her excellent potential, however, Jennifer grew angry with the Lord. She was tired of always being the one who volunteered to work for others. "Haven't I done enough already?" she would ask. When I first worked with her, Jennifer's anger affected her spiritual walk with the Lord. Desiring to see her return to her previous level of commitment, I encouraged her to write her essay on the subject of ways God might use to motivate believers. She agreed to do research in this area.

Some time later, she turned in a wonderful essay, which concluded that God uses both negative and positive motivation in the lives of Christians. During the process of writing the paper, Jennifer realized that she had mistaken God's intentions. Scripture is clear that negative motivators are not always punishments. They are often used to keep believers from wandering further from God's blessings. On the other hand, Jennifer saw that God also promised positive motivators: rewards that are designed not simply to "force" us to obey, but to help us enjoy more fully both this present life and eternity. Once she realized the error in her thinking, she worked on changing her attitude about God. She realized that in growing angry toward God, she had actually been selfish and sinful. She

---

needed God's reminders against wandering, but she also wanted to enjoy more peace in her life as well as God's heavenly reward. Jennifer responded by repenting, and she resolved to follow God wholeheartedly. In so doing, she recovered her first love. She discovered that God had her best interests in mind.

As the Suffering Servant, Jesus has a special interest in all those who have suffered in this life. In the description of Stephen's stoning, Jesus is pictured as standing and waiting to lead the ovation of heaven as His follower is about to come home.[7] Surely, He held the crown of life to adorn the martyred saint for his faithfulness. For Stephen, like us, the best was yet to come.

The following story beautifully illustrates this promise.

Audrey often spent time visiting with an old bedridden saint and was always amazed by her cheerful disposition. Audrey was also friends with a very wealthy woman who always seemed to view things from a negative perspective. Although her friend professed to be a Christian, she always seemed downcast, and Audrey thought it might do her good to meet her other friend, the bedridden saint.

The saint lived in a garret, five stories up. At the bottom of the stairs, the wealthy woman looked around, drew up her dress, and said, "How dark and filthy this is!"

"It's better higher up," said Audrey. When they got to the second floor, however, things were no better, and the woman again complained. But Audrey only replied, "It's better higher up."

The third floor actually seemed worse than the first two, and the woman again complained, but Audrey's response was the same: "It's better higher up."

At last they reached the fifth floor, where the saint's bedroom was located. As they entered the room, the wealthy woman looked around at the thick carpeting, flowering plants in the window, and little birds singing in their cages. And there she also saw the bedridden saint— one of those saints whom God is polishing for His own temple—simply beaming with joy. The wealthy woman said to her, "Isn't it difficult for you to just lie here?"

The saint smiled and said, "It's better higher up."[8]

Summary

Crowns symbolize royalty, authority, honor, victory, and reward. God, the ultimate Promise Keeper, has promised a crown for those who endure suffering. The symbolism is not lost on us when we consider the fact that God's Son, Jesus Christ, wore a crown of suffering.

As Christians, we must expect occasional mistreatment and suffering. More and more, our culture seems to be becoming anti-Christian, and there's a good chance that in this lifetime, we *will* undergo ridicule, affliction, and possibly persecution simply because we bear Christ's name. Suffering is a natural consequence of a consistent Christian witness. It is not easy to suffer, especially when we believe there is no justifiable cause. But our Lord was abused without cause, and we can expect nothing different. God takes pleasure in how we respond to suffering, and He has promised us a reward for our suffering.

CHAPTER EIGHTEEN

God Desires to Be Glorified

Have you ever wanted to be someone else? You might remember a time from your childhood when you pretended that you were a superhero, a great athlete, or some other famous person. My (John's) son, Stephen, found an interesting twist on such a fantasy. One day while my wife and I were sitting together in our family room, Stephen burst into the room with a pair of underwear on his head and his blanket draped around his neck as a cape. As he jumped in front of us, he flexed his arms to make a muscle and shouted, "Underwear Man to the rescue!" Until then, I had not known that Underwear Man existed, let alone resided in my own home.

Such childhood games are cute, but the truth is that we never outgrow wishing we were someone else. You may believe that you are just an average, run-of-the-mill person. But by wishing that you were someone else or somehow different, you are admitting that you believe your life lacks meaning. This might be displayed in thoughts like, *Life would be so much better if only I had his job . . . if only I could sing like that . . . if only I had her background . . . if only I had been given those opportunities.* Such thoughts actually imply that contentment is situational. We believe we need something, but we find it hard to grasp what that *something* is. We want a life that caters to us. We crave paradise; we dream of a life that offers us something special. We secretly dream of being something we are not.

But the truth is that every Christian has the capacity to be someone special. Because of the extraordinary grace of God, we all have the ability to reveal God's glory in and through our lives. We don't need to be anyone else in order to glorify God. Actually, when we allow God's glory to be displayed in our lives, we are *more* than ourselves. We are supernatural reflections of the divine. And the beautiful part is that we don't have to sow our dreams in someone else's garden in order to manifest God's glory.

The Weight of Glory

"What is the chief end of man?" asks *The Westminster Shorter Catechism*. "Man's chief end is to glorify God and to enjoy Him forever."[1] This document of the Reformed Presbyterian tradition reminds us of the real character of our lives. We are to be people who glorify God; and *that* is to be the measure of our lives. It is the golden thread that is to be woven into every aspect of life. But why is glorifying God so important?

God does not need glory, nor does He crave it. He is complete in Himself. His Word, however, commands us to give God glory.[2] The word *glory* means to praise, give distinction to, or give honor to someone or something. Saying "that's heavy" was once a common way of communicating importance. Glory would clearly fall into that category: it is heavy! As a matter of fact, the most common word for *glory* in the Old Testament comes from a root that literally means "to be heavy."[3] In Old Testament times, a person's weight was his glory. Of course, this doesn't refer to physical weight, but rather to what that person was and what he had—honor, reputation, and possessions—the weight of a person's position, the weight of power, and the weight of riches.

When God glorifies Himself, He manifests His "weight," the real nature of His person. The apostle Paul captured the heaviness of glory when he wrote, "For God, who commanded the light to shine out of darkness, hath shined in our hearts, to give the light of the knowledge of the glory of God in the face of Jesus Christ."[4] God wants us to know what He is like by making His glory known. The same God who said, "Let there be light" in creation also said, "Let there be light" in our hearts. When He brings light into our hearts, He manifests something of His attributes, something of His nature. Through His glory being revealed in us, we get a sense of His weight and importance.

Sometimes we associate God's glory with magnificent, lofty cathedral ceilings, stained glass, and ornate woodwork. But God's glory has nothing to do with buildings; His glory resides within the hearts of people. We cannot make it happen on our own accord. It is only through the power of God that we can find the ability to say, "May God be magnified!" And then God shines His glory in us. Our part is simply to acknowledge Him for who He is.[5]

To glorify the Lord means to honor Him, to worship Him, and to give Him the praise He deserves. But the glory of God does not come without a price.

As we've looked at the many purposes for suffering revealed in the Bible, we've seen how each of these purposes describes unique aspects of God's work in and through the lives of His people. Yet, it is this final purpose that literally captures the central theme of suffering; in fact, all of the purposes we have discussed thus far could actually be summed up into one overall purpose, the fact that God can be glorified in and through our suffering. Of all the reasons that we suffer, none is as central to the person of God as is the glory He receives. Nothing is more important than God being glorified.

The Bible contains many stories about God being glorified through suffering. There are at least two ways in which He receives glory in these situations. Let's take a look at each of them.

God is glorified through suffering

Once Jesus and His disciples came across a man who had been blind since birth. Reflecting the common belief of their day, the disciples asked Jesus if it was the man's sin or the sin of his parents that caused his blindness. Jesus explained that sin had nothing to do with the man's plight. This man had been born blind so that they might see God's glory.[6] The man's blindness was a platform upon which God displayed His character and work. Likewise, it is through our trials and tribulations that God is glorified when His power is at work in and through us.

Later in the Gospel of John, we learn that Jesus' close friend
Lazarus was very ill. In fact, Jesus knew that Lazarus had already
died. But rather than go immediately to Lazarus's side, Jesus stayed
away for two days.[7] Certainly Jesus knew Lazarus's condition, but
he decided to delay help. Picture the confusion and anger Lazarus's
sisters must have felt. After all, Jesus had healed others who were at
death's door without even seeing them.[8] Why would Jesus choose
not to heal His dear friend and spare him needless pain? What kind
of God would call this love and mercy?

When Jesus finally arrived at Lazarus's home in Bethany, He
encountered a grieving family. Both Martha and Mary knew things
could have been different "if only" Jesus had come earlier.[9] But
Jesus had a greater purpose, so He allowed His friend to die! God
allowed Lazarus to die and his sisters and friends to experience the
anguish of loss in order to teach a lesson.

Though Jesus knew of the miracle that was to come, He was so
overwhelmed by grief that He wept.[10] Surely heaven's angels stood
still as the sound of Christ's weeping filled the universe. Such grief
showed the crowd Jesus' great affection for Lazarus and his sisters.
Of course, Jesus did not weep because Lazarus was dead, for He
knew that was only temporary. Instead, He wept because of His
compassion for those whose lives were disrupted by death's cold
grip. Truly we have a High Priest who fully understands what being
human is all about.[11]

The death of Lazarus, along with his sisters' grief, set up a miraculous demonstration of God's power and authority. In the final
analysis, Lazarus's suffering would prove to be the vehicle by which
God would be glorified. To the mind of Christ, suffering is a means
to a greater end. In some sense, it seems that God hurts with our
hurts; at least Jesus suffered the pain of others.[12] But from the finish
line looking back, the pain and suffering are inconsequential. It is
only through the darkness of life that the light of God shines the
brightest. So it is with us. God may delay coming to our rescue
in spite of our pleas for deliverance. He may wait two days, two
months, two years, or longer in order to glorify Himself through
a different means.

God is glorified by our responses

When God allows us to suffer, the affliction is never the point. It is simply a tool that allows God to be glorified through the seemingly impossible, as well as through His ability to change us, mold us, and refine us. We are never to glory in ourselves or find confidence in our own abilities or faith in our own spiritual advancement. God frustrated the comfort of Mary and Martha in order to bring them to the brink of brokenness. Then He redirected their focus from their pain to the glorious, miraculous power of God.

We cannot make something glorious out of suffering; only God can do that. But we *can* declare the glory that He has created through our pain and find joy.

In addressing the suffering the readers of his first epistle were enduring, the apostle Peter penned these words:

> Beloved, do not think it strange concerning the fiery trial
> which is to try you, as though some strange thing happened
> to you; but rejoice to the extent that you partake of Christ's
> sufferings, that when His glory is revealed, you may also
> be glad with exceeding joy. If you are reproached for the
> name of Christ, blessed are you, for the Spirit of glory and
> of God rests upon you. On their part He is blasphemed,
> but on your part He is glorified. But let none of you suffer
> as a murderer, a thief, an evildoer, or as a busybody in other
> people's matters. Yet if anyone suffers as a Christian, let him
> not be ashamed, but let him glorify God in this matter.
> For the time has come for judgment to begin at the house
> of God; and if it begins with us first, what will be the end
> of those who do not obey the gospel of God? Now "If the
> righteous one is scarcely saved, where will the ungodly and
> the sinner appear?" Therefore let those who suffer according
> to the will of God commit their souls to Him in doing
> good, as to a faithful Creator.   1 Peter 4:12-19

History tells us that believers in the first century were burned at the stake and their bodies used as human torches. The persecution they experienced was unimaginable. How could they possibly be prepared for such persecution? First, Peter had earned the right to be heard on the matter. He was no stranger to persecution. His life was shrouded in suffering. Peter knew that the believers must accept the reality of suffering and to expect it ("do not think it strange"). Those words might have concerned the readers, but likely did not catch them off guard. They were suffering.

What follows, however, would have hit them between the eyes: "but rejoice." It is one thing to accept that life is painful, but rejoice in it? Peter's words penetrated to the very heart of what enables a person to endure suffering: attitude. Sometimes Christians assume that Christ's suffering on Calvary in our place protects us from having to suffer. We think we should be able to bask in the blessings that His suffering brings without having to experience pain. But Peter knew better. He knew that if we are to experience joy at Christ's appearing we must share in His suffering now.

Peter's theology of suffering included the notion that suffering was related to our eternal rewards but also to our current experiences with Christ. What better way to develop intimacy with Him than to know the fellowship of His suffering. Being mentally ready for difficulties requires accepting it as a common reality and experiencing joy in being connected with our Savior. The result is glorifying God in and through our suffering. Remember, Peter was told that his death (by crucifixion, it turned out) would bring glory to God.[13] The apostle Peter learned that suffering is redemptive, even in death. This occurred on more than one level: Peter's death brought glory to God, it was an encouraging example to others, and it added to his rewards after death.[14]

God can even use circumstances unrelated to our Christian witnesses for His glory. In chapter 13, we saw how Tom Whiteman learned that God could be glorified through painful circumstances like divorce. Through his Fresh Start Seminars, Tom continues to share God's glory with people all over the world as he helps them deal with their shattered marriages. The greatest tragedy in Tom's life resulted in God's glory. Our grave circumstances, disappointments, and embarrassments always hold promise for His honor and glory.

We have hope because God is at work through it all, and such confidence motivates us to move forward in spite of the terrible pain that we may feel. Hope requires us to risk and to open our hearts to the possibility of something bigger and better than comfortable circumstances. As Solomon said, "Hope deferred makes the heart sick."[15] Adversity tries to dash our hopes for the future by bringing misery and despair to our present. Yet if we allow it to, adversity can open us up to a greater, deeper future and a new sense of God in the present.

Indeed, we must learn that even adversity is included when we speak of all things being subservient to our chief end. Whatever comes to pass in our lives has been allowed by God. We must bear the yoke of our burdens and understand them to be light compared to the heaviness of God's glory. The chaff of affliction blows away, but the kernel of God's glory remains because only it is substantial.

Remember that God did not create us for our own sakes, to fashion whatever sense of happiness we can find. Neither does God exist solely for our benefit. We were created for His pleasure.[16] Therefore, our chief aim is not to obtain great estates or status. We are not to be consumed with comfort, predictability, and fairness. Glorifying God is to be our chief aim. It is only then that we can find rest in whatever set of circumstances God has carved out for us.

Giving glory to God has nothing to do with our circumstances; it is a matter of the heart. And God is glorified when we are thankful to Him and praise Him for all He does. We are not to be blind to our painful ordeals, but to experience His glory *regardless* of it. Our ability to magnify God is not based on what we can do to help God, but on what God can do in and through us. Through His Son Jesus Christ, God can work through any situation to reveal His incredible, glorious nature.

Summary

Believing that God can be uplifted through the sufferings of His people is one of the greatest paradoxes. Yet consider the words of the psalmist who penned the heart of God, "Call upon Me in the day of trouble; I will deliver you, and you shall glorify Me."[17]

When we glorify God, our souls are uplifted. Even though we may not have a special talent or be some exclusive person like Underwear Man, God can do something in us beyond our imagination. As we become people changed by the glory of God, we find ourselves able "to enjoy Him forever."

CONCLUSION OF SECTION TWO

At one time educators believed that frustration impeded learning. A Columbia University psychologist, Herbert Terrace, however, claimed that it is not frustration but a lack of it that hinders learning. Dr. Terrace argued that avoiding frustration failed to prepare students for the real world. In life, we don't always get rewarded for doing the right thing, and we have to learn how to cope when we make a mistake. To prove his view, Dr. Terrace taught pigeons to distinguish the color red from the color green. When the pigeons pecked in response to the red light, they were rewarded with food, but food was withheld when they pecked at the green light. The pigeons were divided into two groups. The first group of pigeons got food every time they pecked at the red light, but the second group got food only some of the time. When the pigeons trained by the consistent method were switched to the erratic method, they went to pieces, hitting their heads against the walls, flapping their wings, and pecking wildly at everything in sight. By contrast, birds trained on the intermittent system did not go wild when a correct peck failed to produce food. Instead, they stayed calm and continued to peck only at red until they were rewarded with the deserved snack.[1]

God knows that we learn best through hardship and suffering. Through adversity, our natural and fleshly tendencies are frustrated, and the godly parts of us have an opportunity to flourish by depending upon God and not ourselves. While we may not relish His use of suffering in our lives, we can certainly value His profound love, mercy, and grace to us in times of pain.

A PATHWAY THROUGH SUFFERING

It was girls' night out and boys' night at home for the Thomas family. My (John's) son, Stephen, wanted to spend the last part of our evening playing Candy Land. Perhaps you remember that game from your childhood or from playing it with your own children. The object is to move your gingerbread man through the twisted colored road until you finally arrive at the finish. When it's your turn, you draw a card, which usually has either one or two colored squares on it. You then move your gingerbread man that number of colored spaces on the path. The deck also contains various cards that correspond to pictures on the board. If you draw a picture card, you either move forward or backward to the space corresponding to the card's picture.

Since it was close to Stephen's bedtime, I realized we would have to make this a quick game. What I had forgotten was how long it takes to play Candy Land. I jumped off to a swift lead but soon drew a picture card that returned me to an early square on the board. As Stephen neared the finish line, he too drew a card that forced him far back on the trail. And so the game went on. Every time one of us neared the finish, a card would be drawn that would extend play. I thought we would still be playing when Stephen was in college.

This brings me to my confession. In order to finish the game and get my son to bed, I secretly removed all the cards that required moving backward on the board. (I admit that I cheated. But it was for my son's own good.) Finally, with those obstacles out of the way, Stephen was able to reach the finish, proudly winning the game.

Suffering is much like that board game (in fact, that game can cause great suffering, but that is another story). We want our lives to be fun, enjoyable, and comfortable. Unfortunately, pain and agony often surface, causing us to face the fact that life is hard.

Our deepest desire is to rid ourselves of the obstacles that block our path. Just when we think we are about to "make it," we are forced back into pain as if to start all over again.

As we've already seen, overcoming suffering is a lot like running a marathon. It requires the runner to confront the challenges along the road and have the stamina that is necessary to endure the entire race. As such, suffering requires us to work through weariness of soul and body, to find the strength to run one mile after another. Helen Keller noted that the struggles of life teach us that although the world is full of suffering, it is also full of the overcoming of it.

This section is entitled "A Pathway through Suffering," not *around* suffering. No matter how much we want to avoid pain, there is simply no way around it. The only way out of it is to go through it. Our bent toward pride causes us to want lives that are free of suffering—to become absolute overcomers. A careful reading of the Bible, however, shows that God is much less concerned with us living in a place *of* peace than He is with us living *in* peace. It is possible to find shalom, peace in the midst of our suffering.

God wants us to grow from our suffering. When we attempt to avoid suffering, we risk missing God's purpose for the pain. Christians should not suffer in the same way as those who have no hope. Our passion should not be to feel better but to know God better—no matter what hardships we experience.

Friedrich Nietzsche once said, "He who has a why to live can bear almost any how."[1] As Christians we have a reason to live, a basis for meaning in life. For the Christian, Jesus Christ is the pivotal truth and motivation in life. Yet we must wrestle with the problem of having to move through the pain in a way that honors and capitalizes upon the work God is seeking to accomplish in our lives. The challenge is not *if* we will get through our valleys, but *how*.

God promises us His strength, grace, and presence in the midst of our trials and tribulations. He promises us that He is orchestrating a masterpiece in our lives. It is up to us to submit to His will, to allow Him to use us in any way that He deems appropriate. There is a precious pearl within the dark chamber of every calamity, providing we have the courage to seek it out.

This section will help you learn to allow God to work out His purposes in your life, probe your beliefs about suffering, assign your suffering to God, think through and apply a plan of recovery, and help others who hurt by using what you are gaining and have gained through your adversity. Our desire is that these chapters will not be used as a "fix" for suffering. We cannot approach our suffering as we do the common cold: administering relief medicines as fast as possible in order to feel better. Viruses have to run their course and so must suffering. However, whereas viruses offer no hope for moving us toward wholeness, suffering is the vehicle by which God moves us toward completeness.

CHAPTER NINETEEN

Probe Your Beliefs about Suffering

As we will see in the chapters that follow, what we think and how we think are integral in determining the way we suffer. It's easy to rely too much on human perception, logic, and emotion rather than on God's Word—the basis of truth.[1] If our thinking is congruent with Scripture, however, we will be able to work through the pain and allow God's purposes to be realized in our lives. If our thinking is false, we will have difficulty responding to trials in a way that will help us learn and grow from them.

Unfortunately, we have all bought into various myths regarding suffering. These unbiblical views have the potential to derail us from spiritual gain and even cause greater pain. Because false information breeds spiritual and emotional turmoil, it is critical that we begin to examine our beliefs regarding suffering. Emotional and spiritual health will elude us until we examine our beliefs, identify the fallacious ones, and replace them with God's truth. Such notions and myths must be eliminated if we are going to successfully trust God through our trials and hardships.

Myth #1: Spiritual People Don't Experience Suffering

Of all the myths about suffering, the idea that all suffering is sin related is perhaps the cruelest, since it heaps guilt and shame upon an already-wounded soul. This myth takes on many forms. One links suffering to a lack of faith. Of course, we saw this in chapter 14 when Christ rebuked His disciples for their lack of faith during the storm that hit while they were crossing the Sea of

Galilee. Faith does play a role in suffering, but suffering in and of itself does not mean that we are not spiritual or living godly lives. Remember Shadrach, Meshach, and Abednego? Their faith may have gotten them out of the fiery furnace, but it was also what got them thrown into the furnace in the first place.[2]

A second form of this myth says that those who suffer or feel pain are sinning. Job's friends who attempted to "assist" him with his adversity evidenced this belief. Sometimes such thinkers assume that God abandons those who lack commitment to Christ. In response to this myth, the sufferer believes that he or she did something wrong to justify the pain. This perceived infraction could be either sin or poor judgment. The sufferer believes that he or she is responsible for the peril even in the absence of evidence that any violation has been committed. Subsequently, the sufferer feels a sense of guilt and a deep sense of shame.

It is true that suffering may result from someone's sin, mistake, or fault, but this is not always the case. Jesus Himself felt pain and experienced feelings of abandonment. He was the Suffering Servant, and because He suffered without sin, we know that we, too, can suffer without sinning. Just as God never forsook His Son, we know He has not forsaken us either.[3]

The truth of God's Word is that the rain falls on the just and unjust.[4] We cannot manipulate God into indulging our self-serving craving for control. If Christians were spared pain and suffering when it falls on others, Christianity would be degraded to nothing more than an insurance policy. The ultimate end of Christianity is transformed lives, not stress-free followers.

Myth #2: Reading the Bible Solves Every Problem

In some Christian circles, the Bible has been elevated so much that it is considered even more important than having a close relationship with God. In other circles, parishioners are indoctrinated with the belief that intimacy with God is synonymous with Bible reading.

Certainly, reading the Bible is critical to spiritual development. God's Word provides us with the spiritual nourishment we need, not just when we're in the valley of affliction but also when we're on the mountaintop. Discipline in reading and studying God's Word helps us build our spiritual and emotional immune systems. It insulates the mind and strengthens the soul so that we can ward off despair in times of adversity. In fact, it is during periods of suffering that what we have read and learned from our Bible reading, church attendance, and spiritual teaching are ultimately revealed. Clearly it's impossible to have a close relationship with God without reading the Bible and praying. But it is possible to diligently read the Bible and still not come to know Christ.[5] In the same way, simply reading the Bible does not mean you'll have all you need to address the entire emotional and spiritual side of suffering.

As mentioned earlier, I (John) love the game of tennis. I can read all the books about tennis that I want and even read the Tennis Association's rule book, but it's not the same as playing the game. I need to know the rules to accurately play the game, but the game is bigger than the rules. The same can be said about God's Word and our spiritual lives. God's Word provides us with what we need in order to live the Christian life and deal with suffering. But the Christian life and recovering from emotional and spiritual pain require more from us than just reading.

Reading the Bible is a necessary element of the Christian life. It teaches us about God and leads us in our walk of faith. But we are not just to read God's Word; we must also obey it.[6] Reading the Bible is not the same as submission, obedience, faith, and intimacy with the Lord.

By all means, spend time daily with God through Scripture reading and study. But also use other available means such as prayer, meditation, and talking with a Christian friend to work through your pain and struggles.

Myth #3: You Can Handle It Alone

Rugged individualism and the pioneer spirit have long characterized our culture. We have been taught to be self-sufficient. This is particularly true of men. Asking for help is too often seen as a sign of weakness.

John Donne, the famous English poet, once said that "no man is an island, entire of itself."[7] Unfortunately, even Christians buy into self-sufficient thinking, especially when they hurt. Perhaps out of fear or pride, some people are reluctant to open up, choosing instead to privately battle their way through the pain. Others are hurt and disillusioned about the sincerity of other Christians' desire to help. Sadly, many wounded people push others away or do not reach out for help when they need the caring community of God's people most.

Former missionary Elisabeth Elliot once wrote, "Not many of us are much good at being Christian all by ourselves—we're supposed to be a flock or a body. We've got to have help . . . somebody to lift us up when we're down."[8] Because we are all part of the body of Christ, unified together, it is impossible to do anything or experience anything that does not affect the rest of the body.

Research plainly shows that sufferers who have sound social support get through tough times far better than those who go through painful situations alone.[9] In fact, the German army typically divided families in concentration camps as a way of worsening prisoner morale. Those in charge knew that isolation actually intensifies suffering.

Even if it were possible to get through a struggle alone, why put yourself through that added stress? We have already seen how suffering provides an opportunity to illuminate the value of the body of Christ. Suffering gives the church an opportunity to show, not only the world, but other believers as well, that we are Christians by the way we love and the way we mourn.[10]

If you are suffering today, one way to break free from the grip of despair is to share your pain with others and learn from someone who has been there.

Myth #4: God Owes Us

Some people operate on the "heaven's reward" concept, believing that if they do the right thing, God will grant them their desires. To support their logic, some quote Proverbs 3:5-6: "Trust in the LORD with all your heart, and lean not on your own understanding; in all your ways acknowledge Him, and He shall direct your paths." Simply stated: trust God and He will give you what you want.

I (John) once counseled a hurting man named Max who believed that since God hated divorce, his ex-wife would come back to him. In fact, not only did he expect that she would come back, but that God was obligated to restore their marriage because He could not contradict His Word. Max didn't want a divorce, and since he felt he was "doing the right thing," he believed God would reward him with his ex-wife's affection.

Max saw himself as a victim, but he failed to consider the facts. He minimized the years of physical abuse he had inflicted on his wife—abuse so severe that it had resulted in several hospitalizations. He argued that his actions were often provoked, though he did admit that sometimes he had allowed the "flesh to reign." Max said, "I am no longer controlled by the flesh. She should know that." He did not accept free will, believing that God could and would return his wife to him even if she didn't want to be there. No amount of counsel or Scripture seemed to budge this man from his adamant reasoning. Unfortunately, he left counseling bitter at God, his ex-wife, and me. To my knowledge, he has little to do with church or God today.

Just as God reminded Job that the Creator of the world owed him nothing, neither is God indebted to us.[11] God does not owe us smooth sailing. He is not a servant who dutifully carries out our bidding, a genie who pops up to grant our capricious wishes, or an indulgent parent who complies with our selfish demands and desires. In fact, just the opposite is true. If we got what we truly deserved, we would be eternally separated from Him.

Consider the kind of world we would have if God did everything we demanded. In that world, God would be nothing more than a tool for our self-interest. Remember, Adam and Eve's disobedience was in part related to their desire to "be like God."[12]

We need to be thankful that God has sent His Son to provide an avenue that we may spend eternity with Him. He has not abandoned us but has provided us with a Comforter, the Holy Spirit.[13] The abundant life Jesus promised is not about landing a guest spot on *Lifestyles of the Rich and Famous.* Rather, it is a promise that we will truly know what life is. The word translated *life* is the Greek word *zoe*, which means quality of life in a spiritual sense. The abundant life has purpose, meaning, and direction, and when we live it, we are filled with joy and peace because of the indwelling Holy Spirit. No matter how the course of our lives change, we can still exhibit contentment.[14] *That* is authentic, abundant life.

Myth #5: Pain and Suffering Are of No Value

Our culture indoctrinates us to the belief that we should never suffer. Pain medicines, air-conditioning, smooth-riding automobiles, and even euthanasia are all designed to help us avoid discomfort and pain. This idea that suffering is of little value has permeated theology as well.

Some people believe that pain and suffering are simply the results of a broken, sinful world, and therefore they provide no positive benefit to our lives. According to this way of thinking, we must simply endure and try to find relief in whatever way possible. Our only hope is found in heaven, away from such misery.

Maintaining our focus on eternity is certainly a significant way to deal with the groaning of this world and our earthly bodies. But God has not left us without hope in this world. For Christians, this earthly life is actually the beginning of heaven. After all, the abundant life and eternal life begin at salvation. Therefore, we should be living in expectant anticipation of eternity with Christ, living for others, and laying up treasure in heaven.

Aristotle once said that we couldn't learn without pain. God uses this world and our life experiences to teach us a wide array of lessons, and suffering is without a doubt one means by which God achieves the very things we deeply long for.

Former baseball great Roy Campanella tells of his stay at the Institute of Physical Medicine and Rehabilitation. As one of the first African American ballplayers, he was a survivor and thriver who faced difficult challenges. Now Roy was trying to beat the greatest foe of his life: living in a wheelchair. He was discouraged and depressed by the loss of his career and mobility, and he struggled to find any hope in the future. Blinded by his own self-pity, Roy rolled his wheelchair each day down the hallway past a bronze plaque riveted to the wall. It wasn't until he had been at the institute for many months, however, that Roy finally stopped to read the plaque. What he read transformed him. Written by an unknown Confederate soldier, "A Creed for Those Who Suffered" said this:

> *I asked God for strength, that I might achieve.*
> *I was made weak, that I might learn humbly to obey.*
> *I asked for health, that I might do great things.*
> *I was given infirmity, that I might do better things.*
> *I asked for riches, that I might be happy.*
> *I was given poverty, that I might be wise.*
> *I asked for power, that I might have the praise of men.*
> *I was given weakness, that I might feel the need of God.*
> *I asked for all things, that I might enjoy life.*
> *I was given life, that I might enjoy all things.*
> *I got nothing I asked for—but everything I had hoped for.*
> *Almost despite myself, my unspoken prayers were answered.*
> *I am, among men, most richly blessed!*[15]

Campy, as he was known, read that plaque over and over again. He claimed that after reading it, a powerful glow began to warm him from the inside out. The experience was so real that he had to hold tightly to the arms of his wheelchair. Following his release from the hospital, Campanella became more famous for the thirty-six years he spent in a wheelchair than he had been as a professional baseball catcher. Vince Scully said that Campy looked at life like a catcher: "He was forever cheering up, pepping up, counseling people." He saw the value of his disability in his *ability* to help others who had experienced similar ordeals."[16]

Myth #6: The God of Love Would Not Allow Us to Suffer

This is one of the most prevalent beliefs about suffering. But of this myth, C. S. Lewis wrote:

> The problem of reconciling human suffering with the existence of a God who loves, is only insoluble so long as

we attach a trivial meaning to the word "love," and look on
things as if man were the centre of them. . . . God does not
exist for the sake of man. Man does not exist for his own
sake. . . . Because He is what He is, His love must, in the
nature of things, be impeded and repelled by certain stains
in our present character, and because He already loves us
He must labour to make us lovable.[17]

As human beings, we tend to view all of life from our own self-
serving vantage point. God, however, operates on a different level
altogether. As we have seen, God uses suffering for a variety of purposes, and all suffering has value and merit in the life of the believer.
It is *out of* God's love that He seeks to use suffering to improve us;
the fact that we so passionately seek comfortable, stress-free lives is
an indication that we still do not understand this concept. God's
love does not lie in His extinction of suffering. Rather God's love
is evident in that He embraced suffering in order to identify with
us. His goal is not to abolish suffering, but to channel it in order
to develop the sufferer.

Corrie ten Boom shared her struggle with believing in a God of
love while experiencing the horrific conditions of concentration-
camp life.

I remember one occasion when I was very discouraged
there. Everything around us was dark, and there was
darkness in my heart.

I remember telling Betsie that I thought God had
forgotten us. "No, Corrie," said Betsie. "He has not
forgotten us. Remember His Word: 'For as the heavens are
high above the earth, so great is his steadfast love toward
those who fear him.' There is an ocean of God's love
available. . . . There is plenty for everyone."[18]

Summary

It might seem that God has abandoned you as well. Your head may
know better, but your heart challenges those beliefs with immense
force. If this is where you are today, it is necessary to really assess

what you truly believe about suffering. Consider your current or past trial, particularly one that you deem undeserved. Maybe, like Corrie ten Boom, you believe that God has abandoned you. Perhaps you believe that if you had been good enough, you would not have felt such dreadful hurt. It could be that fallacious beliefs about suffering are programmed into your heart. If you struggle with questions about how God could allow you to suffer or if you need the truth of God's Word to cope, the chapters that follow will help you.

CHAPTER TWENTY

Assign Your Suffering to God

God has at least one objective in mind for our suffering that will transform our lives if we allow our pain to run its course. For God to accomplish His plan, we must turn our suffering over to Him. We must surrender to His will and recognize His lordship.

In this chapter we will examine seven Rs to assist us in placing ourselves and our struggles into God's trustworthy hands. We will use Psalm 143 as the basis for examining each of these steps.

Release Your Feelings to God

It's natural for feelings to emerge when we experience adversity. In order to cope, some try to suppress distressing feelings and keep the hurt at bay. Fearful of opening up to the varying layers of their hurt, they try to rationalize their emotions or distract themselves from them. Perhaps they're afraid that if they allow their hurt to stream forth, they'll unleash a flood of never-ending tears or, even worse, go crazy. The problem with avoiding our feelings, however, is that when we swallow them, we swallow them alive. Feelings that are not dealt with do *not* go away; instead they become distorted and lie in wait. Like a jack-in-the-box, they have a way of rearing their ugly heads when least expected and ultimately lengthening the sentence of suffering. In fact, latent feelings influence everything we think or do.

Many people find it easier to brace themselves against hurt than to embrace it. Very few have been taught how to handle hurt so that it can lead to a better place. Hence, we've become masters of distracting ourselves from pain, holding it at arm's length.

Admitting our pain is the doorway to healing, but we cannot admit what we do not know. First, we must acknowledge the reality of pain's presence and power. Unless we are willing to face the depth of our pain, we will stay trapped in the pit of despair.

Let's look at two important aspects of releasing our feelings to God:

Get real!

Many advertising campaigns use the phrase "Get real!" But those simple words can be pretty difficult to apply to ourselves.

One of the greatest things about the psalms is that they reflect a naked, honest heart before God. In the opening verses of Psalm 143, the writer bears his soul:

> Hear my prayer, O LORD, Give ear to my supplications!
> In Your faithfulness answer me, and in Your righteousness.
> Do not enter into judgment with Your servant, for in Your sight no one living is righteous. . . . Therefore my spirit is overwhelmed within me; my heart within me is distressed.
> PSALM 143:1-2, 4

The psalmist genuinely relates to God with all the passion that is within him. He does not approach God piously or pretentiously; instead, he candidly speaks what is in his heart, knowing that because God is faithful and righteous, He will answer him.

But suffering has a way of drawing out our deep-seated core beliefs and revealing that our hearts aren't always focused toward God. Even though Job did not sin in his initial response to his affliction, he clearly felt overwhelming despair.[1] In the pit of anguish, Job even accused God of trying to destroy him, of being unjust, of oppression, and of killing hope.[2] Because he believed that God had been unfair, Job felt he had a right to complain.[3] Evidently, Job believed that he could reason with God.[4] In defending himself against his friend's accusations, Job was brutally honest. He was real about what he felt and thought.

Suffering often produces more than just despair; those in pain experience the full range of feelings. The prophet Jeremiah understood this when he authentically poured his heart out to God: "I have suffered much because God was angry"; "I am the only one He punishes over and over again without ever stopping"; "Even when I shouted and prayed for help, He refused to listen"; "God has turned my life sour."[5] Jeremiah was experiencing despair, anguish, rejection, and helplessness. And he wasn't the first to feel this way.

The shepherd David sang songs that would put most country-and-western songs to shame. He groaned and cried all night because of his grief and brokenness.[6] The Psalms are filled with these raw expressions of anguish, depression, trouble, fatigue, and isolation. Like Job, the writers accuse God of abandoning them—of causing their hopelessness and pain.[7]

Some people advocate that sufferers should simply "grin and bear it," but that idea is contrary to Scripture. This type of thinking actually encourages us to derive strength solely from ourselves. But as we've already seen, biblical authors didn't do this. They expressed their hearts honestly to the Lord and sought their strength from Him.

Dealing with suffering requires getting real with our thoughts and feelings, and getting honest with God about the truth of our pain. Let's face it: we cannot conceal anything from God so we might as well be honest with Him—even if it means sharing the fact that *He* is the one we're most angry with. Many Christians have a problem admitting they are angry with God. Afraid that God might send a bolt of lightning or something worse, they conceal their feelings of anger. But nowhere in the Bible do we see God zapping someone for being honest.

Even the Psalms express anger toward God. In one passage, He is indicted for selling Israel to heathen nations and making no profit on the deal.[8] In another, He is accused of mistreating the psalmist by removing him from his friends and causing them to hate him.[9]

Yes, it is true that none of us has the right to be angry with God. The point is not that we *need* to get angry with Him, but that we *do* get angry with God. We often blame Him for hard times, and since He already knows what is on our hearts, we might as well admit and express our true feelings.

Being real with God is actually an act of trust. A prudent person does not usually reveal his or her deepest thoughts and feelings to someone who is untrustworthy. When we choose to open up to someone about how we feel, we are implying that the person is able to handle our most ugly and intense feelings—especially if those feelings are directed toward that person. Likewise, when we open up our hearts to God, we are showing our trust in Him.

Let us be clear again about the issue of telling God what is on our minds. It is possible to cross a line; being honest with God is not a license to say anything we want. God acknowledged Job's integrity when He noted that Job did not sin or blame Him in his suffering.[10] Remember, while it is normal and natural to feel anger when we are hurting, it is *not* God's will for us to stay there.

As we discussed in chapter 2, one of the main reasons we become angry with God is because He is not conforming to our plans. We demand that He make life comfortable, easy, predictable, and orderly for us. According to God, however, the only time we can demand our way and negotiate with Him is when we are able to tilt the world on its axis and keep it spinning at just the right speed.[11]

Our willingness to struggle with God must be open and genuine. If we choose to be dishonest, we will only distance ourselves from Him. Marriages grow distant and cold when marital partners believe they are unable to speak honestly and forthrightly with one another. In counseling, husbands have told me (John) that they cannot tell their wives certain things because they will upset them. In other words, they assume that their wives can't handle the news. For that reason, I think the marital vows ought to include something about trusting the other partner enough to always tell the truth.

In the same way, we must trust God with the truth of our feelings—no matter what they are. God is "man" enough to handle it. And when we admit our hurt, anger, frustration, and disappointment, we deepen our ability to trust in God the next time.

David realized that God was able to tolerate heartfelt feelings when he wrote, "For He has not despised or disdained the suffering of the afflicted one; he has not hidden his face from him but

has listened to his cry for help."[12] James encouraged us to ask God
when we need wisdom because He will not mock, belittle, or shame
us when we come to Him.[13] God does not backhand us across our
mouths, saying, "Shame on you for saying that or thinking that!"
We can come boldly before the throne of grace.[14] So it's time to
get real.

Sometimes in the midst of suffering, we have a hard time getting
real because we simply don't feel anything. This numbness may be
an indication that we have not yet moved beyond the shock stage in
the grief process. At other times, however, it may reflect an unwill-
ingness or inability to face the sadness of life. We'd rather psychologically anesthetize the pain. Beneath the surface, however, is often
deep-seated anger. By avoiding our true feelings, though, we aren't
seeing things as they really are, but as we prefer them to be.

Having a biblically sound view of pain and suffering doesn't
mean we won't hurt or that painful feelings will simply evaporate. It
does, however, provide a frame of reference for moving beyond the
pain. Before we can intellectually resolve our afflictions, we must
reckon with our emotions.

Exposing our feelings to the light is critical to avoid being controlled by them. Even Sigmund Freud illustrated the importance of
getting things off one's chest when he borrowed the word *catharsis*
from Aristotle.[15] *Catharsis* comes from the Greek and means "puri-
fication." It was used to speak of the discharge of painful memories
and emotions. While the term has broad significance to psychotherapy, it underscores the importance of releasing our hurtful feelings to other caring individuals, including our heavenly Father.

The psalmist recognizes the value of opening his heart to God.
"I cry out to the LORD with my voice; with my voice to the LORD
I make my supplication. I pour out my complaint before Him; I
declare before Him my trouble."[16] God can provide us with the
ability and the security to face the most awful truths and feelings
about ourselves. He can give us the courage to traverse the unex-
plored ground of our pain so we can heal and grow. We may not
know what lies ahead, but God can help us avoid turning back and
retreating to the familiarity of our pain.

Understand the truth about feelings

It is important to remember in facing our feelings that they, too, were affected by the Fall. Of course, not every feeling or thought is sinful. Our feelings, however, are not amoral; they have the potential to take us in directions away from God. For this reason we have to guard against our tendency to wallow in self-pity.

Jesus protected Himself from falling into self-pity by heading it off at the pass. At one point Jesus prophesied about His upcoming crucifixion. Alarmed by his Master's words, Peter boldly entreated Christ to avoid crucifixion. Without missing a beat, Jesus rebuked Peter, "Get behind Me, Satan!"[17] Jesus knew how easy it would be to give in to temptation and *not* go to the Cross. In addition to the pain of dying this way, Jesus would bear the sin of the world. But anything that interfered with the Cross or salvation was of Satan. In essence, Jesus was associating self-pity with the devil.

Review the Nature of Your Suffering

Regardless of the cause of the pain, adversity generally creates suffering. Before we can respond to the pain, however, we must understand the cause, since that will dictate what we must do.

Examine why you are suffering

The psalmist realized the need to review why he was suffering. "For the enemy has persecuted my soul; he has crushed my life to the ground; he has made me dwell in darkness, like those who have long been dead."[18] David was suffering at the hands of his enemy, and his pain was the result of the choices and actions of others.

It's important that we come to understand the nature of our suffering if we are going to do something about it. For instance, if suffering is caused by other people, we really have little choice but to accept it. Of course, we should do what we can to deal with those who are harming us, make changes to prevent further harm, or find ways to minimize their efforts. But even then, we might not be successful in stopping them from hurting us further. Sometimes we must simply cope with circumstances in our lives because they are outside our realm of control. In fact, the word *cope* literally means to "embattle" and suggests war. Obviously, coping is not a simple process. Christ knew victimization but did not allow Himself to be a victim. As we have seen, He didn't run from the Cross but instead faced His realities.

While the psalmist experienced suffering because of others, Jeremiah acknowledged that he and the people of Israel were suffering because of their own actions: "We have transgressed and rebelled; You have not pardoned."[19] There is always a message in suffering. Sometimes it informs us that there is something we need to learn or attend to.

When we bring on our own suffering, we should take the proper steps to correct the situation. Sometimes this requires brokenness and repentance about sin. Sometimes it means acknowledging our wrong choices. Like the children of Israel, we sometimes do what we want, the way we want, when we want without giving God much thought. In dealing with Israel's sin against God and the subsequent punishment, Jeremiah cried out to God, affirming the sin. God promises that He is near to those whose hearts are broken and contrite, and He will forgive our sins.[20]

Suffering strips away the pretense that life is comfortable, orderly, and fair, a delusion that keeps us looking in all the wrong places for satisfaction. The fact that we seek fulfillment apart from God is the major reason we experience sociological problems, psychological maladies, and even physical illnesses. We are bent on looking away from God to find wholeness. Of the many truths we can extract from the Garden of Eden, one is that a life free of suffering will not guarantee that a person will choose God.

Examine yourself

People respond to mirrors in different ways. Some individuals spend hours examining themselves in a mirror in order to find ways to cover up all the imperfections they perceive. Some take only a causal look, preferring not to see any problems that might need attention. Others try to avoid mirrors altogether. God wants us to inspect ourselves in the mirror of His Word and in light of the suffering we are experiencing. Regardless of the reason we are suffering, God wants us to uncover areas in our lives that are not completely turned over to Him. He wants us to acknowledge our imperfections. It is not evident, based on Scripture, that Job did anything to bring about his suffering. Yet God used Job's pain to expose the arrogance of his heart. In the same way, we need to use the painful circumstances of our lives to deepen our spiritual walks. We need to become more consumed with our unholiness than we are with our discomfort and pain. As we respond to suffering by examining our hearts, we will find unholiness. And as we face our unholiness, we will grow as Christians. Over the course of our lifetimes, we should find that as we examine our souls, we see more and more the image of Christ reflected back to us and less and less our own flawed images. Take time to examine yourself to see what you depend upon for satisfaction.

Recognize the Ways God Works to Accomplish His Plan

David's sincerity and contemplation bring him to consider the activity of God. "I remember the days of old; I meditate on all Your works; I muse on the work of Your hands."[21] The psalmist reflects on the good things God had done for him; he declares the wonderful works of God. And in the midst of his pain, he ponders the mysterious ways of God.

God seems to thrive on surprises. Just when we think we understand how God acts, He shows us that we were badly mistaken. As long as our microscopes are too narrowly focused, the meaning of our suffering may always remain a mystery. Although we will never understand the ways of the Almighty, there are some things that we can know about Him.

God is unchanging

Sometimes it's difficult to relate to the way God worked in the lives of various Bible characters. Even if we wholeheartedly believe the Bible, the level of intimacy God had with people like Abraham, Moses, and David seems far removed from the way we experience Him today. But the God who did business with these saints is the same God who works with us now. God does not change.[22] The very person, character, and Word of God are today—and always will be—exactly what they were in biblical times.

God's purposes never change,[23] but our understanding of Him does. Because we are so limited in our capacity to grasp the supernatural, our comprehension of God will unfold as we get to know Him. In the same way that husbands and wives grow in their understanding of one another over the years, so, too, do we grow in our understanding of God. The more life we experience, the more we will be confronted with "new" aspects of God's eternal nature.

God is untamable

In C. S. Lewis's *The Lion, the Witch and the Wardrobe*, God is represented in the character of Aslan the lion, who had a tendency to show up unexpectedly. When asked about Aslan, Mr. Beaver's description beautifully captures some aspects of God's nature: "If there's anyone who can appear before Aslan without their knees knocking, they're either braver than most or else just silly."

When Lucy asks, then, whether or not Aslan is safe, Mr. Beaver responds: "Safe? . . . Who said anything about safe? 'Course he isn't safe. But he's good. He's the King, I tell you."[24] The God of the Bible cannot be reduced to a set of principles. He is predictably unpredictable, yet absolutely good.

It's difficult to understand how God can be so unpredictable and yet so good at the same time. It's nearly inconceivable how He can allow so many bad things to happen in this world, yet still be considered good. When we are hurting, that goodness is very hard to grasp.

Nevertheless, the Bible makes it very clear that God is good and good is God. God continually shatters our understanding of Him. After all, a God we can understand is not a God at all.

God is mysterious

Just as God is unpredictable, He is also mysterious.[25] Our God is an enigma that we will never figure out.

In chapter 2, we discussed one of the main questions sufferers ask during times of trouble: "Why me?" If you believe in a world of chance, it makes no difference why something happens. It simply does. If, however, you believe in a powerful and loving God, it makes all the difference. While there may be one or more purposes for our suffering, God's ultimate plan is to change us spiritually.

The Bible seems to imply that God typically waits to use negative circumstances until He has tried other avenues to get our attention first. In the physical world, we usually experience pain immediately—as when we are burned by a hot stove. Imagine if God dealt with us in the same fashion. If we chose to disobey, we would quickly be punished. In such a world, God would be the tamer and we would be His trained animals.

But instead God has given us the ability to choose, and sometimes we don't experience the consequences of wrong choices for years. He may send various messengers or expose us to sermons, music, or other people's situations in order to get our attention. Sometimes it is only when we do not respond to Him that He begins using painful circumstances.

Certainly, when God disciplines us He wants us to understand His purpose. I (John) knew a man who adamantly believed that his chronic illness was from God. He was a former deacon, Sunday school teacher, and regular singer at his church, and his fall from the Lord had been very public. This man believed that his illness was God's hand of discipline for leaving his wife. Whether or not that was true, at least his illness caused him to return to the Lord with a repentant heart. God is not obligated to explain Himself.

As in the case of Job, God may never tell us what the storm means. An elderly acquaintance of my (John's) family lost his wife in a car accident after the birth of their second son. He has lived these past forty years never knowing why God "took" his wife. In spite of his loss, however, this man never doubted that God knew what He was doing. The point is that we can still love and trust God without ever knowing why.

As we've already seen, it's human nature to want an explanation and cause-and-effect reason for our pain. We look backward for a connection between some action and our present suffering. This is wise, since some personal sins or poor choices might have been the cause of our problems. Confession and learning from experience are essential in order to move ahead. But the Bible typically points us to the end result of suffering: the future. God wants us to look forward in hope and to seek explanations, not so much for the origins of our troubles, but for what He wants to do through our pain.

Researchers have found that rather than asking, "Why me?" trauma victims are better off asking, "For what end?"[26] And as believers, we must even go beyond that question and ask "Who?"—that is, "Who is behind and in the trauma?"

Consider the story of a lone shipwreck survivor who was washed up on an uninhabited island. After a while, he managed to build himself a hut in which he placed the meager belongings he had salvaged from the wreck. The man prayed for deliverance and anxiously scanned the horizon each day to hail any passing ship. One day upon returning from a hunt, he was horrified to find his hut in flames—everything had gone up in smoke. Broken and dejected, the man slumped next to a tree by the coast to await death. After sleeping through the night, the man was startled to feel someone touch him. As he looked up, he saw the face of a man. "We saw your smoke signal," said the man, the captain of a passing ship. "We came to see if you needed help."[27]

If our lives are in God's hands, all things truly do work together for good.[28] As if creating a complex tapestry, richly embroidered with innumerable intersecting threads, God weaves the contours of human experience into a masterpiece of His design. The late Mother Teresa insightfully captured the creative talents of God when she said, "We are pencils in the hands of a loving God."[29] She truly lived out that belief. Just as a piece of yarn cannot comprehend the plan of the weaver, so we, too, are equally ignorant of our mysterious artisan, God.

Sharon, one of my (John's) clients, told me that she needed to forgive God for taking her husband of over twenty years. At first, I wanted to tell her that God does nothing wrong, so she didn't need to forgive Him. Yet Sharon blamed God, and she concluded that in order to heal, she needed to let God off the hook. I realized that Sharon did not need to forgive God in order to release Him from the guilt of wrongdoing, but to release herself from holding God responsible.

God can turn His power on like a faucet wherever and whenever He wishes. We may sense how much we need His comfort, power, and guidance, yet our attempts to compel Him by prayers, confessions, and zeal only reveal that God cannot be manipulated. He will be silent when He chooses to be, and He will be active according to His own purposes. Faith in God glorifies Him as He reveals Himself in and through our circumstances.

When God rocks our world, we are forced to pick up the shattered pieces of our core beliefs. No longer is anything the way it used to be, including our views of God. But it is only as we struggle to see God in a new light that we can once again draw close to Him and move through our pain.

Reaffirm Your Desire to Know God

David released his feelings of sorrow to God, reviewed why he was suffering in order to deal with the problem, and recognized that God had many ways of accomplishing His plan. Now he needed to reaffirm his desire to know God: "I spread out my hands to You; my soul longs for You like a thirsty land."[30]

Do you long to know God?

It is impossible to fully trust anyone we do not know deeply. We will never come to the place where we can depend upon God to get us through adversity unless we take the time to get to know who God really is and what He is truly like. Clearly, David felt this passion for God: a passion to know God in a deeper and more profound way. But this passion emanated from God's goodness.

The wonderful weeping prophet Jeremiah voiced a similar longing: "Deep in my heart I say, 'The LORD is all I need; I can depend on him.' "[31] This prophet knew persecution and suffering. Like Job, he came to know that in spite of his adversity, God was vital to his life, completely good, and dependable. While it is true we can be so heavenly minded that we are no earthly good, the greater problem is often that we're so earthly minded that we are no heavenly good. We must seek God as if we were looking for a priceless antique in a dark attic filled with junk. We know He is there, but sometimes it seems impossible to find Him. There is too much clutter to get through. At times we might spot Him buried under the disarray of our lives, but sadly, He still seems out of reach.

Paul told the Philippians that he had willingly lost all things "that I may know Him and the power of His resurrection . . ."[32] Such words reveal the passion of the apostle's heart and encourage us to get to know God in a deeper way. But Paul did not stop with that sentiment. He continued, ". . . and the fellowship of His sufferings, being conformed to His death." If we were ordering from this menu, we would request the knowledge of God à la carte. Sometimes, however, the only way we can know God and understand the power of His resurrection is through suffering.

Just as an author's biography helps readers better understand his or her point of view as they read, our knowledge of God will help us to accept His creative purposes as they unfold in the story of our lives. The more time we spend with God and the more we worship Him, the better we will be able to grasp His benevolence.

Do you really know God?

As we saw in the section on recognizing the ways God works, we are limited in our understanding of God. Part of the problem is that we think we know God, but the notions of God that we embrace are typically not accurate. Often, we don't even embrace the God who is portrayed in the Bible.

As a counselor in training, I (John) was fascinated by C. S. Lewis's brief narrative *A Grief Observed,* which gives an account of a committed Christian and scholar agonizing over something he could not control. A bachelor until midlife, Lewis found great enjoyment in his marriage. After four years of marriage, Lewis's wife, Joy, died of cancer. As a means of coping with his loss, Lewis turned to his gift of writing to express his heartache. In *A Grief Observed,* Lewis candidly expressed his fears and doubts. Seeking comfort in God, Lewis felt the door being slammed in his face and double bolted from the inside. Early on, he wrote with searing honesty of his personal journey: "Not that I am . . . in much danger of ceasing to believe in God. The real danger is of coming to believe such dreadful things about Him. The conclusion I dread is not, 'So there's no God after all,' but, 'So this is what God's really like. Deceive yourself no longer.'"[33]

Suffering tends to test and change our views of God, challenging our earthly notions of who God is and what He is like. We can't understand why God would seem to contradict His own nature. Like Lewis, we struggle to grasp God's role in suffering and pain. Job realized that God could not be at odds with Himself, and therefore resolved the apparent contradiction by realizing that the problem was between his idea of God and God as He really is.

Early in the book of Job, God seemed hostile and unjust. Yet in his misery Job recognized that there was another side of God—that He forgave sin, that He did not neglect His creation, and that He was and is a witness in heaven, an advocate on high, a pledge for all those who are scorned.[34] Through his ordeal, Job sensed that in spite of his despair, his Redeemer lived and would at last stand on the earth.[35] In fact, it was not until he arrived at this declaration about his Redeemer that Job wanted someone to take a pen and write his story. It is not the depth of our pain that ought to stop the presses, but the realization that we have a Redeemer.

Suffering transforms our head knowledge of God into an experiential knowledge. The decisive break with the old ideas of God did not come easily for Job. It took immense suffering for Job to radically shift his notions of God.

> I know that You can do everything, and that no purpose of Yours can be withheld from You. You asked, "Who is this who hides counsel without knowledge?" Therefore I have uttered what I did not understand, things too wonderful for me, which I did not know.[36]

Job came to understand that knowing about God and truly knowing God are not one and the same. Upon coming to grips with the sovereignty of God, Job's response was one of repentance: "Therefore I abhor myself, and repent in dust and ashes."[37]

Helmut Thielicke, an influential theologian from Hamburg, Germany, pointed out that a fabric viewed through a magnifying glass is clear in the middle and blurred at the edges. But in spite of how it appears, we know the edges are clear because of what we see in the middle. Life, he says, is like a fabric. Many edges are blurred; many events and circumstances we do not understand. But they are to be interpreted by the clarity we see in the center—the Cross of Christ. We are not left to guess about the goodness of God from isolated bits of data. He has clearly revealed His character and dramatically demonstrated it to us in the Cross. As Paul wonderfully expressed, "He who did not spare His own Son, but delivered Him up for us all, how shall He not with Him also freely give us all things?"[38] Meditate on who and what Jesus Christ is and what He has done for you through His life, death, and resurrection. If ever you doubt His love, consider the Cross. No other symbol better signifies love, let alone hope!

We must rid ourselves of myths about God, such as "God helps those who help themselves." Our minds must be saturated with the truths of God that are found in His Word if we are going to survive perilous times. A Christian who was also a recovering alcoholic attended an Alcoholics Anonymous meeting where the topic was surrendering to a higher power. After listening to a lot of discussion about this higher power, the man said that he did not believe in a loving God. His father had been a stern, abusive parent who told him that God would punish him if he disobeyed. This young man learned that God was not someone to approach but someone to be avoided, or at least appeased. A gentleman from the meeting said, "If that was my God I would fire Him." At first, the Christian was put off by that notion, but then the gentleman went on, "Since you need a God, why not try mine?" It was then that the man realized that his "god" was not the God of the Bible.

Children are often very anxious and fearful of doing something wrong. All too often, parents use the threat of God and punishment

to control childish behavior. This fear of displeasing God then mag-
nifies our growing sense of guilt and shame. There are some truths
in these statements (i.e., God *does* punish, and it is possible to dis-
please Him), but some of us only see and hold to this lopsided, half-
truth view. These distorted images of God then shape our views of
Him. When that happens, we must fire the god we've created in our
image: the god who abandons us, holds grudges, is not approach-
able, has no mercy or grace, plays games with our lives, and belittles
us at every turn. These unbiblical concepts must be replaced with
the whole of Scripture on the nature of God, which includes His
enduring love for us.

Sometimes, as C. S. Lewis wrote, our god isn't evil, but neither
is he strong or powerful. That god is more like a benevolent grandfather than a father.[39] Fathers want to enjoy a relationship with
their children but primarily seek to raise healthy, mature, and well-
balanced people. Grandfathers, on the other hand, tend to overlook
their grandchildren's faults and avoid interfering in their lives. But
the God portrayed in the Bible is not a sentimental, beard-stroking
grandfather in the sky. Make sure that the God you get to know is
the God of the Bible.

God, who is merciful, patient, and long-suffering, loves us so
deeply that He is willing to put up with us.[40] Because God is good
and wise, He can make anything we encounter work out for our
good, at least in the end.[41] His plans are to help us rather than harm
us.[42] Finally, because He is faithful, changeless, and dependable, He
has promised never to leave or forsake us.[43]

Even the names of God speak to His wondrous nature. He
is *Jehovah-Jireh*, the God who provides all our needs and supplies relief.[44] He is *Jehovah-Rophi*, the miraculous healer.[45] One
of the most revered of divine titles to Jews and Christians alike
is *Jehovah-Shalom*, the Lord who is peace.[46] He is also *Jehovah-
Ra-ah*, meaning "the Lord the Shepherd," which speaks to His
guiding, providing, and protecting His followers.[47] Finally, He
is *Jehovah El Shaddai*, the Almighty God who gives strength and
satisfies His people.[48]

Even as you read these words, Jesus is making intercession for you at the right hand of the Father, and the Holy Spirit is indwelling you, sealing you, and providing you comfort.[49]

All of the promises in the Bible are based upon the character of the Promiser, God Himself. He is rich in promises, and they are as sure as His unchanging nature, backed by His faithfulness. This is the God we all need to come to know.

Reassess Your Dependency and Trust in God

Someone has said that "adversity is a means of introducing a man to his real self." While there is truth in that statement, it is incomplete. Adversity also reveals the genuine nature of an individual's faith and dependency in God. God's hope is that adversity will give us a deeper and richer view of Himself.

The psalmist cried out, "Answer me speedily, O LORD; My spirit fails! Do not hide Your face from me, lest I be like those who go down into the pit."[50] David realized he needed God because he could not meet his own needs. It is as if he said, "God, if you don't answer me, I will die!"

He knew that he had not been fully dependent upon God but turned to God as a last resort. It is interesting that when we suffer, most of us eventually arrive at God's doorstep. In the end, the "why" questions always bring us back to God.

What is my real God?

The greatest wrestling match in a time of suffering occurs when we consider our relationship with God. While we cannot control our circumstances or God's purposes, we can control our trust and dependence in and on Him.

Trust is a relational term. When someone does not fully trust another person, there is an inherent relational deficit. Trust is based on the strength of the relationship. It will not grow or flourish unless tested and ultimately worked through. This idea of trust is the same when it comes to our relationship with God. Consider your response when a significant tragedy befalls you, something you believe you don't deserve. If you believe God should have intervened, that He should have done something to prevent you from experiencing such an awful ordeal, you probably do not trust the character of God. Do you believe that God is still good and gracious to you even when you suffer?

When we're in pain, we tend to look to anything tangible to give us hope. I (John) remember reading a story about a man condemned to solitary confinement in a pitch-black cell. After hours of boredom and isolation in his dark chamber, he progressively became more and more panicky. Knowing he would not survive his punishment long if his emotions spun out of control, the man sought to solace himself. He realized that he had a marble in his pocket, so he began to occupy himself by repeatedly throwing the marble, his only companion, against the wall. The ill-fated man spent hours listening to his marble bounce and roll along the cold stone floor. Then he would grope in the darkness to find it. In a strange way, this activity gave him comfort and purpose during his confinement. One day the prisoner threw his marble into the air as he always did, but this time it failed to come down. He was naturally disturbed about its disappearance. He combed the cell looking for his marble, but he never could find it. The more he looked, the more panicky he became. Broken by the strange disappearance of his only source of comfort, the prisoner became uncontrollable, pulled out his hair, and died. When the prison officials came in to remove the body, one of the guards noticed something caught in a huge spider's web in a corner of the cell. "Now look at that! How did a marble get up there?"[51]

We so readily place our trust in things that cannot be relied upon. Some depend upon their education or bank accounts. Others rely on their independence or ability to make things happen. But none of these things will prove themselves 100 percent reliable. They are temporal, finite, and limited. Yet God is eternal, infinite, and dependable beyond our definition and imaginations, and He asks us to place our trust in Him. Sadly, we struggle to comply.

The great patriarchs of the Old Testament put their confidence in things they couldn't see.[52] Why then do we struggle so much to relinquish our destinies into God's hands? Charles Haddon Spurgeon is credited with saying, "When you can't trace God's hand, trust His heart."[53] Trust requires us to live with our unanswered questions.

How can I trust God?

Before we can place our dependency on God, we must reconcile two questions: First, do we truly believe that God is totally committed to our welfare? If that is true, then do we believe that He is good and right in doing whatever He deems necessary to accomplish His will?

God's goodness doesn't change. The God who raised Jesus from the dead so that we can know eternal life did so because He is good and gracious. This same God, who has the power over death, is still good today even when we hurt.

I (John) knew a couple who was having a difficult time with their toddler. In spite of a well-executed bedtime routine, the child refused to sleep by himself. The frustrated parents would then put the screaming youngster in bed with them in order to get some sleep themselves. With another child on the way, these parents knew something had to change. After spending time loving and comforting their child before bedtime, the parents realized they had to let him cry, and not allow him to get into their bed. It took all their strength to listen to their youngster scream from his crib and not rush in to rescue him. Yet for their son's own good and development, the parents painfully endured his tears and ignored their hearts' desire to ease his pain. Obviously, their son did not understand why they weren't responding, but they rested in the fact that it was best to do nothing. Because these parents were committed to the long-term welfare of their son, they had to leave him alone in his bedroom. The same is true with God. It may seem that He is hiding, but His purpose is to grow us. While we might not fully understand why He would allow our pain and misery to continue, we can rest assured that it will be best for us in the long run.

If we are going to trust God, we must not put our faith and dependence in understanding. While it is appropriate and acceptable to pray that God will give us understanding, God wants us to place knowing Him, believing Him, and accepting His plans as our priority and passion. He never expects us to fully understand His ways. Even if God did give us His rationale, we probably wouldn't really accept His answer as justification for our suffering anyway.

We need to trust Him with the innocence of a child. You may explain to a child all the reasons he must be immunized, but when the doctor gets ready to give the shot, none of those reasons matter. And what does the child do when the needle strikes? He screams for his mommy. Comfort comes, not in knowing the reasons, but in knowing the Comforter.

I (John) have an acquaintance who lost his spouse about four years ago. While in her forties with three young children, she was diagnosed with a rare form of cancer. She endured almost a year of painful treatment to no avail. Even though it has been four years since her death, my friend still does not know why God allowed her to die such a painful death while their children were so young and vulnerable to her loss. He says, "God gives and God takes away. God didn't have to send His Son to die for me or raise Him from the dead so that my wife and I could enjoy eternal life. God was not obligated to explain Himself then, and He is not obligated to explain Himself now." There is not much more that needs to be said. With that attitude, it is not surprising that a look of hope radiates from this man's face whenever I see him.

Relinquish Your Destiny into God's Trustworthy Hands

As a student in college, I (John) traveled with a group to Haiti to help build some schools and to conduct Bible studies and concerts. One of the meetings was high in the mountains, so we rode donkeys to get there. As we traveled along the windy trails, at many points along the way we were literally riding next to a cliff. Our instructor told us to sit balanced on the donkey, even though our minds were telling us to lean in toward the mountain. The guide tried to reassure us that donkeys are sure-footed animals and that they do not slip. As I looked down over the edge, I thought, *Yeah, but they are also dumb.* Nevertheless, if we were going to be safe, I knew we had to trust that the donkeys were sure. Obviously, the donkey, dumb or not, survived the trip. But it was difficult to place trust in that animal!

The psalmist David did not desire to place his life at the feet of a donkey but in the hands of a loving God. "Cause me to hear Your lovingkindness in the morning, for in You do I trust; Cause me to know the way in which I should walk, for I lift up my soul to You."[54] David knew he had struggled in the past, but now he was ready to place his trust in God and affirm the Lord's goodness.

Similarly, the prophet Jeremiah wrote a letter to a group of early exiles in Babylon seeking to encourage them with a message from God: "For I know the thoughts that I think toward you, says the LORD, thoughts of peace and not of evil, to give you a future and a hope."[55] If you are suffering, this is a great verse to memorize. It speaks volumes about God's enterprise. In the Hebrew, the word for "thoughts" means "plans." God has a plan for us; we can trust that it is a good plan because it is designed to give us a future and hope.

When my (John's) wife and I were married, I brought her to my one-bedroom apartment in Orlando, Florida. As we neared the apartment complex, I lovingly told her that while I had made many preparations to our new home, it was hers to do with as she wanted. We arrived, unloaded the last of our possessions, and settled in for the night. The next morning I kissed my bride good-bye and wished her a pleasant day as I left for work. When I came home that evening, I was shocked to find that my wife had rearranged everything in the apartment. I had to look at the number on the door to make sure I was in the right place!

My wife gave me a huge kiss and enthusiastically told me that she had fun making my apartment *our* apartment. But I was hurt that she had made so many changes, and I told her so. In fact, I criticized most everything she did (yes, the honeymoon was definitely over!). While you may think little of me for treating my wife poorly, consider how we typically respond to the way God arranges our lives. If you are a Christian, you made a willful decision to turn your life over to the Lord. You gave Him permission to do with you whatever He pleased. You probably even sing "I Surrender All" on Sundays. When, however, God does with you what He pleases, do you find yourself complaining rather than surrendering? It is so much easier to talk and sing about surrender than it is to exhibit it when God stomps on our comfort.

One of the great paradoxes of the Christian faith is that we are never completely free until we have become totally dependent. When we want answers, God offers Himself as the answer to our pain. And until we are willing to accept that, and only that, we are not yet totally dependent.

Genuine trust is independent of understanding. This was true for Daniel's three friends, who affirmed their confidence that God could save them from the furnace. Of course, they did not have the foggiest idea how God would do it, but these three ordinary men were able to face their ordeal with extraordinary composure because they placed their faith in an extraordinary God.[56] While they may not have entirely understood the awesome power of their God, they knew enough to know that they could rest in His care. The apostle John wrote, "For whatever is born of God overcomes the world. And this is the victory that has overcome the world—our faith."[57]

Through Christ all enemies are defeated; the victory is ours, we need only to appropriate it. Of course, that's the hard part. We appropriate faith when we accept it, believe it, and act upon it. Many biblical characters resisted following God's will (e.g., Abraham, Jonah, Samson) only to later regret their decisions. That is why God encourages us not to rely on our own understanding, but in every situation to depend on Him.[58] Put another way, we are to resist following our own plans. Being dependent on God means being willing to accept what He has promised, even when we cannot always explain what He has said. We accept life's mysteries and suffering because God knows them and we know Him. Of course, this does not mean that we are to resign ourselves to our situation. In fact, in the next chapter we'll talk about developing a plan of recovery. The point here is that we are to put our trust in God above our own plans. Because God is the First and the Last, the Everlasting to the Everlasting, we need not fear.[59] It is okay to seek answers, but when none are forthcoming, we must trust. That is why faith is so foundational, not just to salvation, but to day-to-day living.

There is a popular story of a man who went mountain climbing.

As he made his way over the rough mountain terrain, his rope gave way and he began to fall. Barely holding on, the panicky climber cried out, "Is anybody there?" Suddenly and miraculously a voice from heaven bellowed, "I am the Lord Your God. I am here and I will rescue you from this mountain. But for Me to help, you must trust Me to save you. Let go of your rope and I will catch you. Just release your grip and my powerful hands will be under you to carry you safely to the ground." After what seemed a long time of silence, the climber yelled, "Is anyone else out there?"

Are you able to say, "When my life seems to break loose, I will trust God no matter how difficult it becomes?" Remember, no matter what circumstances you face, God has promised never to abandon you.[60] Job came to the realization that life has meaning and purpose no matter what is lost here on earth. Our meaning and purpose are always secure because they are not rooted in what we have but in who we are in Christ.

Five helps to trusting God

For most of us, trust is not something that comes easily. The following five steps can be helpful when learning to trust God and relinquish our lives into His hands.

1. *Get to know God.* This is the most important step to developing and nurturing a trusting relationship. We examined the importance of getting to know God in the last section. While we may acknowledge the importance of knowing God intimately, many obstacles stand in our way. One obstacle is caused by our experiences. Knowing God can be very difficult for people who have come from dysfunctional backgrounds where they experienced emotional, mental, physical, or sexual abuse, abandonment, and/or rejection. While transferring human experiences with our parents onto other authority figures is normal, it need not destine us to repeating negative patterns with every person in authority. Likening God to our parents is normal, but it can have devastating consequences. No parent measures up to the attributes and

character of God. Therefore, every child must move from earthly expressions of love, mercy, and grace to what those attributes are like as they emanate from God. Because of their backgrounds, this step is harder for some. Their inability to grasp who God is blocks their fellowship with God and their ability to trust Him with the control of their lives. If trust is a problem for you, you may need to seek professional Christian counseling to help you work through this obstacle.

2. *Accept what happens as God's way of helping you to grow.* He does not needlessly allow us to go through painful experiences. God's goal is always to produce some greater work in our lives. Accomplishing His purpose was so important that God even took the lives of Job's children, as well as allowing Job and his wife to go through emotional and mental torment. It does not seem fair that God might choose to hurt a person as a way of helping someone else. But God seeks conformity to His image, not comfort. He wills faithfulness, not fairness, and holiness over happiness. Therefore, learn to ask, "For what end?" rather than "Why?" Remember that knowing the "Who" will make all the difference in the world.

3. *Focus on your response to the problem rather than the cause of it.* Jesus declared that "in the world you will have tribulation; but be of good cheer, I have overcome the world."[61] We can make an idol of our ability to reason and figure things out. Therefore, surrender the need to know everything. Certainly examine your life for any reason that might explain the why. If your teeth fall out, for example, it might be helpful to know it's because you failed to brush them.

4. *Focus on God's presence.* When we're hurting, our first inclination often is to run from God. But the truth is, there is no greater prescription for suffering than the

presence of the Lord. So immerse yourself in Him and rest in these words:

"When you pass through the waters, I will be with you; and when you pass through the rivers, they will not sweep over you. When you walk through the fire, you will not be burned; the flames will not set you ablaze. For I am the LORD, your God, the Holy One of Israel, your Savior."[62] "So do not fear, for I am with you; do not be dismayed, for I am your God. I will strengthen you and help you; I will uphold you with my righteous right hand."[63] "And those who know your name will put their trust in You; for You, LORD, have not forsaken those who seek you."[64]

5. *Make a willful decision to trust the Lord.* You may find it difficult to allow God to be fully in charge of your life, but if the alternative is misery, God's authority might be easier to accept. The key is to make the decision, commit to that decision, and trust the outcome to God.

Curt Richter, a psychobiologist from Johns Hopkins, became interested in the consequences of stress after watching so many people give up and die when overwhelmed by pressure.[65] Although stress is often purely psychological, Richter realized that it often caused the patient's body as well as his or her mind to collapse. So he began a series of rather dramatic—and even unkind—experiments to measure the physiological consequences of various highly threatening situations. In one particular study, Richter placed a rat into a large tub filled with water. Since rats are usually great swimmers, it was not surprising that the little fellow stayed afloat by paddling for over eighty hours before succumbing to exhaustion and going under. If the water was too cold or too hot, the rat would give up after less than thirty hours. If a research assistant handled the rats roughly before putting them into the water or blew a jet of air into the animal's face while it was swimming, the rats became exhausted even more quickly. Therefore, Richter found that the more stressful the situation, the greater the rat's suffering. Interestingly, Richter discovered that if he pulled the drowning rat out of the water and let it rest on a table for several minutes, the animal could make a remarkable recovery. Once the rat rested and gathered its wits, it seemed to realize that it could, in fact, survive the traumatic situation. If Richter tossed it back into the water, the rat would swim again for many hours. It seems that hope truly does spring eternal, but apparently only if one has been given a reason to hope.

As Christians, we have every reason to hope because our hope is not based upon happenstance or ourselves. It is based on the Creator of the universe. Therefore, we can confidently trust God with our worries, anxieties, questions, problems, and crises.

Paul Tournier said that the Christian life is sometimes like a trapeze act. You can swing on the bar, exercising and building muscles all you want. But if you want to excel, you have to let go and reach for the next bar—even when there's nothing beneath you. As they say in Alcoholics Anonymous meetings, "Let go and let God!"

Rejoice in How God May Use Your Suffering

While preparing his patient for ear surgery, a physician was explaining the various procedures and associated risks. In trying to calm his anxious patient's fears, he said, "I may hurt you, but I won't injure you." Likewise, our Great Physician speaks the same truth to us. He recognizes that, when used by His skilled hand, pain and suffering provide great benefit. As Friedrich Nietzsche said, "That which does not kill me, makes me stronger."[66]

David understood this. Regardless of his emotional state, he desired to follow after God, knowing that the result would be good. "Teach me to do Your will, for You are my God; Your Spirit is good. Lead me in the land of uprightness. Revive me, O LORD, for Your name's sake! For Your righteousness' sake bring my soul out of trouble. In Your mercy cut off my enemies, and destroy all those who afflict my soul; for I am Your servant."[67] The good things God is doing that we cannot see are far greater than the circumstances we can see. While God may not seem to respond to our every cry, He promises to use trouble and calamity for our good if we allow Him.

Corrie ten Boom wrote, "Praise lifts your eyes from the battle to the victory, for Christ is already Victor in your heart that you might have His victory in your life."[68] There is nothing remarkable about praise when life is going smoothly. But when we are able to worship God in the midst of a storm, *that* is truly extraordinary.

Some people, including Christians, live with chronic unhappiness and feelings of inferiority. These believers incorrectly assume that unless their self-esteem improves, they are doomed to a life of misery. But solving self-esteem problems is not the answer to having hope and peace. It is possible to have inner joy even with low self-esteem because true peace and joy come from knowing and believing in God's goodness.

Paul put it this way, "Rejoice in the LORD always. Again I will say, rejoice!"[69] At the root of the word *rejoice* is the word *grace*. We can rejoice in suffering because of the grace bestowed upon us through Jesus Christ. Joy is not a response that can be mustered by one's own efforts.

In essence, suffering speaks to the future. But discovering meaning in our sufferings will not necessarily change us. After we have discovered meaning in and through our sufferings, we need to develop a vision for what we can become as a result of that suffering.

Before you strive to rid yourself of pain, take the time to look for the meaning God has in it. Once you understand the significance, you can then take action to achieve the vision God has for you, a vision about what might be and what you can become. Then with the power of the Holy Spirit, you can take steps to achieve that vision. And it doesn't stop there. As you take new actions, you generate new meaning. And so the cycle goes.

God seeks to use broken hearts to draw people to Himself, to deepen fellowship with Him. Perhaps that is why James told us to be joyful when we suffer and the writer of Hebrews cautioned us not to "despise" the chastening of the Lord.[70] While this counsel deals with discipline, it is applicable to any kind of suffering. Suffering is an opportunity to grow and to know God in richer ways; such transformation would never be possible apart from pain.

People who have experienced and survived difficult ordeals often report that they are truly different people afterward. They have a newfound appreciation of life and a sense of gratitude. I (John) once spoke with a physician who suffered a massive heart attack while in his midthirties. He reported how much more sensitive he is now to his patients' complaints and pains. When we come to understand, as Job did, that God can do anything, we are able to experience God in a different way. Just as a brook would lose its song if God removed all the rocks, so we would lose our ability to experience and demonstrate the power and majesty of God if He removed all the stones of suffering in our lives.

A couple of nights ago, my (John's) sleep was interrupted by a terrible sound. It was a buzzing noise, and though I couldn't pinpoint the source of the sound in my sleepy state, I knew it was annoying. I soon realized it was the clock, which I quickly turned off so that I could roll over to get more rest. Unfortunately, my day got off to a later start than I had planned. As unpleasant as that alarm was, it was a signal that I needed to get up. It didn't matter how comfortable I was in that warm bed, I needed to rise to the occasion. Pain in our lives is a lot like that alarm clock. Sometimes we work so hard to rid ourselves of the pain that we miss the message and the opportunity to become better people.

When suffering hardships, our focus is on the solution, but the strength we gain in finding the solution and working our way through it is equally important. Perhaps this is what the prophet Isaiah had in mind when he said that God would "give them beauty for ashes,"[71] or as the Contemporary English Version says, "give them flowers in place of their sorrow, olive oil in place of tears, and joyous praise in place of broken hearts." Only a supernatural God who is profoundly committed to us is capable of making masterpieces out of misery. As Oswald Chambers wrote, "If through a broken heart God can bring His purposes to pass in the world, then thank Him for breaking your heart."[72]

CHAPTER TWENTY-ONE

Apply a Plan of Recovery

A counselor once asked a group of people, "Why is it that some folks go through agony and become gentle, sensitive, loving, thoughtful, and compassionate—the kind of person anyone would want as a friend? But others experience the same turmoil and become embittered, hardened, callous, cynical, and despondent?" One elderly lady, sitting comfortably in the back of the class, raised her hand. When the counselor acknowledged her, the woman smiled, leaned forward in her chair, and said, "Young man, the older you get the more you get into a rut."

That woman captured an important truth about human nature. Life change must be purposed and intentional. We must strive to grow and be different, or we will become hardened and more comfortable with a world we were not intended to call home. We must resist our self-defeating, automatic responses and consciously and willfully choose better ways to face hardships. These new ways of thinking and behaving are unfamiliar and frightening, but they offer a new life. We must persistently practice the adopted "new reflexes" in order for them to become both familiar and natural. We shape our futures through the decisions we make today, and these choices involve purposing our hearts, changing our perspectives, and preventing undue stress.

Many paths can lead to recovery. As you read this chapter, do not allow yourself to become overwhelmed with the numerous strategies that are recommended. It is not necessary to master each of the "new reflexes" or skills that we will discuss. My (John's) daughter is very creative. When she cuts the grass she makes patterns with the mower that can only be described as art. One of my neighbors likes to mow diagonals across his lawn. When I mow, my objective is to finish the job as quickly as possible so I employ the tried and tested box method. No matter which mowing pattern is used, the end result is the same: the grass is cut. Likewise, there is no specific pattern or strategy to respond to suffering. Some of the strategies will fit you better than others. Simply find and use those tools that you believe will contribute to your own emotional and spiritual maturity.

Purpose Your Heart

A history professor had been teaching his class about the French-English wars. One of his students asked how the English were able to win all those wars. The history professor explained that it wasn't because the English had wiser generals, better equipment, bigger armies, or even better-trained soldiers. The English won because they "learned how to hang on one day longer than the French."

In the face of adversity, especially during long-term trials, sometimes even hanging on to the day feels beyond our reach. If we are to get through, however, we must purpose our hearts to recover. Purposing involves four things: accepting reality, deciding to grow from our pain, developing the lines of communication with God, and using a support system.

Accept reality

During times of suffering, we all want a quick fix, a parachute that will take us back into the land of normalcy. One client told me (John) that he wanted the shortest cut, easiest road, and the no-pain approach to feeling better. He didn't want a process; he wanted to fly right into health. The idea of having to walk through a valley in order to reach the promised land of healing was not only foreign to this gentleman, it was simply unacceptable.

Quick fixes, shortcuts, and no-pain approaches almost never work. In fact, the result of not accepting adversity is actually greater suffering. Carl Jung believed that all psychological problems were the result of avoiding legitimate suffering.[1]

There are several ways people avoid the truth. One is by denying personal responsibility and blaming someone or something for the way we feel. Another is by exaggerating and overstating the situation. By making the problem bigger than life, we continue to justify our "right" to self-pity.

But as long as we point the finger of blame or wallow in self-pity, we are helpless in the face of suffering. For the committed believer, self-pity has no place. If ever one was justified to feel sorry for Himself, it was Jesus. Yet He displayed no self-pity because He knew His mission. Are we, then, to be exempt from such a process?

Ultimately, we must wrestle with the vexing monsters of the valley if we want to reach the promised land. When we accept this reality, we can finally grow. Dealing with hardship requires that we gain awareness of what happened and accept the reality of it. This acceptance is the key because it gets us to stop living in the problem and to start finding the solution. We must get honest with ourselves, give up self-pity, and allow the circumstances to change us rather than attempt to change our circumstances.

Decide to grow from your pain

Dr. Viktor Frankl observed that prisoners' attitudes and outlooks on life were the result of a decision, not concentration-camp influences. All of us, even under such formidable circumstances, can decide what shall become of us—mentally and spiritually. In other words, while we may have been victimized, we do not have to remain victims.

The focus of Dr. Frankl's therapy was to reorient his patients' focus away from their circumstances toward meaning. This reorientation required that the person take responsibility for recovery and for faith, and understand that in the larger scheme of life, suffering is valuable. As Christians we know that true meaning comes from a personal relationship with Christ. We must reorient ourselves from the trials we face to God's higher purposes. Consider the words of Dr. Frankl once again: "Man does not behave morally for the sake of having a good conscience but for the sake of a cause to which he commits himself, or for a person he loves, or for the sake of his

God."[2] That is why having a reason for living gives us the ability to endure any circumstance. When we begin to view things from God's perspective, we recognize that knowing Him gives us the ability to endure any trial.

We may never know why we suffer in certain circumstances, but we can harvest something from the study of affliction. According to Dr. Frankl, knowing that there can be meaning in suffering totally transforms the situation from a burden to a quest. He wrote, "Once the meaning of suffering had been revealed to us, we refused to minimize or alleviate the camp's tortures by ignoring them or harboring false illusions and entertaining artificial optimism. Suffering had become a task on which we did not want to turn our backs. We had realized its hidden opportunities for achievement."[3] It seems bizarre that these prisoners did not want to run from their suffering. But as we saw in the last chapter, to run from pain is to run from the chance to advance our emotional and spiritual character. Maturity means facing adversity head-on.

When we stop spending energy on avoiding pain, we can direct that energy to bring something new into being. Accepting our circumstances and committing ourselves to grow offers hope. Realizing that the ordeal serves a larger purpose redeems it. Many victims of suffering report positive changes in themselves as a direct result of their hardships. Some describe themselves as more compassionate, caring, patient, and loving individuals. Other victims realize they have untapped strengths they never knew of before facing trials. All in all, these individuals are better people now, as difficult as their paths have been. As such, suffering builds character. It also builds us spiritually. Suffering helped Job develop a more personal faith. Paul discovered that he could be content in the midst of dire circumstances. Jonah learned lessons about God's character and the consequences of disobedience.

Call to mind difficulties from your past. What did you learn from those experiences? At the time, you may have believed nothing good could come out of such ordeals. But now, years later, are you able to harvest a great deal of learning from each situation? Some people, like Job, see God in a bigger and more personal way.

Others, like Joni Eareckson Tada, develop a more real and genuine faith. Some sufferers develop unfeigned patience. Many find that they are able to minister to other people like never before as suffering provides a more heartfelt compassion for their fellow human beings.

To the Christian, suffering is an opportunity that requires us to do more than bear it. We are called to use it. If you purpose your heart, you, too, can glean a harvest from your pain. Poet and author Robert Louis Stevenson, who contracted pulmonary tuberculosis, shared his philosophy for dealing with chronic disease: "Life is not so much a matter of holding good cards, but sometimes of playing a poor hand well."[4]

Opportunity speaks to the future, not the present. It envisions possibilities. Remember that the ultimate aims of the Christian life are becoming like Christ and giving glory to God. We will not arrive there overnight, but we can hold on to the fact that we can eventually be more emotionally and spiritually attuned. If we have an injured leg and remain bedridden to avoid any additional pain, our leg muscles will atrophy and contract. But if we exercise too vigorously, we may reinjure the leg even more severely. Instead, we begin by limping—putting just enough weight on the leg to build strength gradually, but not so much as to strain it and prevent healing. As the muscles strengthen, we are able to bear more and more weight. In the same way, emotional healing is a process that requires us to challenge ourselves to move forward toward growth.

Develop the lines of communication with God

God said, "Call upon Me in the day of trouble; I will deliver you, and you shall glorify Me."[5] Victorious Christian living requires that we relentlessly communicate with God. Of course, most Christians have some level of communication with God, perhaps praying at meals or reading the Bible from time to time. But such limited communication will not sustain our spiritual lives in the good times, let alone during times of affliction and adversity.

Prayer is the glue that keeps us close to God, and Scripture is the truth that keeps us grounded in Him. Spending time in prayer

gives us an opportunity to seek God's plan for us. When we communicate with God, we need to do so with intensity, honesty, and
humility. In adversity, we are driven to pray, to cry out to God
from the depths of our hearts and to invite His involvement. Bear
in mind the promise that God gives us when we fervently seek
Him with all of our hearts: we will find Him.[6] If you believe that
God is silent or has abandoned you, the answer is to pray with all
your might.

It is not just the frequency or fervency that is an issue with prayer.
What we pray is most important. When we experience pain and
suffering, our tendency is to pray for deliverance, relief, answers—
anything that will bring a sense of comfort. Instead, the nature of
our prayer lives should be worshipful, praising God. When our
prayer lives becomes characterized by praise, we will rise above our
circumstances. A friend of ours has said that when going through
a difficult time, he spends 95 percent of his prayer time praising
and worshiping God.

As we saw in the previous chapter, we need to release our feelings to God. Prayer allows us to strip away pretense by revealing
our passions, hurts, and longings. Since sin blocks fellowship with
God, we need to first confess any sin. As we admit our wrongs to
the Lord, we will find that His unconditional love forgives us and
cleanses us.[7]

Studying God's Word will help us in many areas. For instance,
Psalm 119 shows us that Scripture is more than adequate to help us
in addressing any concern. According to this passage, God's Word
protects us from sin, provides enlightenment, counsels us, comforts
us, offers hope, gives wisdom, guides, and provides peace.[8]

Through Bible study we can get further instruction from God.
Because the Bible is a lamp, it promises illumination and guidance.[9]
It promises rest to the weary[10] and sustenance to the starving.[11]
Since the Bible is brimming with God's promises, it is imperative
to spend time in daily Bible reading. In the Old Testament, we can
find promises made to the great patriarchs, kings, prophets, and the
world at large. In the New Testament, the promises are set forth
to the church. God's promises are not ambiguous. They are stated

in clear, simple terminology that even a child can understand. You cannot feed on the promises of God and remain hopeless and hapless. Among other disciplines, a regular regimen of prayer, Bible reading, solitude, fasting, and meditation makes it clear that relief from pain is a day-to-day reprieve.

Use your support system

Social support plays a powerful part in our psychological and spiritual well-being because we were created as interpersonal beings. Other people play key roles, not only in shaping our attitudes, but also in helping us adjust following a tragedy. Sufferers receive feedback about themselves and the world around them from the impact of their own behaviors as well as from the responses of those around them. It has been well established that the way people respond to the sufferer dramatically affects that person's adjustment. Research has concluded that social support protects people from the potentially adverse effects of stressful events,[12] and even in the absence of stress, social involvement has beneficial effects on people.[13] In fact, research has even demonstrated that a strong support group can lessen the effects of many physical illnesses such as the common cold.[14] Finding and maintaining a positive support system, a group of fellow believers with whom we can share our struggles, is critical. This need is one reason that regular church attendance is so vital. We need the Word of God *and* the fellowship and encouragement of other Christians.[15]

Sometimes we can benefit even more from being with people who have suffered similar tragedies. Alcoholics Anonymous is based on this idea; sobriety is maintained by helping another alcoholic to stay sober. As a counselor, I (John) have strongly encouraged grieving people to get together regardless of the nature of their losses, so that through their interaction, everyone can heal. Thank God for the growing movement in the church to offer support groups for different kinds of hurting people.

The Bible encourages us to minister to suffering people. Hence, when we are in need, we allow the body of Christ to work when we go to particular godly individuals for wisdom and guidance.

Once we have our support systems, we must share our hearts with them. Even Shakespeare recognized the importance of sharing one's hurts: "Give sorrow words. The grief that does not speak whispers the o'er-fraught heart, and bids it break."[16]

Research clearly spells out the benefits of talking.[17] Disclosing our feelings to caring people unloads the weight of the painful emotions associated with a trial. Talking also helps us organize the experience so that we can make sense of it. Initiating a dialogue and beginning to talk about the pain might initially cause an increase in distress, but over the long haul, those who talk fare much better than those who do not.

Some people have a difficult time admitting they need help. This reluctance is typically nothing more than pride and self-reliance. We always need input from others, especially during times of adversity. There is a favorite saying among the addicted recovering community: "You are only as sick as your secrets." Shame and fear prompt people to hide in order to avoid being open and honest with others. But silence only leads to greater sickness. A caring community of support creates feelings of acceptance, reduces the shame and isolation, and provides a healing remedy for recovery.

Opening up to others means letting people know that we hurt, and it's crucial that we find someone to talk to who is capable of giving godly advice. Some of us feel comfortable talking with our ministers; others should seek the counsel of a mature Christian we trust.

Change Your Perspective

Abraham Maslow once said, "If the only tool you have is a hammer, you tend to see every problem as a nail."[18] We must widen the windows of our minds to see life from varied angles. Our perspectives are not fixed or unchanging. In fact, perspective can change instantaneously, resulting in a new set of thoughts, feelings, and actions. The way we experience life is based upon a convergence of circumstances, perceptions, and interpretations.

A cute story is told of two boys who were asked to participate in a study. One of the boys was known for his strong, positive attitude, and the other was equally known for his incredibly negative attitude. The pessimistic boy was taken to a large room filled with countless toys and encouraged to do anything he wanted for one hour. The other boy was put in an adjoining room with only a huge pile of dung heaped on the floor. After an hour, the researchers went to the boy in the toy room and found him sitting on the floor amidst the toys.

"What did you do?" the researchers inquired. "Nothing." said the boy. "I was afraid that if I played with anything it might break and I would get in trouble." When the research team arrived at the room filled with dung, they opened the door to find the young lad shoveling his way through it. "What are you doing?" they asked with a puzzled grin. The boy kept on digging and said, "With all this dung, I figured there had to be a pony in here somewhere."

We might laugh at such a silly illustration, but the point is clear: the circumstance itself has little to nothing to do with our attitude.

When we learn to see life, or a particular circumstance, through new "lenses," we are better equipped to deal with pain and suffering. This fresh vision is akin to watching an old horror film on television that you haven't seen in years. The movie, once so frightening on the big screen, seems tamer, even silly on a small screen with the lights on and the suspense taken away. New perspectives offer ways to translate hopelessness into hope and despair into optimism.

Examine Your Attitude

Two seriously ill men were in the same room of a large city hospital. The room had one small window. As part of his treatment, one of the men was allowed to sit up in bed for one hour. The other man had to spend all his time flat on his back. Every time the first man was propped up for his hour, he passed the time by describing what he could see through the window. He described a park where there was a lake with ducks and swans, a place where children came to sail model boats. The elderly man described young lovers who walked hand in hand through the park. There were flowers and stretches of

grass, games of softball, vendors of all kinds, and the most beautiful trees imaginable. Through the trees, the man was able to see a
wonderful view of the city skyline. The man on his back listened
intently as the man described the picturesque scenery.

One afternoon, frustrated that his roommate had the pleasure of
seeing outside while he remained flat on his back, the second man
thought, *I, too, should have the chance.* He felt ashamed, but the
more he tried not to think like that, the more he wanted to switch
places with the other man.

One night the lonely, envious man sleeplessly stared at the ceiling. Suddenly, the patient by the window awoke, coughing and
choking. Because of his negative attitude toward his roommate,
the man did not call for help—even when the sound of the other
man's breathing stopped. In the morning, the nurse found the man
by the window dead.

As soon as it seemed decent, the envious man asked if he could
be switched to the bed by the window. The minute he was alone, he
painfully and laboriously propped himself up on one elbow to look
out the window. To his amazement, all he could see was a blank
wall.[19] It was what the first patient could envision with his attitude
that created beauty.

Attitude is one of the most underappreciated aspects of life.
With the right attitudes, all the hardships in the world cannot make
us despondent. With the wrong attitudes, all the help in the world
will not make us joyful. Attitude creates a unique reality in the
same way a film creates an image on a movie screen. It predisposes
us toward specific thoughts, feelings, and behavior. Attitudes are
rigid and limiting because we believe our attitudes are reality, and
attitudes are self-validating because we see what we want to see.
They can just as easily lock us into a perspective of peace and joy
as they can a perspective of unrest and despair.

Clearly, attitudes are something within our ability to control.
William James, who is called America's first psychologist, held that
the greatest discovery was realizing that if we can change our attitudes, we can change our lives.[20] Some people say that in life, we
must deal with the hand that we have been given. The issue is not

if we will accept our difficulties, but *how*. No matter how bad the hand we've received, it must be played. We can fold and hope for a better hand next time, or we can accept the hand and recognize that, skillfully played, we can still win.

Viktor Frankl said that the last human freedom is choosing one's attitude. He noted that those who survived the Nazi concentration camps were not those who had better constitutions, but those who had positive attitudes. He wrote, "When a man finds that it is his destiny to suffer, he will have to accept his suffering as his task; his single and unique task. . . . His unique opportunity lies in the way in which he bears his burden."[21]

Frankl tells of an elderly doctor who remained intensely depressed for two years after the death of his wife, whom he had loved above all else. Dr. Frankl asked the grieving patient what would have happened if he died before his wife. After momentary reflection, the doctor replied that his wife would have suffered even more greatly than he had. Dr. Frankl pointed out that by surviving and mourning her loss, he had spared his wife's suffering. The doctor stood to his feet, shook Frankl's hand, and calmly left the office. Dr. Frankl artfully writes, "In some way, suffering ceases to be suffering at the moment it finds a meaning, such as the meaning of a sacrifice."[22] Abraham embraced this attitude when God asked him to sacrifice his son, Isaac. He understood that he needed to invest his life to serve God's higher purposes, not his own.

Have a grateful attitude

One of my (John's) friends was diagnosed with a well-known physical disease, but he demonstrated no fear, sadness, or anger. When I asked how he was dealing with the "tragedy" at such a young age, he responded, "This is not a tragedy; this is a reality."

One of the most significant beliefs that makes up our attitude is gratitude. Think about what life would be like if we considered what we have, rather than what we don't have. An interesting study found that people who kept gratitude journals fared far better than those who wrote down unpleasant experiences or those who simply recorded events. Gratitude-journaling participants were more likely to help others and to be the recipients of kind acts. Also, grateful people felt better about their lives as a whole, had healthier habits, and were more optimistic about the future. Researchers found that these people were grateful regardless of whether circumstances were good or not.[23] A familiar hymn encourages us to "count your blessings, name them one by one; count your blessings, see what God has done." Such an activity has the power to change our attitudes, even in the midst of suffering. We are not to praise God *for* the circumstances, but *in* them. Such thinking will eventually eradicate self-pity.

A great way to influence and change our attitude is through music. Most of us do not sing like the professionals, but we can make a joyful noise to the Lord. Praise choruses, hymns, and other popular Christian songs can take us out of self-pity and despair and help us focus on Christ. In short, they can change our attitudes.

Have a teachable attitude

An old Taoist parable tells the story of a student who seeks out a gifted master to learn wisdom. Willing to share his ways, the master began to converse with the student over tea. Interestingly, every time the master started to explain a point, the student would abruptly interrupt him. "Oh, I know that," the student would reply, or "No, that is not a problem for me because . . ." After a few such interchanges, the master stopped talking and picked up the teapot. He began pouring tea to fill the student's empty cup. He continued to pour until the cup was overflowing and spilled out. The student hollered, "Stop! The cup is full." With a wise grin, the master replied, "Yes, your cup is full; therefore I cannot teach you anything until you empty it."

The point of the story is clear: to be teachable we must be open to learn. And to be open we must be humble enough to learn from another. The psalmist penned it this way: "The humble He guides in justice, and the humble He teaches His way."[24] Jesus thanked the Father for hiding His ways from the wise, but not from babes. With childlike openness and humility, we can be taught by others.

Parents know that as children develop, they may become less open and humble to learning. It seems that rather than learning a lesson the first time, they continue to do the same wrong things over and over again, perhaps each time hoping that the outcome will be different this time. But their attempts rarely produce a different outcome. Unfortunately, we are the same way with God. It is impossible to teach people who don't think they need to learn anything new. Pride will block God's ability to teach us His truths during times of adversity.

As our divine parent, God constantly reminds us not to forsake Him, to live for Him, and to obey Him. But we continue to miss the point. As we saw in chapter 7, we must learn to accept God's discipline and ways. Like any parent, God wants us to be teachable, learning the lesson the first time. The bottom line is this: learning only takes root in fertile ground.

God has a lesson to teach through every circumstance. Just as successful people know that they must continue to learn, successful Christians accept that all of life is a classroom.

Maintain a sense of humor

Dr. Frankl called humor "the soul's weapon in the fight for self-preservation."[25] In order to rise above the horrific conditions of the concentration camp, he and other prisoners tried to share at least one amusing story every day.

I (John) used to have a screen saver on my computer that announced, "Fun is not what you do, but how you experience what you do!" We all need to learn to create fun in our lives—even in the midst of affliction. Find things that make you laugh, and adopt an attitude of playfulness. Read cartoons. Do whatever it takes to lighten things up.

I (Gary) purposely spent time watching *The Three Stooges* on television when my wife was first diagnosed with cancer. I was not so much trying to avoid the encroaching darkness of the situation as I was looking for a way to keep a positive perspective on life. You don't have to be outrageous; just allow your mind to be open to positive thoughts. Humor is like a shock absorber for the soul; it will not patch the potholes that lie ahead, but it will provide a smoother ride.

Let heavenly rewards motivate you

We all expect to be rewarded when we work. We want to be recognized for a job well done, especially by those who are in authority over us and in a position to provide compensation or promotion. The apostle Paul understood this when he wrote these lines about pursuing a heavenly prize:

> Not that I have already obtained all this, or have already been made perfect, but I press on to take hold of that for which Christ Jesus took hold of me. Brothers, I do not consider myself yet to have taken hold of it. But one thing I do: Forgetting what is behind and straining toward what is ahead, I press on toward the goal to win the prize for which God has called me heavenward in Christ Jesus.
> PHILIPPIANS 3:12-14, NIV

And in his letter to Timothy, Paul again talks of future reward:

> Now there is in store for me the crown of righteousness, which the Lord, the righteous Judge, will award to me on that day—and not only to me, but also to all who have longed for his appearing.   2 TIMOTHY 4:8, NIV

As Christians, the size and scope of our heavenly rewards are determined by the quality and quantity of our earthly service to the Lord. And when we are going through hard times, this service is based upon our attitudes.[26] Is our service done out of obligation and habit, or is it an expression of gratitude and faith?

In chapter 17, we saw that God has no problem using rewards as a means of motivating us. The writer of Hebrews said that God rewards those who diligently seek him, and Jesus told us to lay up treasures in heaven.[27] In fact, Hebrews also tells us that Christ looked ahead to the reward that was before Him when He endured the Cross.[28] As excruciatingly painful as the crucifixion would be, the reward that awaited Him was greater.

Yes, we will receive crowns in heaven. But heaven is a reward in and of itself. Jesus told His disciples that He was going to prepare a place for them, one apparently still under construction. But Jesus assured His followers that when it was finished, He would take them there.[29]

I (Gary) like to describe heaven as greater than the most wonderful experience you can imagine. It is greater than the feeling that comes when you lower your aching body into a swirling hot tub. It is greater than the most sensuous sex.

Just as expecting parents await the birth of their first child, we should anticipate our entrance into heaven. The reality of heaven's reward should arouse our hearts' deepest hunger, soon to be satisfied with the most extravagant meal. In the midst of suffering, remind yourself of heaven. It is our present comfort and our eternal hope.

The truly ultimate reward, however, is to fellowship with the Godhead for all eternity. Revelation 22:4 says that we shall see His face. The beauty of the Godhead is beyond words and certainly beyond our imaginations. One day we will bathe in the splendor of God's presence. Nothing we can do on this earth earns us the right to enjoy heaven and the presence of God. That is simply the result of God's voluntary goodness for those who have repented of their sins and trusted Jesus as their Savior.

When my (John's) children were small, I used to have them grab onto my clothes in crowded places. "Hold on to my clothes," I would tell them, "and I'll get you safely through the crowd. Even if you cannot see me, you will not lose me if you hold on to me." As we experience the difficulties this fallen world has to offer, we can lay hold of the fabric of heaven's promises and not lose our way. The rewards of heaven are a great attitude adjuster when we find ourselves giving way to self-pity and pessimism.

Change Your Emotions

As we discussed in the preceding chapter, our emotions play a major role in both the experience of suffering and in the way we try to cope. As we saw, it is important and critical for sufferers to honestly express their deepest feelings to God as well as to others.

The problem with feelings

One problem with feelings is that some people do not understand them. Our feelings seem to come out of nowhere, but feelings actually arise out of our deep-seated beliefs. They are a compass that indicates the quality of our thinking. Feelings do not provide information about life or our circumstances, but rather about who we are deep inside. Feelings reveal our insecurities and the intentions of our hearts.

Many counselors say that feelings are amoral; they are neither right nor wrong. But while feelings are a God-given, natural part of our psychological makeup, they also are part of our fallen nature: flawed because we are flawed.

People generally handle feelings in one of two ways. Some indulge their feelings and experience a downward spiral of negativity. They place too much importance on how they feel. Others run from their feelings to distract themselves from their internal pain—so much so that in time they become hardened to it. Like thoughts, feelings grow when we pay attention to them. I (John) like to compare feelings to goldfish: their growth depends on the size of the pond and how much they are fed.

Consider a mirage. Scientists tell us that the angle of the sun, a person's vision, and the slope of the ground can converge and cause someone to see water where none exists. Viewed from the senses, the mirage is real. Viewed from a higher, broader perspective, the mirage is clearly exposed as an illusion. In the same way, feelings can be illusory. Just as sun exposure leads to sunburn, most people believe that adversity leads to emotional turmoil. But Jesus experienced adversity, yet never allowed it to defeat him emotionally. His spiritual perspective acted as an internal sunscreen, protecting Him from the harmful rays of harsh conditions. Emotions are to be our servants, not our masters. When we are emotional, we do not think logically. Consequently, we cannot rely on feelings as indicators of what we need to do. We must work hard to keep our emotional lives in perspective. When our emotions are out of control, we will not be able to work our way through our hardships.

How sufferers experience emotions

When life is hard, it's natural to experience profound feelings of shock, hurt, sadness, disillusionment, anger, guilt, fear, fatigue, loneliness, emptiness, and helplessness.

In the initial stages of suffering, shock and numbness typically occur, often experienced as denial or a lack of any feelings at all. Shock is a God-given emotion absorber when the magnitude of our emotions is simply too overwhelming. Numbness serves as an internal psychological novocaine. It protects us from being flooded with feelings.

If suffering is due to the actions of another person, we feel hurt and a sense of sadness that might even lead to depression. Sometimes we cry and other times we feel that there are no more tears. Crying is one of God's ways of helping us release the intensity of our pain.

In the midst of difficulty, it's also common to feel disillusioned with the church, God, family, the medical profession, or friends. Eventually, anger may result. Since anger is the root of many psychological problems, it's important that we understand this stage of the process. If the anger is not adequately acknowledged and faced, it can lead to significant problems. Anger may be displaced onto someone or something else. If someone else can be blamed for our pain, then there is a logical reason we hurt and we are not at fault. Thoughts like this rise out of the core beliefs discussed in chapter 2.

When we turn anger on ourselves, we get depressed. Sometimes when anger is directed this way, it is manifested in the form of guilt or self-reproach. We may feel overly responsible, needlessly accepting blame. Guilt and anger have a way of keeping the focus on the problem, not the solution. It is easy to become stuck within these emotions.

Fear, a major culprit in preventing us from achieving inner peace, is perhaps the single common denominator that can make a painful experience feel unbearable. Christians need not feel worry or fear because our security is in Christ. Of course, we often will feel fearful because we are human, but we can use that fear as a cue to turn to God. "Whenever I am afraid, I will trust in You. In God (I will praise His word), in God I have put my trust; I will not fear. What can flesh do to me?"[30] In his fear, David was driven to God, and in His Word he found comfort. Because he trusted the Lord, he had no need to fear man. Corrie ten Boom said, "Worry does not empty tomorrow of its sorrow, but it empties today of its strength. It does not enable us to escape evil. It makes us unfit to face evil when it comes."[31]

Perhaps the gravest feeling one might experience is hopelessness, the greatest predictor of suicide and a major factor in depression. In certain situations, we find ourselves feeling hopeless, as if we are living in a kind of swamp, bogged down in marsh. Left in the lurch with no evident means of escape, it's easy to languish in our dark thoughts. When faith seems lost, our only view of the future is a continuation of the past or present entanglement. Hope is so foundational to the Christian life that without it we are most miserable.[32] For that reason, Satan often works to rob us of our hope. In so doing, he purloins our joy, trust, and peace. For that reason, we must really work on our thinking and develop a solid biblical basis in which we root our hope in Christ rather than circumstance.

The feelings that seem most natural are not always correct. A proper perspective will help us avoid becoming trapped in emotional despair. In John Bunyan's *Pilgrim's Progress*, the Giant of Despair captured Christian and Hopeful. Locked up in the dungeon of Doubting Castle, with no apparent means of escape, the two pilgrims were disheartened. Soon they were in deep despair. Yet, somehow Christian remembered that he had the Key of Promise in his pocket that would unlock the dungeon door.[33] Though it seemed as if there was no hope of freedom, they had the means to liberate themselves the entire time.

There are many ways to keep your emotions in proper perspective. One exercise that will help you transcend your pain is writing in a journal. Record what you feel and think. If you don't like to write, speak into a tape recorder. The advantage of translating your feelings into the written or recorded word is that you can read or play back what you have expressed and learn more each time the exercise is revisited.

You can also talk about your feelings with a close friend. Consider singing praise songs, even if doing so feels contrived. The best way to maintain a proper perspective in your emotional life is to convert painful and unpleasant emotions to more positive and pleasant ones. You do this by changing your thinking.

Change Your Thinking

Although thinking is part of attitude, it deserves special attention. Thinking is the steering wheel of personality. It is like breathing—we do it continuously from birth to death. Each thought creates a feeling that makes the thought seem real. One school of psychology believes that it is not so much what happens *to* us, as what happens *in* us; in other words, what we *think* has happened to us actually governs what *will* happen to us. When life looks a certain way to us, we assume that life really is that way. Cognitive psychology, however, reminds us that events or circumstances are mediated by our thinking.

Two general types of thinking characterize people who are suffering. Some think that compared to others, their suffering is not so bad. While you can typically find someone worse off, minimizing your pain may prevent you from dealing with it. This is fine as long as it's not an attempt to deny the reality of the situation. Whether you are run over by a car or a tractor-trailer, there will be resultant pain and damage.

Others believe that no one could possibly understand how bad their pain is. They see themselves as perpetual victims. Our tendency to evaluate life in absolute extremes can be a great obstacle to dealing with suffering. Instead of viewing life in extremes, we must balance our thinking. We can neither afford to catastrophize our situation, which leads to self-pity, despair, and hopelessness, nor can we ignore it, which prevents us from learning. We must think soberly, looking for God's hand through our pain.

Certainly, it is human and normal to ask "why?" when we experience adversity. But if we keep asking questions when there are no clear answers, we will experience frustration and confusion, possibly even leading to despair. As we saw earlier, no one can know the mind of the Lord.[34] We simply must trust and ask, "For what end and for Whom?" Like Job, we know enough about God to trust Him in those things we do not understand. Such thinking requires a right attitude and a willingness to challenge our thinking. Whenever we notice wrong beliefs coming into play, we can learn to challenge them and begin to replace them with more accurate understandings—ones that may not be as comforting but will certainly prepare us for greater growth.

Examine Your Expectations

As I (John) was writing this section, I suffered from a bad cold with flulike symptoms. My doctor told me that I had a virus and though I could take medicine for the symptoms, there was no remedy for the virus itself. After spending a week on the couch, I called the doctor again to review my symptoms. I guess I wanted him to reconsider his diagnosis and give me something to make me better. Once again the doctor kindly reminded me that I had a virus and would need to wait it out. Obviously, this was news I didn't want to hear but needed to accept.

When we are sick, we want a clear diagnosis and an effective treatment regimen to make us feel better. Regrettably, we live in a world full of illnesses with no cures. We do not want problems, and when they come we want them gone. All too often, however, there are no solutions. If we are to overcome misery, we must adjust our expectations of what this world can and will offer. The world is broken and fallen; it offers no guarantees on most things. We will experience pain and suffering, even when we expect ease and comfort. Clearly, while we cannot control our circumstances, we can control our expectations, beliefs, and attitudes.

In writing to the church at Thessalonica, Paul encouraged his readers not to be unsettled by their trials because they were destined for them.[35] In other words, they were to expect trials, hardships, and adversity. We will not be so easily shaken during bad times when we expect and accept them and take the necessary and appropriate actions. Researchers from the University of Chicago and Southern

Illinois University studied victims of tornado damage across the country.[36] They studied a phenomenon related to what psychologists call "locus of control." People with an internal locus of control believe that they are in control of their own fate, whereas externalizers believe outside sources control the outcome.[37] The study found that people who lived in the South suffered a higher frequency of tornado-related deaths than Midwesterners and had developed a fatalistic attitude toward disaster: "If it hits, it hits; there's nothing I can do to stop it." In contrast, whenever severe warning was predicted, Midwesterners listened to weather reports, secured loose equipment, and went to a safe place to wait out tornado warnings.

The writer of Proverbs said, "Trust in the LORD with all your heart, and lean not on your own understanding; in all your ways acknowledge Him, and He shall direct your paths."[38] Examining our responses to suffering will help us determine if we are leaning on the Lord or on our own understanding. If we are leaning entirely on the Lord, we will not panic and demand answers of God. This response does not mean we exercise blind faith. Rather, it implies that we willingly rest in God's reliable character. In short, leaning on God means we will not be insisting that He owes us an explanation.

God's timetable is so different from ours. During a difficult time in my (John's) life, a friend wrote the following verse on a note of encouragement: "But when the fullness of the time had come, God sent forth His Son, born of a woman, born under the law."[39] I looked at that note in amazement. *What does that have to do with anything?* I wondered. Later, I came to realize the depth of truth in those words. After settling in Egypt, the people of Israel had waited four hundred years for God to speak, but God was in no hurry. You would think that by this point in Jewish history, the Israelites would have become accustomed to God's timetable. In fact, they were in bondage approximately 430 years before God sent Moses to deliver them (and He had to develop Moses for forty years before he was ready to tackle that job!). My friend used Galatians 4:4 simply to remind me that God has a timetable to accomplish things in my life. My job was to be patient and wait for God to act. Interestingly, one of my favorite Bible verses in college was

Philippians 1:6: "Being confident of this very thing, that He who has begun a good work in you will complete it until the day of Jesus Christ." God will not fail us, though it might seem that way.

Assess your expectations and make sure that they are realistic and biblical. Expect God to deliver on His promises in His time, no more and no less.

Have a Proper Perspective on Your Life

There are two requirements for having and maintaining a proper life perspective. First, we must stay focused on today and live in the present moment. Second, we must keep our minds on eternity. While these statements may sound like a contradiction, they are actually two sides of the same coin.

Focus on today

When I (John) was suddenly hit with that kidney stone I mentioned in chapter 2, the only thing I could think about was getting rid of the pain as soon as possible. I wanted it to go away; I wanted instant relief. I prayed for the Rapture, death, or instant healing. I would have done anything to ease the constant intensity of that pain. While in the emergency room, I thought that I would never see the doctor and get the necessary painkiller. It took everything I could muster to focus on the immediate moment.

So it is with other kinds of suffering. Our driving goal is to get things back to normal. But the truth is that things will never be back to normal. With each passing day, good or bad, life is forever changed. Broken bones mend and infections dissipate, but soul scars may never completely heal.

As days of suffering turn to months and months become years, our resolve to stand strong weakens. When the future seems bleak, we begin to lose hope and wonder if we will even be able to make it through the day. God, however, remains our timeless refuge. When we are wondering whether the pain will ever cease, the eternal God is already in the future seeing the outcome.

I (John) have a friend who loves to climb mountains. He has told me there is nothing like working his way up a mountain to experience both the feeling of accomplishment and the view from its summit. While the top of the mountain is the goal, my friend appreciates all the vistas along the way. He can look up, keeping his goal firmly in view, and look down to recognize his progress. Such a balanced view allows him to rest, look around, and admire the view from wherever he is at that moment. Unlike climbing a physical mountain, the climb we make in this life never ends at the pinnacle; we simply continue to climb upward every day. Along the way, however, we can all learn to appreciate the journey.

Therefore, we need to avoid becoming consumed with time. A wonderful phrase often found in the Bible is, "And it came to pass . . ." Truly, everything will eventually come to pass, maybe not in this life but certainly in heaven. Our best option is to focus only on today, and if necessary, only on the moment. With God's help, we can handle today, so we shouldn't worry about tomorrow. As we trust God for the grace and strength to make it through this day or moment, we'll be able to deal with whatever suffering comes our way. The apostle Paul had this truth in mind when he said that we should not lose heart because our inner man is being renewed day after day.[40]

Focus on eternity

Heaven has relevance for our lives today, and it has special significance in addressing our hardships. Paul was obviously well versed in suffering. He wrote:

> Therefore we do not lose heart. Even though our outward man is perishing, yet the inward man is being renewed day by day. For our light affliction, which is but for a moment, is working for us a far more exceeding and eternal weight of glory, while we do not look at the things which are seen, but at the things which are not seen. For the things which are seen are temporary, but the things which are not seen are eternal.   2 CORINTHIANS 4:16-19

We won't give up our self-focused demand for ease, predictability, and fairness until we have an equally compelling yearning.

For the Christian, that yearning is to know God and to look toward the hope of heaven.

Heaven is not just something to look forward to, but something that can be experienced today. We are told to live life in light of eternity and set our minds on the things that are above. This hope was the mark of the Old Testament heroes of faith. Though heaven had not been realized, they had a definite view toward their future lives. In fact, we are told that they longed for the better country that God had prepared for them.[41] As we saw in chapter 14, we are only in the waiting line of heaven. We are not to see ourselves as earthly dwellers but as pilgrims. And as the psalmist penned, "So teach us to number our days, that we may gain a heart of wisdom."[42]

God has placed eternity in our hearts, and this focus gives us hope and peace. One of Satan's best weapons against the Christian is to rob us of our eternal purpose. But by maintaining an eternal vision, we can keep Satan from using a calamity to engulf us in a sense of hopelessness. Just as a Thanksgiving feast makes us salivate, so God's extravagant table should be something we eagerly anticipate. I (Gary) call this having a "Christmas morning" view of eternity: we do not know all that God has planned for us, but we do know it will be fantastic.

Eternity gives us more than just the hope that we will one day no longer suffer. It also gives us something that we can be assured of, something to embrace in our trials today. As we focus on the heavenly city, we gain a sense of renewal and refreshment in our spirits—in spite of our outer hurts, aches, and problems. What hope! What comfort! The best is yet to come!

Prevent Undue Stress

During times of suffering, people are often tempted to make major life decisions or take on additional responsibilities. But times of adversity are, more than ever, occasions when we need to limit our activities. These are times when it is best to be still and know that He is God.[43]

Given our emotional state during times of suffering, we are not in the best position to make rational decisions. Unless your situation demands certain immediate changes or it's clear God is attempting to use your adversity to get you to make major life changes, it's usually best to wait until you have been through the suffering to make any significant decisions.

When your life has been turned upside down, you need to take whatever energy is left and channel it in constructive ways. In the movie *Apollo 13*, the astronauts are in danger of lacking sufficient power to return to earth. In order to conserve as much amperage as possible, the engineers tell the astronauts to shut down their power until they can devise a plan. To help them find a solution, the engineers contact one of the astronauts who had been prohibited from the flight due to illness. Together they fervently work in a simulator to determine a procedure that would allow the astronauts to power up all the necessary reentry equipment with the limited amperage.

In times of crisis, we also are in danger of lacking enough energy to survive. Like the men in *Apollo 13*, we need to conserve sufficient energy to accomplish the things that must be accomplished. All day, every day, we make choices. Ultimately, we choose to do the things we value, but all too often, our values go awry, and therefore our choices do not serve our best interests. It is hard to prioritize, but now more than ever, we must channel our energies where they will serve us best. Taking care of what God has given us is good stewardship, so it is important to attend to our own needs—physical, emotional, mental, social, and spiritual—during times of difficulty. Often people feel overwhelmed when going through a crisis, and in order to survive the ordeal, they have to step away from dealing with daily life for a time. One woman I (John) counseled felt so overwhelmed at everything she had to do that I encouraged her to list things she did *not* need to do. I told her every time she looked at the list, she could say, "Hey, there is something I don't need to do!" This comical, but realistic, perspective helped my client feel more in charge of her life.

Attending to yourself physically includes good nutrition, exercise, and hygiene. You may not have an appetite or you may crave unhealthy food. It is necessary, however, to give your body proper fuel. You probably won't feel like getting off the sofa and taking a brisk walk, but do it anyway. Research has clearly shown that exercise will affect your brain chemistry in a way that will help you recover faster.[44]

As we've already seen, growing spiritually means spending time with God in order to know Him in a deeper way. And growing socially involves avoiding isolation. Get with God's people, open up, and be honest.

CHAPTER TWENTY-TWO

Redeem Your Suffering

There is a saying commonly heard at Alcoholics Anonymous: "You have to give it away to get it."[1] This motto applies to most problems of life. By helping others we are constantly reminded who we are, where we came from, and what we could become again.

Spiritual growth has limited impact unless we take what we've received from God and use it to help others. Think of how many people have been encouraged by the life of Job. Had you told Job during the days of his ordeal that countless people throughout history would receive comfort and hope from his trials, it probably would have offered him little relief. After the ordeal, however, Job probably found great comfort in the thought that, through his pain, he could help others.

Redeem Your Pain

A major help in recovering from suffering is to be able to redeem the experience. We can redeem suffering by growing through it and giving it meaning in our lives. Many Vietnam veterans redeemed their war experiences by adopting Vietnamese children, providing assistance to fellow veterans who were struggling with the emotional aftermath of the war, or lobbying for war-related causes. In Old Testament days, the people of Israel often built stone markers to symbolize the significance of a particular event in their journey.

In chapter 14, we read about Belinda, the young woman who was abused by her youth pastor. Today, Belinda would tell you that reaching out to others in need was a major factor in her recovery.

She was able to redeem her years of sexual abuse and begin to glorify God through ministry. Belinda is living out Paul's challenge to
comfort those with the comfort she has received from God.

Open Yourself to Others

Sometimes when we're suffering, the people around us are not
positive or supportive. Often, we decide it's easier to simply act
cheerful and optimistic than to open up and be real. We fear being
truly known because we fear being criticized or rejected. Putting
on a happy mask protects our raw wounds, the places where we are
most vulnerable to negative responses, the places where we need
encouragement and reassurance the most. We want to be known
and accepted for everything we are experiencing, but we fear the
thought of being rejected. So we build fortresses of protection. But
this dilemma between being real and hidden is in itself traumatic
for someone who is already suffering. We often vacillate between
expressing our true feelings and putting on a mask to hide the pain,
and this ambivalence makes it even more difficult for those who do
care and desire to be supportive. They simply do not know when
or how to approach us.

Ultimately, hidden suffering makes us feel even more isolated
and alone. This is one of Satan's best tools against the wounded
believer. And as we've already seen, isolation actually intensifies suffering because there is no outlet for the pain. In studies of various
crises, social support has consistently been associated with better
adjustment.[2] It was not necessary that the helpers had been through
similar experiences, as long as they demonstrated empathetic concern and support for the sufferer. This is offering a "ministry of
presence" to those who are hurting, in order to bear the burden
that they cannot bear alone.

Reach out to Help Others

As Belinda learned, ministering to others is a key to recovery. The
point of reaching out is not to avoid your own pain, but to take the
inner turmoil you have experienced and connect it with someone
else's struggle.

Psychologists have found that getting clients to see themselves as helpers and givers, rather than takers and receivers, produces healing. As we've seen, Viktor Frankl, Betsie ten Boom, and Corrie ten Boom found great strength in comforting other prisoners, even when they were subjected to similar maltreatment.

The word *compassion* comes from the Latin *com*, meaning "together," and *pati*, meaning "to suffer." Compassion is defined as "sorrow for the sufferings or trouble of another, accompanied by the urge to help." However much we may have suffered, we can find meaning in it by transforming pain into compassion. There is great satisfaction and benefit in bringing order into lives beset by pain and turmoil. Helping hurting people see how God's grace is sufficient speaks to your own unresolved questions and issues.

God has commanded us to provide care for struggling souls. "Brethren, if a man is overtaken in any trespass, you who are spiritual restore such a one in a spirit of gentleness, considering yourself lest you also be tempted. Bear one another's burdens, and so fulfill the law of Christ. . . . For each one shall bear his own load."[3] "To restore" is to "mend, to furnish completely" or to "set a bone."[4] Since it is used here in the present tense, the healing and mending of others who are hurting is to be an ongoing process. But in order to help, we need to know what we are to mend. At first glance, this passage seems to present a conflict by urging us to bear other people's burdens while telling each of us to take care of our own. But in encouraging us to take care of our own burden, the Greek term *phortion* actually means knapsack and refers to the daily load that someone carries. The burden that we are to bear for others refers to boulders (*baros*), or problems that seem crushing and heavy. These words are also used to speak of the future state of Christians as an "eternal weight of glory."[5] We are not to take on the responsibilities of others, but we are to help those who are stricken with a grievous, weighty load.

In the last chapter we talked about the danger of overtaxing ourselves. Sometimes helping other people can cause us to take on too much responsibility, believing we are responsible to fix their problems. But we are not the Redeemer or Savior; that job is filled.

If one or more people are becoming overly dependent upon you, refer them to a pastor or professional Christian counselor. It is okay to let them know that you are still vulnerable yourself and simply not able to provide all the adequate support necessary to carry them through their own ordeal.

How could I possibly help?

People who have pain of their own often find it difficult to reach out to others. They simply lack the initiative, energy, or knowledge of how to meaningfully touch someone else's pain. But even if you are hurting yourself, sharing God's comfort with someone else will not only help that person, it will help you as well.

You might be someone who has never gone through a significant time of suffering. You might be reading this book to learn what you can do to help a close friend or family member. This section will help you in knowing what to say and do to provide beneficial help.

1. *Give the wounded individual the ministry of your presence.* Simply taking the time to be with someone who is hurting does wonders. Job's friends spent seven days sitting with him on an ash heap in silence. In fact, their helpfulness ceased when they opened their mouths. We could learn much from this. We do not have to know exactly what to say. Just being there can provide a tremendous lift. In being with someone who is suffering, it is helpful to also use appropriate touch. When people are hurting, they are vulnerable, and an appropriate touch can convey a physical presence. When I (John) visited with my friend Dave Sours in the hospital following the death of his son, Nathan, there were no words that could have had any meaningful impact at that time. When I saw Dave, we hugged long and hard. Throughout our encounters, I often just put my arm around Dave's shoulder, and I could tell my compassionate touch was important to him.

2. *The best help that anyone can render in a time of crisis is an empathetic listening ear.* In the course of several years, the

Joe Bayly family lost three of their children. In his book
The View from a Hearse, Bayly shared his experience of
being helped by two different individuals. "I was sitting
there torn by grief. Someone came and talked of God's
dealings, of why it happened, of hope beyond the grave.
He talked constantly. He said things I knew were true. I
was unmoved, except to wish he'd go away. He finally did.
Another came and sat beside me. He didn't talk. He didn't
ask me leading questions. He just sat beside me for an hour
and more, listened when I said something, answered briefly,
prayed simply, and left. I was moved. I was comforted.
I hated to see him go."[6] By listening, we enter into the
suffering of our loved ones. Research shows that sufferers
rank listening as the gift that is most meaningful during
times of difficulty.[7] Do not worry if you don't know what
to say. There is no need to give advice, offer trite Christian
slogans, or quote Scripture. Simply listen. Sometimes
sufferers do not want you to talk at all. True and attentive
listening is hard work. It means allowing the hurting person
to express himself or herself in whatever way needed. People
who are hurting often have a need to tell others what it
is like and what has happened to them. Your listening
ear helps your loved ones to sort through and face their
feelings.

3. *Accept what has happened to the individual and the way that
   person is responding to the trial.* Even if you experienced
   a similar problem, your experience is different. Perhaps
   you were quicker to acknowledge the goodness of God.
   Perhaps this person is feeling things and doing things that
   you would never have imagined. Remember, it takes time
   to heal. When someone is hurting, it is not the time to
   be judgmental. You are not the authority on that person's
   responses. God accepts and hears the cries of our hearts.
   Bite your tongue and acknowledge the living hell that
   the person may be experiencing. In one study of cancer

patients, 87 percent reported that they tried to cope by
keeping their thoughts and feelings to themselves to avoid
bothering or upsetting loved ones.[8] But people need to
be able to share their thoughts and feelings without being
criticized or minimized and without worrying how the
other person will handle what they have to say.

4. *Whenever it is expected or appreciated, you can still seek to
   instill hope.* The hope might come from how you made it
   through your own experience. It might come from your
   attitude toward your situation, or it might arise from the
   bond that occurs between you and the sufferer. Ultimately,
   hope comes from the Lord, and you can help direct that
   person toward Him. No matter how it is communicated
   or felt, this hope is critical to recovery.

5. *Pray.* Do not simply say, "I will pray for you." Rather, ask
   specifically *how* you can pray. Take time to pray with the
   hurting person right then if possible. When I (John) was
   going through a difficult time, a friend asked me how he
   could best pray. After my vague response, he simply put his
   arm around me and prayed for me at that moment. I felt so
   touched by the sincerity and genuineness of my friend.

6. *Be practical in your help.* Typically, well-meaning individuals
   tell those who are hurting to call if they need anything. But
   we all know that call is rarely made. It's better to anticipate
   what the person might need, and if you are not able to take
   care of the need, arrange for someone else to do it. When
   my (John's) father died, I returned home from the funeral
   to find my grass cut, weeds pulled, and hedges clipped. I
   cried when I learned that a neighbor whom I didn't even
   know had done such a wonderful thing for me.

7. *Be aware of your attitude as you attempt to help another
   person.* Often when people have gone through a great
   deal of suffering, they will either approach others with a
   sense of superiority ("Look what I have been through!"

or "That's nothing compared with what happened to me!") or inferiority ("Given what I feel, I can offer you very little"). Whether you are currently in the midst of a trial or down the road of recovery, it is fine to share your experience whenever it is appropriate, but remember that your objective is not to elicit sympathy for yourself. Now is the time for you to give, not receive. This principle is beautifully illustrated in the hours preceding Christ's death. As the guests were arriving at the Last Supper, Jesus was preparing a basin of water to wash His disciples' feet. As Jesus moved around the room humbly washing the dust from their feet, He said, "If you know these things, blessed are you if you do them."[9] In reaching out to sufferers, you need to maintain your focus on them and their problems. Therefore, be brief in what you share. Do not minimize what the other person may be feeling by swapping war stories. Be compassionate and attempt to understand.

8. *Adopt an attitude of love and acceptance toward the hurting.* Because we have a need to explain the whys of life, we sometimes speculate as to whether a person brought a problem on himself or herself. If we decide the person is responsible for his or her own pain, we think, feel, and act differently toward that person than if we view him or her as an innocent victim. Research shows that innocent victims are often wrongly blamed for playing a contributing role in their own victimization. Put simply, if something bad happens to someone, we wonder what the person might have done wrong. Like Job's friends, we jump to conclusions without having all the facts. But just as Jesus accepted the woman at the well, the woman caught in adultery, and everyone else He encountered, we must display grace and acceptance. By demonstrating unfailing love to those who are hurting, we earn the right to eventually advise and challenge them.

9. *Stay in contact with the individual by making phone calls and sending e-mail messages or cards throughout the ordeal, as well*

as over the next year or so. One family who experienced the
death of their son said that after the funeral no one from
the church, including the minister, ever spoke to them
again about their loss. The hurt was still evident on their
faces five years later. If the person is having a difficult time
coping, you might recommend that the person talk with a
minister or competent Christian counselor. If you received
help from that person, share your experience. While some
people are reluctant to see professional counselors, even
Christian counselors, they *will* talk to a minister. It the
person doesn't have a minister, refer him or her to yours.
You might even go with the person if he or she is afraid
of talking to a stranger.

As you move through your own recovery, helping others will
become a more natural part of your life. The trauma to your soul
will be redeemed from the hands of the evil one and be used to
further the Kingdom of God.

Our motivation in life should not be to pursue our own comfort and happiness, but to love and serve both God and man. Yes,
sometimes in the heat of the fiery furnace we need someone with
cold water and a fire extinguisher to assist us. But when the flames
have died down, we need to reach out to others who are in need
of help.

CONCLUSION OF SECTION THREE

In your adversity, you may feel as if you have melted. Perhaps you have been unable to find your way through the maze of pain. In spite of your best efforts to recover, you are unable to find God in your affliction. Do not lose heart—we serve a God who is victorious over life and death. Get help from someone who will walk with you down the road of recovery. Remember that nothing is impossible with God. Your powerlessness is the place where God wants you because it is there that you most recognize your lack of control. And when you realize you are not in control, God is finally able to have control of your life. Take your "why me?" mentality, turn it over to Him, and find the "what for?" of your pain.

The bottom line of this entire book is that our responses to suffering matter. Job could never have grasped the historical significance of his response to the incredible adversity that came upon him. But Job 42 shows that he realized there was something bigger and greater than his comfortable, predictable, and orderly life. Expanding his vision of God and coming to know Him in a new and fresh way was sufficient to satisfy all of Job's questions, to clarify his confusion, and to provide hope instead of despair. His story has provided inspiration and comfort to millions. While our stories are not yet complete, we must realize that there is a great deal at stake in our own responses to suffering. Like Job, our questions may never be answered, but the fact that God can use our suffering and that we can come to know Him in ways beyond our imagination is reason enough to respond in worship.

God is more committed to changing us than He is to making us comfortable. Therefore, we should not expect God to make us comfortable, but to make us *holy*. God's purposes and lessons are profoundly more important than getting our own way. He is not obligated to explain Himself; His reasons for allowing us to experience hardship may be something known only to Him.

The development of our souls depends upon our understanding of what the soul is and what it can become. No soul is ever complete. No work of the soul ever finished. Our prayer is that God will use your pain to remake your soul into His image.

Acknowledgments

This work is a testament to the wondrous work of God in the hearts and lives of people. The faces of friends and clients have been before us as we have penned this book. The stories of their struggles with suffering have enriched our lives both professionally and personally. These individuals have left indelible footprints in our lives, honoring us with the joy of walking their healing journeys with them.

A work of this magnitude is never accomplished single-handedly. It would be extremely ungracious to go to print without publicly and humbly noting our gratitude to all those who have offered invaluable contributions to this book.

Our first debt is to Tyndale and their incredible staff, who helped bring this project to published completion. Thank you, Sharon Leavitt, Sarah Atkinson, and Lisa Jackson. You have been a joy to partner with.

I (John) am indebted to Billy Coffey and Donna Honeycutt for their valuable role in shaping and painstakingly scrutinizing the manuscript. You both were a real blessing. Pastor and counselor Walt "Nifty" Wilson's friendship was priceless; he blessed me with comfort during painful times and offered a taste of God's grace, tenderly calling me to honor Christ. My dear brother in Christ, Larry French, challenged me to consider the implications of my words. His relentless pursuit of sound biblical reasoning stretched my intellectual and spiritual resources. I also appreciate the insights of Teresa Sours and Dr. Dan Gregg; they both contributed to the manuscript and to my spiritual journey. Without the vantage points of all these people, the endeavor of this book would have been unthinkable.

Most specially, I would like to express deep appreciation to my best friend and companion, Denise. Her ever-present support and exceptional patience have richly blessed me. Additionally, I am indebted to her careful editing and wise comments, which I have had good cause to respect over many years.

Like John, I (Gary) chiefly acknowledge all those who have helped shape my view of a biblical notion of suffering. Besides

Scripture itself, nothing is more valuable then hearing the experiences of those who hurt. After all, even much of the biblical content itself is concerned with the similar experiences of God's people. Making sense of this suffering is a difficult but necessary task, even in my own family. Watching my wife succumb to cancer at a very young age had a profound affect on my family and me. I continue to deal with these issues, as my young nephew was recently diagnosed with cancer. I have come to see that not only does God not promise us a "bed of roses," but God's Word repeatedly explains that suffering is more often than not the experience of God's own people, in both the Old and New Testaments. To miss this is to overlook a large percentage of the picture. As members of the body of Christ, we suffer together (1 Corinthians 12:26). As we approach the solution, it must be consistent with the clear and well-evidenced truths of Scripture.

Endnotes

INTRODUCTION: MELT IN THE MOUTH
1. Exodus 17:7
2. Psalm 100:5; 103:8; 1 John 4:16
3. Isaiah 55:8-9
4. Hebrews 12:11

SECTION 1: THE PAIN OF SUFFERING
1. Matthew 5:45
2. John 16:33

CHAPTER 1: THE PERILS OF PAIN
1. This story is used with the permission of Dave and Teresa Sours.
2. Hosea 7:14
3. Virginia Woolf, *The Waves* (New York: Harcourt Brace Jovanovich, 1931), 263.
4. I first heard this analogy from my friend and colleague Larry French, and I've found it very helpful in understanding the unnerving effects of suffering.
5. 2 Corinthians 7:10; Isaiah 1:18; 1 John 1:9; James 5:16
6. 1 Corinthians 12:23-28
7. Hebrews 11
8. Romans 8:36, NASB
9. John 11:25-26; 16:33
10. Romans 6:9-10
11. Isaiah 53:4; Hebrews 2:14-15

CHAPTER 2: THE BEDROCK OF SUFFERING
1. Philip Yancey, *Where Is God When It Hurts?* (Grand Rapids: Zondervan, 2002), 5.
2. You may find similar ideas from the following sources: Ronnie Janoff-Bulman, *Shattered Assumptions: Towards a New Psychology of Trauma* (New York: Free Press, 1992); Melvin Lerner, "The Desire for Justice and Reactions to Victims: Social Psychological Studies of Some Antecedents and Consequences," in *Altruism and Helping Behavior*, eds. J. Maculay and L. Berkowitz (New York: Academic Press, 1970); C. Parks, "What Becomes of Redundant World Models? A Contribution to the Study of Adaptation to Change," *British Journal of Medical Psychology* 48 (1975): 131–37.
3. Psalm 14:3; 51:5; 58:3; Romans 3:23-24; 7:20-21
4. C. S. Lewis, *The Problem of Pain* (New York: Macmillan, 1967), 26.
5. Romans 8:21
6. Job 16:12-14
7. 1 Samuel 1:4-28
8. Corrie ten Boom, *Clippings from My Notebook* (Minneapolis: World Wide Publications, 1982), 56.
9. M. Scott Peck, *The Road Less Traveled* (New York: Phoenix Press, 1985), 15. Throughout this manuscript we are not attempting to critique Scott Peck's controversial work and theories but to pull from his work concepts that are relevant to our points.
10. 1 Peter 4:12-13
11. Melvin Lerner, "The Desire for Justice and Reactions to Victims"; M. J. Lerner and G. Matthews, "Reactions to the Suffering of Others under Conditions of Indirect Responsibility," *Journal of Personality and Social Psychology* 5 (1967): 319–25; M. J. Lerner and C. Simmons, "Observers' Reaction to the 'Innocent Victims': Compassion or Rejection?" *Journal of Personality and Social Psychology* 4 (1966): 4, 203–10.
12. Ecclesiastes 8:14, NLT
13. Unless otherwise specified, all characters in the stories used in this book are composites of individuals.

CHAPTER 3: SUFFERING AND THE HAND OF GOD

1. Job 1:1
2. Job 1:1-12
3. Job 2:1-7
4. C. S. Lewis, "Peace Proposals for Brother Every and Mr. Bethell," in *Christian Reflections*, ed. Walter Hopper (Grand Rapids, MI: William B. Eerdman Publishing, 1967), 33.
5. Viktor E. Frankl, *Man's Search for Meaning: An Introduction to Logotherapy* (Boston: Beacon, 1967), 67.
6. Ten Boom, *Clippings from My Notebook*, 18.
7. Ecclesiastes 2:1-11
8. Lewis, *The Problem of Pain*, 93.
9. Genesis 3:17-18
10. Ecclesiastes 1:15
11. Romans 8:22
12. Matthew 9:33; 12:22; 17:15-18; Mark 5:15; 9:25
13. Luke 13:11-16
14. John 17:15-17
15. Job 1:12
16. Job 1:10-12
17. Genesis 4:7-8; 37:12-36; 2 Timothy 4:14-16
18. 2 Timothy 3:12; 2 Corinthians 1:7
19. John 13:34-35
20. Galatians 6:7-9
21. Romans 6
22. Acts 9:1-6, 22, 26
23. Acts 5:27-42
24. Oswald Chambers, *My Utmost for His Highest* (New York: Dodd, Mead & Company, 1935), 310.
25. Ecclesiastes 11:5
26. Isaiah 55:8-9; 1 Corinthians 2:10-11
27. H. G. Wells, *Mr. Britling Sees It Through* (New York: Macmillian, 1916), 406.
28. John 11:35
29. Galatians 4:4
30. Exodus 3:7
31. Psalm 56:8
32. Hebrews 4:15
33. Isaiah 53:3
34. Hebrews 2:17-18; 4:15; Isaiah 53:2-5
35. Job 38:4-41
36. Taken from a sermon, October 25, 1998, at Wayne Hills Baptist Church in Waynesboro, Virginia. Used with permission.
37. Job 19:25-27
38. Romans 8:6-8; 1 Peter 1:3-9; Revelation 20:12-15; 21:4
39. Matthew 5:11-12; 2 Corinthians 5:1-2, 8; Revelation 7:16-17; 14:12-13; 21:3-4
40. Romans 10:9
41. Jim Hill, "What a Day That Will Be," in *Hymns for the Family of God* (Nashville: Paragon, 1958), 314.

CONCLUSION OF SECTION 1

1. Most notable among these studies are: Martin Seligman, *Helplessness: On Depression, Development, and Death* (San Francisco: Freeman, 1975); E. J. Langer, "The Illusion of Control," *Journal of Personality and Social Psychology* 32 (1975): 311–28; P. K. Presson and V. A. Benassi, "Illusion of Control: A Meta-Analytic Review," *Journal of Social Behavior and Personality* 11 (1996): 493–510. These ideas were culled out of the work of the following: Melvin J. Lerner, *The Belief in a Just World: A Fundamental*

Delusion (New York: Plenum Press, 1980); Melvin J. Lerner and Sally C. Lerner, eds., *The Justice Motive in Social Behavior: Adapting to Times of Scarcity and Change* (New York: Plenum Press, 1981).

SECTION 2: THE PURPOSES OF SUFFERING
1. Stephen J. Freeman and Sharon Ward, "Death and Bereavement: What Counselors Should Know," *Journal of Mental Health Counseling* 20, no. 3 (1998): 221.
2. Deuteronomy 29:29
3. Lewis, *The Problem of Pain*, chapter 6, and Alvin Plantinga, *God, Freedom, and Evil* (William B. Eerdmans, 1977), 57–9.
4. Matthew 5:45
5. One of the classical works on this subject is John Hick, *Evil and the God of Love* (New York: Harper & Row, 1996).
6. 2 Corinthians 1:3-6
7. Hebrews 4:15
8. Hebrews 5:8
9. James 1:2-4
10. Ecclesiastes 7:2-3
11. From chapter 16, "How Repentance Is Given," of Charles Haddon Spurgeon's book *All of Grace*; see http://www.spurgeon.org/all_of_g.htm.

CHAPTER 4: GOD DESIRES A PURIFIED FAITH
1. Michael P. Green, ed., *Illustrations for Biblical Preaching* (Grand Rapids, MI: Baker Book House, 1989), no. 1410.
2. 1 Peter 1:6-9; see also Isaiah 48:10
3. Romans 5:3
4. Ten Boom, *Clippings from My Notebook*, 124.
5. Joni Eareckson Tada is a powerful example of how suffering can better us. You can read her story in her autobiography: *Joni: An Unforgettable Story* (Grand Rapids, MI: Zondervan, 1996).
6. This is a true story and is used with permission. Some details have been changed, however, in order to provide anonymity.
7. Romans 10:17
8. Hebrews 11:35-38
9. 1 Kings 17:1-24
10. 1 Kings 18:20-40; 19:1-8
11. 2 Corinthians 1:9
12. Hebrews 13:8

CHAPTER 5: GOD DESIRES A HUMBLE HEART
1. 2 Corinthians 12:1-10
2. Revelation 2:1-7
3. 2 Corinthians 12:9

CHAPTER 6: GOD DESIRES TO TEST OUR FAITHFULNESS
1. Deuteronomy 8:2-3
2. Psalm 119:71, 78; Matthew 25:14-30
3. 2 Corinthians 12:9
4. C. S. Lewis, *Mere Christianity* (New York: MacMillan, 1952).
5. Genesis 22
6. Hebrews 11:8-9
7. Genesis 12:1-20
8. Genesis 16
9. Genesis 22:12
10. A. W. Tozer, *Man—The Dwelling Place of God* (Camp Hill, PA: WingSpread Publishers, 1996), chapter 25.

CHAPTER 7: GOD DESIRES WELL-BEHAVED CHILDREN

1. Hebrews 12:5-6; 1 Corinthians 11:28-34
2. Galatians 6:7-8
3. Numbers 12
4. 2 Samuel 12:15-23
5. Acts 5:1-11
6. Hebrews 12:5-6
7. Walter Bauer, *A Greek-English Lexicon of the New Testament and Other Early Christian Literature*, 2nd ed., rev. by F. W. Gingrich and F. Danker (Chicago: University of Chicago Press, 1979).
8. Acts 22:24
9. Psalm 103:8-10
10. Leviticus 26:14-21
11. Judges 2:7-16
12. Jonah 4:2
13. 1 Samuel 15:22
14. Psalm 119:71
15. Luke 15:18-21
16. Proverbs 20:30
17. Habakkuk 1:5-11
18. Habakkuk 2:20
19. Hebrews 12:6
20. Hebrews 12:10-11
21. 1 Peter 1:16
22. Paul Lee Tan, *Encyclopedia of 7700 Illustrations*, 3rd ed. (Rockville, MD: Assurance Publishers, 1980), no. 6884.

CHAPTER 8: GOD DESIRES TO MATURE US

1. Hebrews 2:17-18; 5:8-9
2. See http://www.brainyquote.com/quotes/quotes/v/victorhugo152539.html.
3. Romans 5:3-5; 1 Peter 5:10
4. Tan, *Encyclopedia of 7700 Illustrations*, no. 6900.

CHAPTER 9: GOD DESIRES FOR US TO BE CHRISTLIKE

1. Helen Keller, *The Story of My Life* (New York: Bantam Classics, 1990).
2. See http://www.bestinspiration.com/quotes-1/of/Helen_Keller.htm.
3. 2 Timothy 3:17; Hebrews 2:10; 13:21
4. Howard A. Rusk, *A World to Care For* (New York: Random House, 1972), 281.
5. Acts 4:13
6. Tan, *Encyclopedia of 7700 Illustrations*, no. 6893.
7. From a presentation by Diane Langberg at the American Association of Christian Counselors (AACC) Conference in 1996
8. Hebrews 12:11
9. Galatians 4:19, NIV

CHAPTER 10: GOD DESIRES FOR US TO HAVE A PERSONALIZED FAITH

1. Chambers, *My Utmost for His Highest*, 306.
2. Psalm 6:9; 42:1-2
3. Job 42:5
4. Job 42:1-6
5. Charles H. Spurgeon, *Spurgeon at His Best*, compiled by Tom Carter (Grand Rapids, MI: Baker Books, 1988), 218.
6. Psalm 34:17
7. Exodus 32:11-14
8. Jeremiah 29:11-13
9. Romans 8:26-27

10. 2 Corinthians 12:9
11. Joseph Scriven and Charles Converse, "What a Friend We Have in Jesus," in *Hymns for the Family of God*, ed. Fred Bock (Nashville: Paragon Associates, 1976), 466.
12. Ten Boom, *Clippings from My Notebook*, 25–6.

CHAPTER 11: GOD DESIRES TO BUILD HIS KINGDOM

1. Acts 16:25-34
2. Philippians 1:13
3. Courtney Anderson, *To the Golden Shore: The Life of Adoniram Judson* (Valley Forge, PA: Judson Press, 1987).
4. We read their story in Daniel 3.
5. Luke 22:42
6. 2 Timothy 2:8-10
7. For the second-century account of his death, see "The Martyrdom of S. Polycarp," in *The Apostolic Fathers*, ed. and trans. J. B. Lightfoot and J. R. Harmer (Grand Rapids, MI: Baker Book House, 1992), 101–17.

CHAPTER 12: GOD DESIRES A STRONG AND CARING CHURCH

1. Green, *Illustrations for Biblical Preaching*, 150.
2. 1 Corinthians 12:7-31
3. Romans 12:15; Galatians 6:1-2
4. Acts 2:44
5. Acts 12:5-16
6. Galatians 6:2
7. Proverbs 17:17
8. John 13:35

CHAPTER 13: GOD DESIRES TO MINISTER THROUGH US

1. The story of Tom and Maria is based on an interview with Tom Whiteman. Used with permission.
2. 2 Corinthians 1:4
3. 2 Corinthians 1:5
4. 2 Corinthians 1:4
5. Letter to Sheldon Vanauken, April 22, 1953; quoted in Sheldon Vanauken, *A Severe Mercy* (New York: HarperCollins, 1977), 134.
6. From a sermon, October 27, 1998, at Wayne Hills Baptist Church, Waynesboro, Virginia. Used with permission.
7. 2 Corinthians 1:6

CHAPTER 14: GOD DESIRES THAT WE SEE HIS TRUE CHARACTER

1. Job 38–39; 40:4-5
2. Job 42:1-3
3. Job 16:6-22
4. Jeremiah 32:17
5. Jeremiah 32:27
6. Corrie ten Boom, *The Hiding Place* (Grand Rapids, MI: Chosen Books, 1971), 63.
7. Ibid., 217.
8. Mark 4:35-41
9. Job 2:10

CHAPTER 15: GOD DESIRES TO PREPARE US FOR A BLESSING

1. Job 1:21
2. Job 42:10
3. Genesis 50:19-20

4. From the movie *Star Trek: The Wrath of Khan*. See http://www.imdb.com/title/
   tt0084726/quotes.
5. Ecclesiastes 7:8

CHAPTER 16: GOD DESIRES TO GIVE BELIEVERS DYING GRACE
1. Steve Goodier, "Good Friends Are Good Medicine," see http://www.allthingsfrugal
   .com/g.friends.htm.
2. Philippians 1:20-23
3. Romans 12:1
4. Luke 9:23
5. Philippians 1:20
6. Debbie's story is told in Gary R. Habermas, *Forever Loved: A Personal Account of Grief
   and Resurrection* (Joplin, Mo: College Press, 1997).
7. Philippians 1:21
8. Philippians 1:23
9. Romans 8:30; 2 Corinthians 5:2, 4
10. Isaiah 55:8-9

CHAPTER 17: GOD DESIRES TO REWARD THOSE WHO ENDURE
1. Lewis, *The Problem of Pain*, 144.
2. James 1:12
3. Bauer, *A Greek-English Lexicon of the New Testament and Other Early Christian
   Literature*.
4. 2 Corinthians 4:17-18
5. Frankl, *Man's Search for Meaning*, 74.
6. Gary Habermas and J. P. Moreland, *Beyond Death: Exploring the Evidence for
   Immortality* (Eugene, OR: Wipf and Stock, 2003), chapter 15.
7. Acts 7:54-56
8. This story is based on an illustration in D. L. Moody, *Anecdotes and Illustrations of
   D. L. Moody* (Chicago: Rhodes and McClure, 1881), 132.

CHAPTER 18: GOD DESIRES TO BE GLORIFIED
1. See http://www.reformed.org/documents/wsc/index.html.
2. There are many passages that deal with God's glory; here are but a few: 1 Chronicles
   16:28-29; Isaiah 6:8; John 15:8; Romans 15:5-6; 1 Corinthians 10:31; Ephesians
   3:21; Philippians 1:11.
3. Bauer, *A Greek-English Lexicon of the New Testament and Other Early Christian Literature*.
4. 2 Corinthians 4:6, KJV
5. 2 Corinthians 4:15
6. John 9:1-3
7. John 11
8. Matthew 8:5-13; 15:21-28
9. John 11:21, 32
10. John 11:33-35
11. Hebrews 4:14-16
12. John 11:35
13. John 21:18-19
14. 1 Peter 1:3-9; for Paul's thoughts on this, see 2 Corinthians 4:7-18
15. Proverbs 13:12
16. Revelation 4:11
17. Psalm 50:15

CONCLUSION OF SECTION 2
1. Herbert Terrace, "Discrimination Learning with and without 'Errors,' " *Journal
   of Experimental Analysis of Behavior* 6 (1963): 1–27; also see Herbert Terrace,

"By-Products of Discrimination Learning," in *The Psychology of Learning and Motivation*, ed. G. H. Brower (New York: Appleton-Century-Crofts, 1950).

SECTION 3: A PATHWAY THROUGH SUFFERING
1. Nietzsche, as quoted in Frankl, *Man's Search for Meaning*, 76.

CHAPTER 19: PROBE YOUR BELIEFS ABOUT SUFFERING
1. 2 Timothy 3:16-17
2. Daniel 3:19-30
3. Isaiah 53; Matthew 26:36-46
4. Matthew 5:45; see also Luke 13:1-5 and John 9:1-3 for additional examples.
5. John 5:39-40
6. James 1:22-25
7. From his work: *Meditation XVII*. Find this quote at: www.brainyquote.com/quotes/authors/j/john_donne.html.
8. Elisabeth Elliot, *The Mark of a Man* (Grand Rapids, MI: Fleming H. Revell, 1981).
9. Many studies confirm the value of a caring social support. The reader is offered the following examples: C. A. Dunkel-Schetter, "Social Support and Cancer: Findings Based on Patient Interviews and Their Implications," *Journal of Social Issues* 40 (1984): 77–98; S. Cohen et al., "Social Ties and Susceptibility to the Common Cold," *Journal of the American Medical Association* 277, no. 24 (June 5, 1997): 1940–44; J. D. Lindy, M. C. Grace, and B. L. Green, "Survivors: Outreach to a Reluctant Population," *American Journal of Orthopsychiatry* 51 (1981): 468–78; Robert Putnam, *Bowling Alone: The Collapse and Revival of American Community* (New York: Simon & Schuster, 2000); D. Myers, "The Funds, Friends, and Faith of Happy People," *American Psychologist* 55, no. 1 (2000): 56–67.
10. Romans 12:15
11. Job 38:21
12. Genesis 3:4-5
13. John 14:16-18
14. Philippians 4:11-13
15. Jack Canfield and Mark Victor Hansen, eds., *Chicken Soup for the Soul* (Deerfield Beach, FL: Health Communications, 1993), 263.
16. *Encyclopedia of World Biography* (Farmington Hills, MI: Thomson Gale, 2005).
17. Lewis, *The Problem of Pain*, 47–8.
18. Ten Boom, *Clippings from My Notebook*, 56.

CHAPTER 20: ASSIGN YOUR SUFFERING TO GOD
1. Job 1:22; 3:3, 11
2. Job 6:8-9; 10:3, 10, 18, 20-21; 14:19; 19:7
3. Job 7:11; 23:4-5
4. Job 13:3
5. Lamentations 3:1, 3, 8, 15, CEV
6. Psalm 6:6-7; 55:4-5
7. Psalm 88:2-4, 8, 14-16, 18
8. Psalm 44:12
9. Psalm 88:8
10. Job 1:22; 2:3, 10
11. Job 38
12. Psalm 22:24, NIV
13. James 1:5
14. Hebrews 4:16
15. Adnan K. Abdulla, *Catharsis in Literature* (Bloomington: Indiana University, 1985).
16. Psalm 142:1-2
17. Matthew 16:23

18. Psalm 143:3
19. Lamentations 3:42
20. Psalm 34:18; Jeremiah 31:34
21. Psalm 143:5
22. Psalm 90:2; 93:2; Isaiah 48:12; 1 Timothy 6:16; Hebrews 13:8; James 1:17
23. 1 Samuel 15:29; Psalm 33:11
24. C. S. Lewis, *The Lion, the Witch and the Wardrobe* (New York: Collier Books, 1956), 75–6.
25. Romans 11:33-34
26. For a sampling of research the reader is directed to the following sources: M. Webb and K. J. Otto Whitmer, "Abuse History, World Assumptions, and Religious Problem Solving," *Journal for the Scientific Study of Religion* 40, no. 3 (September 2001): 445–53; Yvonne Tauber and Elisheva van der Hal, "Transformation of Perception of Trauma by Child Survivors of the Holocaust in Group Therapy," *Journal of Contemporary Psychotherapy* 27, no. 2 (February 1997): 151–71; Sherry A. Falsetti, Patricia A. Resick, and Joanne L. Davis, "Changes in Religious Beliefs following Trauma," *Journal of Traumatic Stress* 16, no. 4 (2003): 391–98; Mark Waysman, Joseph Schwarzwald, and Zahava Solomon, "Hardiness: An Examination of Its Relationship with Positive and Negative Long Term Changes following Trauma," *Journal of Traumatic Stress* 14, no. 3 (2001): 531–48.
27. Illustration can be found on the following Web site: http://www.bible.org/bits/bits-155.htm.
28. Romans 8:28
29. See http://www.geocities.com/Athens/Acropolis/7989/quotes.html#archive.
30. Psalm 143:6
31. Lamentations 3:24, CEV
32. Philippians 3:10
33. C. S. Lewis, *A Grief Observed* (San Francisco: HarperCollins, 1989), 18–9.
34. Job 7:10-21; 10:8-22; 16:19; 17:3
35. Job 19:25
36. Job 42:2-3
37. Job 42:6
38. Romans 8:32
39. Lewis, *The Problem of Pain*, 40.
40. Exodus 34:6; Psalm 36:7; 86:15; 103:8; Daniel 9:9; John 3:16; Romans 5:8; 15:5; Ephesians 2:4-5; 1 John 4:16
41. Exodus 34:6; Job 9:4; Psalm 86:5; 100:5; 139:2-4; Isaiah 55:9; Romans 8:28
42. Jeremiah 29:11
43. Psalm 36:5; 40:10; 88:11; 89:1; 92:2; 119:75; Isaiah 25:1; Lamentations 3:23; Hebrews 13:5, 8
44. Genesis 22:14; Philippians 4:19
45. Exodus 15:26; Psalm 41:4; 103:3; Matthew 12:15; Luke 4:18
46. Judges 6:24
47. Psalm 23
48. Genesis 17:1; 28:3; Exodus 6:3
49. John 14:16-17; Ephesians 1:13
50. Psalm 143:7
51. Story found in James Dobson, *When God Doesn't Make Sense* (Carol Stream, IL: Tyndale House, 1993), 45–6.
52. Hebrews 11:13
53. See http://www.worldofquotes.com/topic/Cliches-and-One-Liners/23.
54. Psalm 143:8
55. Jeremiah 29:11
56. Daniel 3:17-18
57. 1 John 5:4

58. Proverbs 3:5-6
59. Revelation 1:17
60. Matthew 28:20
61. John 16:33
62. Isaiah 43:2-3, NIV
63. Isaiah 41:10, NIV
64. Psalm 9:10
65. For more information on these experiments, see Curt P. Richter, "The Total Self-Regulatory Functions in Animals and Human Beings," Harvey Lecture Series no. 38 (1942–1943): 63.
66. Nietzsche, as quoted in Frankl, *Man's Search for Meaning*, 82.
67. Psalm 143:10-12
68. Ten Boom, *Clippings from My Notebook*, 51.
69. Philippians 4:4
70. James 1:2-4; Hebrews 12:5
71. Isaiah 61:3
72. Chambers, *My Utmost for His Highest*, 306.

CHAPTER 21: APPLY A PLAN OF RECOVERY
1. Carl Jung, *Psychology and Religion* (New Haven, CT: Yale University Press, 1938).
2. Frankl, *Man's Search for Meaning*, 101–02.
3. Frankl, *Man's Search for Meaning*, 78.
4. Quoted in Charles Wallis, *The Treasure Chest* (San Francisco: Harper & Row, 1983), 120.
5. Psalm 50:15
6. Jeremiah 29:13
7. 1 John 1:8-9; Psalm 32:3-5
8. Psalm 119:11, 18, 45-46, 52, 74, 98-100, 105, 165
9. Psalm 119:105, 130
10 Deuteronomy 32:2; 2 Samuel 23:2, 4
11. Psalm 119:103; 1 Corinthians 3:2
12. S. Cobb, "Social Support as a Moderator of Life Stress," *Psychosomatic Medicine* 38 (1976): 300–14; S. Cohen and T. A. Wills, "Stress, Social Support, and the Buffering Hypothesis: A Critical Review," *Psychological Bulletin* 98 (1985): 310–57; R. Kessler and J. McLeod, "Social Support and Mental Health in Community Samples," in *Social Support and Health*, eds. S. Cohen and S. L. Syme (San Diego, CA: Academic Press, 1985), 219–40.
13. S. Cohen et al., "Measuring the Functional Components of Social Support," in *Social Support: Theory, Research, and Applications*, eds. I. A. Sarason and B. Sarason (Martinus Nijhoff, Holland: The Hague, 1985), 73–94; Kenneth Pargament, *The Psychology of Religion and Coping: Theory, Research, Practice* (New York: Guilford Press, 1997). Pargament's book provides wonderful information on coping and the value of social support.
14. Many studies support the role of social relationships in our physical health. An early study known as the Alameda County study followed over 7,000 people for nine years: L. F. Berkman and L. Syme, "Social Networks, Host Resistance, and Mortality: A Nine-Year Follow-Up Study of Alaeda County Residents," *American Journal of Epidemiology* 109 (1979): 186–203; S. Cohen et al., "Social Ties and Susceptibility to the Common Cold," *Journal of the American Medical Association* 277, no. 24 (June 25, 1997): 1940–44; S. Cohen, L. Underwood, and B. H. Gottlieb, eds., *Social Support Measurement and Intervention: A Guide for Health and Social Scientists* (New York: Oxford University Press, 2000); B. N. Uchino, D. Uno, and J. Holt-Lunstad, "Social Support, Physiological Processes, and Health," *Current Directions in Psychological Science* 9, no. 5 (October 1999): 141–8.
15. Hebrews 10:24-25
16. William Shakespeare, *Macbeth*, Act IV, scene 3.

17. James W. Pennebaker, *Emotion, Disclosure, and Health* (Washington DC: American Psychological Association, 1995); L. F. Clark, "Stress and the Cognitive-Conversational Benefits of Social Interaction," *Journal of Social and Clinical Psychology* 12 (1993): 25–5; J. Hunt, "Sole Survivor: A Case Study to Evaluate the Dual-Process Model of Grief in Multiple Loss," *Illness, Crisis & Loss* 12, no. 4 (2004): 284–98.

18. See the following Web sites for more information on Maslow: http://www.maslow.com; http://www.answers.com/topic/abraham-maslow.

19. This story is attributed to Gregg Langill and Jon Antallmi, 1985.

20. William James, *The Will to Believe and Other Essays in Popular Philosophy* (New York: Dover Publications. 1956).

21. Frankl, *Man's Search for Meaning*, 78.

22. Ibid., 114–15.

23. R. A. Emmons, and M. E. McCullough, "Counting Blessings versus Burdens: An Experimental Investigation of Gratitude and Subjective Well-Being in Daily Life," *Journal of Personality and Social Psychology* 84, no. 2 (2003): 377–89.

24. Psalm 25:9

25. Frankl, *Man's Search for Meaning*, 42.

26. 2 Timothy 4:5

27. Hebrews 11:6; Matthew 6:20

28. Hebrews 12:2

29. John 14:1-3

30. Psalm 56:3-4

31. Ten Boom, *Clippings from My Notebook*, 33.

32. 1 Corinthians 15:19

33. John Bunyan, *Pilgrim's Progress* (Grand Rapids, MI: Christian Classics Ethereal Library), section 8.

34. Romans 11:34

35. 1 Thessalonians 3:2-3

36. J. Sims and D. Bauman, "The Tornado Threat: Coping Styles of the North and South," *Science* 176 (1972): 1386–92.

37. For more information on locus of control, see J. Rotter, "Generalized Expectancies for Internal vs. External Control of Reinforcement," *Psychological Monographs* 80, no. 1 (1966): whole no. 609.

38. Proverbs 3:5-6

39. Galatians 4:4

40. 2 Corinthians 4:16

41. Hebrews 11:13, 16

42. Psalm 90:12

43. Psalm 46:10

44. J. A. Blumenthal et al., "Effects of Exercise Training on Older Patients with Major Depression," *Archives of Internal Medicine* 159, no. 19 (October 25, 1999): 2349–56; G. F. Fletcher et al., "Statement on Exercise: Benefits and Recommendations for Physical Activity Programs for All Americans," A Statement for Health Professionals by the Committee on Exercise and Cardiac Rehabilitation of the Council on Clinical Cardiology, American Heart Association, *Circulation* 94 (1996): 857–62; P. Martin, *Sickening Mind: Brain, Behaviour, Immunity and Disease* (New York: HarperCollins, 1995).

CHAPTER 22: REDEEM YOUR SUFFERING

1. See http://www.alcoholics-anonymous.org for more information about their services.

2. In actuality, it is the perceived availability of social support that seems to buffer people from the damaging effects of stress. The buffer may come from emotional support such as feeling cared about or not feeling alone, informational support such as giving helpful advice, and instrumental support such as the practical ways by which people demonstrate their support—cooking meals, cutting grass, etc. Many studies

support this, including: S. R. Jenkins, "Coping and Social Support among Emergency Dispatchers: Hurricane Andrew," *Journal of Social Behavior and Personality* 12, no. 1 (February 1997): 201–06; M. C. Logsdon, J. C. Birkimer, and A. P. Barbee, "Social Support Providers for Postpartum Women," *Journal of Social Behavior and Personality* 12 (1997): 89–102; P. Callaghan and J. Morrissey, "Social Support and Health: A Review," *Journal of Advanced Nursing*, 18, no. 2 (1993): 203; B. W. J. H. Penninx, et al., "Direct and Buffer Effects of Social Support and Personal Coping Resources in Individuals with Arthritis," *Social Science and Medicine*, 44, no. 3 (1997): 393–402.

3. Galatians 6:1-2, 5

4. Bauer, *A Greek-English Lexicon of the New Testament and Other Early Christian Literature.*

5. 2 Corinthians 4:17

6. Joe Bayly, *The View from a Hearse* (Elgin, IL: Cook, 1973), 53–6.

7. The value of listening to troubled people's experiences is not even debated by experts in the field of counseling. Examples of such research are: Boris Drozdek, "Follow-Up Study of Concentration Camp Survivors from Bosnia-Herzegovina: Three Years Later," *Journal of Nervous and Mental Diseases* 185, no. 11 (1997): 690–94; J. J. Wright and D. Davis, "The Therapeutic Relationship in Cognitive-Behavioral Therapy: Patient Perceptions and Therapist Responses," *Cognitive and Behavioral Practice* 1, (n.d.): 25-45; M. B. Gibbons, "Listening to the Lived Experience of Loss," *Pediatric Nursing* 19, no. 6 (1993): 597–99; Christine M. Jonas-Simpson, "The Experience of Being Listened To: A Human Becoming Study with Music," *Nursing Science Quarterly* 16, no. 3 (2003): 232–38.

8. C. A. Dunkel-Schetter, "Social Support and Cancer: Findings Based on Patient Interviews and Their Implications," *Journal of Social Issues* 40 (1984): 77–98.

9. John 13:17

About the Authors

DR. JOHN C. THOMAS is chair of the Center for Counseling and Family Studies and associate professor at Liberty University. In addition, Dr. Thomas provides psychological consultation services to DuPont in Front Royal, Virginia.

Dr. Thomas holds a doctorate of philosophy degree in counseling and a graduate certificate in alcohol and drug studies from the University of South Carolina. He received his master's degree in counseling and bachelor's degree in missions from Liberty University. Dr. Thomas also holds a doctorate of philosophy degree in organizational psychology from Capella University.

Dr. Thomas is a licensed professional counselor (LPC), certified substance abuse counselor (CSAC), and certified employee assistance consultant (CEAP). He has authored articles for many professional publications, conducts marriage enrichment retreats, and speaks on mental health and organizational issues. Dr. Thomas is an active member of Thomas Road Baptist Church in Lynchburg, Virginia. He resides with his wife, Denise, and their two children, Katie and Stephen, in Lynchburg, Virginia.

DR. GARY R. HABERMAS is Distinguished Research Professor and chair of the Department of Philosophy and Theology at Liberty University, where he has taught since 1981. He also teaches in the Ph.D. program in theology and apologetics at Liberty Baptist Theological Seminary. He earned his Ph.D. at Michigan State University and his M.A. from the University of Detroit. He has authored, coauthored, or edited more than thirty books, as well as contributed more than fifty chapters or articles to other books. He has also written more than 100 articles and reviews for journals and other publications. While his chief areas of research (and the topic of about sixteen of his books) are issues related to Jesus' resurrection, he has also published frequently on the subjects of suffering and religious doubt. Some of his publications can be found at http://www.garyhabermas.com.

During the past thirteen years, he has often been a visiting or adjunct professor, having taught courses at some fifteen different graduate schools and seminaries in the United States and abroad. He and his wife, Eileen, have seven children and nine grandchildren, all of whom live in Lynchburg, Virginia.